BLUBBERLAND

BLUBBERLAND

THE DANGERS OF HAPPINESS

ELIZABETH FARRELLY

The MIT Press
Cambridge, Massachusetts
London, England

© 2008 Elizabeth Farrelly
First published by University of New South Wales Press, UNSW, Sydney NSW 2052 Australia.

MIT Press books may be purchased at special quantity discounts for business or sales promotional use. For information, please email special_sales@mitpress.mit.edu or write to Special Sales Department, The MIT Press, 55 Hayward Street, Cambridge, MA 02142.

This book was set in Adobe Caslon Pro by Di Quick and was printed and bound in Australia.

Library of Congress Cataloging-in-Publication Data

Farrelly, E. M.
  Blubberland: the dangers of happiness / Elizabeth Farrelly.
     p. cm.
  Includes bibliographical references and index.
  ISBN 978-0-262-56236-2 (pbk. : alk. paper)
  1. Happiness. 2. Consumption (Economics) 3. Popular culture. I. Title.
BF575.H27F37 2008
306—dc22
                                    2007031408

10 9 8 7 6 5 4 3 2 1

10/08

Contents

For LMF
Who tried to save me from life as a writer

Preface

Mea culpa. Mea culpa.

I, like you, drive too much. I buy too much – of which I keep too much and also throw too much away. I overindulge my children, and myself. Directly as well as indirectly I use too much water, energy, air and space. My existence, in short, costs the planet more than it can afford. This is not some handed-down moral stricture, nor any sort of guilty self-flagellation, but a simple recognition of fact. The consequences are obvious, and near enough now to see the warts on their noses. For my own future, as well as my children's, I must change. And yet – this is what's weird – I, like you, can't. Cannot abandon comfort, convenience and pleasure for the sake of abstract knowledge. Can't stop doing it.

This is interesting. It's interesting because we think we are so rational, so intelligent, and yet we behave, both individually and as a herd, in such unintelligent ways. That's what drove this book into being. A craving, at the very least, to see what the f... is going on with this crazy species.

Introduction

'We animals eat to live. But humans live to eat. Food, food, food.
Do you think they have enough?' They all nod.
'For humans, enough is never enough.'

RJ TO THE OTHER ANIMALS, *Over the Hedge* (2006)

Want used to mean need. Want was life or death stuff, as in 'the lad wants feeding', 'the horse wants putting down'. Now, want has flipped one-eighty to imply an arbitrary and even whimsical desire, unfettered by need, significance or logic. As in, 'I want it because I want it, geddit?' At the same time, and perhaps even because our wanting has become so wilful, human beings have grown insatiable. The more we have, it seems, the more we want, as though desire itself is the thing we cannot forgo. As though, even cocooned by layers of brimming superfluity, we must want or perish. Welcome to Blubberland. You're rolling in it.

Blubber is unused energy, neither good nor bad in itself but a-quiver with potential. Blubber is whale oil for the lamps on long winter nights. It is the egg's white, the fruit's flesh, the yeasty bounce of a baby's thigh designed to sustain life through cold and famine. Blubber is anything spare or surplus. The aedicule, gazebo or porch that adds to a building nothing but graciousness; the purposeless energy of birdsong that is neither mating call nor warning call but pure, simple pleasure; the spare time in the day, or in the tribal calendar, that makes space for creative play. Blubber, in this sense, is the crack where the light gets in.

But blubber is also the very opposite of light: the track-suited, mind-numbed couch potato, the quadruple-garaged McMansion, the idealised fantasy life of the virtual-reality addict, home alone with a flickering screen in a darkened room. It is the bear-pit of reality TV, the pseudo-feminist 'me-ring' that you buy yourself, the neurotic shopaholics aspiring to ever bigger and more perfect apartments just to house all the stuff. Blubber is the world of vast, glittering malls and dreary look-at-me suburbs interspersed with limitless acreage of concrete, asphalt and billboards. It is cashed-up pension funds forcing their market-driven conservatism across the corporate world, terrified women with silicone breasts and plastic relationships locked into the fearful luxury of gated communities, and critic Michael Bywater's dead-hearted towns with 'their grilles and burger joints, their litter and their obese, sportswear-clad, snarling crop-haired families yoked in greed and hatred, their slashed prices, their ugliness, their interest-free deals ...'. All this, less a state of body than of mind, is Blubberland.

This paradox, which might be merely interesting were it not now threatening the very planet beneath our feet, forces us to ask: What is the difference between good blubber and bad blubber? In part, it's a question of degree. As with sunshine or chocolate, so with surfeit. Some is good but too much – superfluous superfluity – is, well, too much. Too much converts blubber's protective layer into an embalming shroud.

But it's not just degree. It's also attitudinal. It is the difference between happiness as a hoped-for side-effect of lives shaped mainly by duty, obligation or necessity, and happiness as a near-universal goal, whose elusiveness only fans the fury of our pursuit. The difference between good blubber and bad blubber is the difference between hope and expectation, between something to be prayed for and sought after, and something to be demanded, litigated, fought for. Between a blessing and a right. This shift, which you might see as the triumph of humanism, or of hubris, has the surprising effect of blinding us to our own core construct, significance.

So where once a desperately needed harvest or successful hunt was imbued, by its very rarity, with deepest significance (not to mention a certain thankful humility), our habituation to excess robs us of the very sense of meaning that we so desperately crave. Blubber-rich but meaning-poor, we are increasingly incapable of using our blubber to build a better world, hell-bent on using it to dig our own grave.

Now, though, Gaia is offering us a chance. As if agreeing with Dr Who that 'these stupid little people have only just learned how to walk, but they're capable of so much more', Gaia has brought us to the brink of crisis. Climate change, and all of its moving parts – from litter to lightbulbs to deforestation – is more than a crisis of survival. It's a crisis of significance, where we must grasp the essential connectedness of everything, and re-invest in our source of meaning, or die.

Everything, as environmentalist John Muir pointed out more than a century ago, connects to everything else. This is the central intuition of most mystical traditions, from Sufism to Jung to the Aboriginal Dreaming. More surprisingly, as matter resolves itself into energy and nuclear physics pursues its latest 'theory of everything', the oneness of things is also becoming a core tenet of science. Because the pattern of connections is neither linear nor planar but three-dimensional, like the neuronal connections in the brain, this is hard for us to grasp, let alone articulate. Language doesn't help, being so infuriatingly linear, nor does our Enlightenment heritage, which has so accustomed us to separation and definition as dominant modes of thought.

Modernism, as perhaps the final flowering of the Enlightenment, became obsessed by the scientific-materialist mindset. Science seeks essences, the common factors that allow the formation of general rules. This search underpinned both modernism's universalising push – democracy, Esperanto, ecumenicalism, welfare and free school milk – and its obsessive separation by definition. The positivist urge to see the world as a uniform field of equal-but-separate entities – be they atoms, species, disciplines, humans or tower blocks – relies on clear definition. So definition became modernism's defining act, and materialism its defining belief. Just as the Renaissance rediscovered Plato, modernism rediscovered old man Aristotle, the father of taxonomy.

Moral philosopher James Flynn, for example, explains his controversial findings that human IQ has been increasing steadily for more than a hundred years by pointing out that a nineteenth century person, asked about the link between dogs and rabbits, would have answered that dogs were used to catch rabbits, whereas a contemporary person would answer that both dogs and rabbits are mammals. What we've got better at, in other words, is not thought per se, but analytical, taxonomic thought of the kind favoured by IQ tests and by the modernist scientists who design them.

This urge to separate permeates our lives. Modernism separated disciplines, genres, city functions, nuclear families, species, cars, elements and houses, much as a child separates colours and textures on the plate. Strangely, postmodernism exacerbated the effect, albeit for the most pluralist of reasons, blowing a succession of pretty bubbles that seduced us with offers of safety, comfort and retreat. There are physical bubbles like the super-mall, the four-wheel-drive, the Mc-Mansion, the home theatre and the MP3 player. There's also a range of cultural bubbles, including hot-desking, enterprise bargaining, personalised truth and the universal expectation of happiness even as we become increasingly fat, bored and miserable. Denizens of our own gated communities, we have become frightened to stay, but more frightened to emerge. So, imperceptibly, does comfort become the enemy and refuge the prison.

Certainly, if reason has any sway, we won't stay here. We'll see that burning our blubber to brighten the truth-and-beauty flame makes us happier than hoarding it, as well as better. That to test ourselves, even at great risk, is something we occasionally need; that the seven lean years are as crucial as the seven fat ones; that connection creates meaning; that to give is actually to receive. And that enough is actually enough.

1 | Desire body: wanting it, all, now

You cain't always get what you want, but if you try sometimes,
well you just might find, you get what you need.

MICK JAGGER AND KEITH RICHARDS (1968)

Desire is a fundamental force of life; probably the fundamental force. Pretty much everything we do is desire-driven, whether at appetite level – for food, love, money, sex or power – or on a higher, more abstract plane – the desire for truth, say, or order, or god. In many ways, desire is simply what we do, our motive force and our *raison d'être*. It's why we get out of bed, how we define ourselves and, to a large extent, how we shape our future. We are because we want, as well as vice versa. As philosopher William Irvine puts it, 'desire animates the world'. So it's hardly surprising that desire also animates our mythic lives. From Luke Skywalker to Becky Sharp, from Ahab to Siddhartha, the character must *want* something. Desire drives plot, just as it drives life. Conversely, absence of desire, which normally only happens to people who are old, sick or Buddhist, is something we dread.

• 'The force that through the green fuse drives the flower'

In evolutionary terms, of course, the 'reason' for desire is clear. The scarcity environment in which humanity evolved prioritised appetite: whoever got the most sex, or food, or stuff was likely to be a successful spreader of the seed. Now, that's all changed. While for most of us – perhaps even for the perpetually dissatisfied Mick Jagger – satisfaction is increasingly achievable, the desires themselves show no sign of waning. On the contrary, they've become, if anything, more voracious. The more we have, the more we seem to want and the more driven we are to want to want. As though we're terrified to see what might happen if we stop desiring, even for a moment. Psychiatrists report that a common response to significant weight loss among the long-term obese is a sense of terror, of unwonted exposure and fragility in the face of the maelstrom; as if even the hated kilos were themselves protective bulwarks. We standard middle-class consumers, facing any reduction in our rate of blubber-acquisition, are struck by the same abject fears. So that now, combined with our satisfaction-skills and our sheer, planet-smothering species-biomass, the very desires that once enhanced our survival now threaten it. Our response? Have another daiquiri.

• Why we over-satisfy

The ultimate point of desire, of course, is happiness. We are hardwired, it seems, not just to desire, but to presume a causal chain from desire to happiness. This linkage is so deeply embedded in Western culture and economy that it is seldom articulated. Spelled out, though, it reads like some sloppy post-hippie mantra: desire impels gratification; gratification equals pleasure; pleasure equals happiness and happiness equals, well, pretty much everything. What else is there? But what if this presumption is wrong? What if one of the links should prove false?

In fact, every step in the desire = gratification = pleasure = happiness chain of reasoning is demonstrably false. Desire needn't always be satisfied. Gratification often brings less pleasure than we expect, and for a shorter time. And pleasure, even when achieved, doesn't bring happiness. Much of the time pleasure is, at best, a distraction from unhappiness and its causes; at worst it simply intensifies our misery.

All this is becoming obvious, as study after study reveals the causal connections between consumption, climate change, obesity and epidemic depression. And yet, in popular culture, the gratification-compulsion chugs on. For must of us, religion is in the reject pile and the Enlightenment was a disappointment, but the pursuit of happiness through pleasure survives as the supreme orthodoxy of our times. Bookstores overflow with how-to happiness manuals. As psychologist John Schumacher notes, 'there are happiness institutes, camps, clubs, classes, cruises, workshops and retreats. Universities are adding Happiness Studies ... Personal happiness is big business and everyone is selling it ... even with the planet in meltdown'.

That Western culture's happiness-addiction has burgeoned in direct parallel with its depression epidemic is as obvious as it is ironic, just as thin-worship has grown in direct parallel with the obesity epidemic. But we consistently refuse to recognise any causal connection, and happiness is still the grail. 'If it makes you happy,' goes the popular song, 'it can't be that bad.' If life were to end now, they'd put this on our gravestone, epitaph to the modern world.

The irony is that it's our very pursuit of happiness that makes such an end a serious possibility. Which begs the obvious question: If it's not making us happy, if in fact it's more likely to precipitate planetary catastrophe, why are we so driven to over-satisfy the wrong desires?

In part it's cultural, with contemporary advertising relentlessly insisting that to satisfy our every desire is not just a right but a kind of duty. Buy it (the superannuation, the lingerie, the holiday), urge the ads, because you deserve it, because you're worth it, but mainly because you want it. Robert Louis Stevenson's 'great task of happiness' has become, for us, little more than a consumer's duty of instant self-gratification.

In part, over-gratification is driven by naughtiness. The urge to transgress is strong, and does have its positive aspects. In desire terms, though, while we do occasionally desire what is good, or good for us, we more reliably, and more intensely, desire what is bad, or bad for us. You might argue that it is only transgression that makes desire obvious. That 'good' desire is ubiquitous and unnoticeable, no more than a constant background hum. That only when desire intensifies into craving – and forbidden pleasures, like chocolate, opium or sex, are the ones we crave – only, in other words, when desire becomes something to resist do we even recognise its presence.

Naughtiness of this kind is institutionalised. Without the seven deadly sins, especially without the desire-sins (gluttony, envy, lust, avarice), civilisations would shrivel and die. Imagine starting a business, a garden or a family without desire. Imagine writing a love-song, running a marathon – or robbing a bank – without desire.

In part, too, our over-gratification may relate to the contemporary dominance of youth culture, since young people tend to be more in the grip of desire-drives than older people. And in part our over-gratification is palliative. Like the fat person comfort-eating, we consume precisely because the implications of our consumption are so terrifying.

The only thing more terrifying is not to desire at all. Absence of desire may be a Zen ideal but it is also one of the things we fear most. The end of desire seems like the end of life. Without desire, there is no reason to get out of bed – or indeed, to get into bed in the first place. As Irvine notes, 'banish desire and you get a world of frozen beings with no desire to live and no desire to die'.

Irvine catalogues people who suffer 'crises of desire', who lose, either temporarily or permanently, not the capacity to feel pleasure but the capacity to take pleasure in pleasure. That is, to desire pleasure. Irvine offers three categories of such crisis. There are those who simply lose desire (writer Larry McMurtry, for example, was devastated to find, after major heart surgery, that he had lost the desire to read, which had been until then the defining desire of his life); those who, like Siddhartha, become disgusted by their own desires and renounce them; and those who, like Tolstoy at the height of his success, continue to feel desire even as they recognise its futility, and simply stop caring whether their desires are fulfilled or not.

Without desire the world goes grey. Even losing your sense of taste to a head cold can remove all sense of colour and purpose. Which is why the longing for desirelessness, which Freud labelled the Nirvana principle, struck him as a form of death-wish, and why St Augustine so famously prayed for God to 'grant me chastity and continence, but not yet'.

Desire itself, then, is something we desire. Are we so addicted to desire itself that we contrive to sustain it even past the point of satiation? Past need, reason or even decency? Or does it work the other way? For historian and social critic Christopher Lasch, writing *The Culture of Narcissism* almost thirty years ago, the 'longing to be free from longing' was also the deep wellspring of the narcissism that, for him, defined the modern era. So is it perhaps a narcissistic urge to be desire-free that explains our relentless determination not only to satisfy our desires but also to sustain these same desires even as they are satiated?

Either way, we have become, as a species, insatiable. This puts the focus squarely on *what* we desire, *how* we desire it and whether, as a species, we can begin – perhaps for the first time ever – to direct our desires for our own collective benefit.

Why we want what we want: pleasure

So what are the things we believe will bring us pleasure? On the whole it's obvious stuff: physical comfort, safety, love (or at least admiration) and envy. Most of our immediate objects of desire – material possessions, physical perfection, freedom – are desired for their capacity, real or imagined, to bring us one or more of these perceived goods.

Our belief, for example, in the direct relationship between comfort and happiness makes us crave the capacity to avoid pain. This, like our urge to pleasure, has clear evolutionary virtues. As Winston Churchill once noted, pain, like criticism, 'calls attention to an unhealthy state of things'. But now, as permanent and total pain-avoidance begins to look genuinely possible, it behoves us to ask: Is our anti-pain impulse as wrong-headed and potentially counterproductive as our pro-pleasure urge? Many of us fantasise a world without pain; a world where mental suffering is at least as extraordinary an experience as physical pain, once commonplace, is for us now. But would we, now that it is a distinct possibility, truly wish a world without pain?

The fantasy approaches. A recent *Scientific American* article by Stefanie Reinberger showed how unpleasant tastes could be eliminated with a new type of food-additive called adenosine monophosphate (AMP). AMP is a 'bitter-blocker' that overrides our ancient sensitivity to bitterness, acquired to protect us from eating toxic substances like strychnine, by preventing communication of the recognition of bitterness from tastebud to brain. The additive has already (2004) been approved by the US Food and Drug Administration; the application of similar principles could mean we never have to taste anything unpleasant. Brussels sprouts could taste like gruyere, or ice cream, or chocolate and still be as good for us as the bitter green cruciform original.

But is this what we really want? Do we, even at the relatively trivial level of taste, want a world where our only sensations are pleasurable ones? Will pleasure still have meaning when that's all there is?

That's at a trivial level. But some take the same thinking much further, and much more seriously. David Pearce's ambitious website *The Hedonistic Imperative* is an example of a movement that is dead serious about the complete abolition of human pain, presenting a detailed manifesto 'to eradicate suffering in all sentient life'. For Pearce, pain has outlived its usefulness and should be removed by whatever means possible – surgery, genetic engineering or discovery of the perfect, side-effect-free drug.

Pearce's presumption is that the age-old equation, every pleasure has its price, no longer holds. We may feel it to be true, that pain is simply the flipside of pleasure, but this intuition of ours is itself outmoded, indicating merely that we are, as a species, 'victims of what our successors will reckon an atavistic mood disorder', an habitual presumption that the downside is inherently part of the upside. This, he argues, is mere perception; life can and some day will be all upside.

In a section called 'The Naturalisation of Heaven', Pearce argues that in the future, whether through drugs, surgery or genome-design, humans will live entirely pain free:

> nanotechnology and genetic engineering will eliminate aversive
> experience from the living world. Over the next thousand years or
> so, the biological substrates of suffering will be eradicated completely
> … Post-human states of magical joy will be biologically refined,

multiplied and intensified indefinitely. Notions of what now passes for tolerably good mental health are likely to be superseded … as the genetic revolution in reproductive medicine unfolds, what might once have been the stuff of millennialist fantasy is set to become a scientifically feasible research program. Its adoption or rejection will become, ultimately, a social policy issue. Passively or actively, we will have to *choose* just how much unpleasantness we wish to create or conserve – if any – in eras to come.

But is this utopia or dystopia? Literature, of course, has long been interested in whether there is a difference. Aldous Huxley's *Brave New World*, published in 1932, was one of the earliest explorations of a pain-free future. In a totalitarian world where pleasure is the primary instrument of tyranny, individualism, melancholy, monogamy and memory are punished, and people are lulled into pleasant acquiescence by hypnopaedia, eugenics and the official drug, soma. The resultant euphoria, far from being utopian, is seen as a threat to knowledge, freedom and pain itself. Happiness, suggests Huxley, is not only unachievable through pure pleasure – it actually depends on pain and adversity as surely as light depends on shadow.

Pearce is unmoved. For him, Huxley's vegetative chemical dystopia simply shows he was onto the wrong drug. Modern euphoriants, argues Pearce, more commonly generate energy than suppress it, and are less likely to generate unwanted side-effects. It is unlikely that this riposte would have satisfied Huxley who, one suspects, was more concerned about dignity and freedom than physical or even emotional pleasure.

It's interesting, however, to read the reflections of swimming-god Ian Thorpe on the rigours of world-class athleticism. It wasn't just a question of 'pushing through the pain barrier', as in the cliché. The pain itself became a positive:

I was addicted to the pain, I used to get into it. I miss that part, I miss pushing myself to the point where it almost brings you to tears … My favourite moment is when I finish a race and my body is virtually collapsing from the pain … and my body tells me 'I'm okay. I've run from the lion and I'm not going to die'.

And it's not only the body. Constant euphoria, argues Thorpe, is unnatural and unsustainable: 'I don't think it's good for you to have those intense highs too regularly … you're meant to have those experiences occasionally, not every week'. Perhaps, implies Thorpe, pain is not pleasure's opposite but its essential other.

Such wisdom, traditionally part of the Christian message but now largely rejected, and ridiculed even by Christianity itself, is beginning to creep through into popular culture. The film *Little Miss Sunshine*, for example, shows a normally dysfunctional family being healed by an experience of adversity and enforced altruism. But for most of us, unable or unwilling to accept such insights, the presumed pleasure = happiness equation persists.

Half a century after the hippie rebellion, we are still trying to subvert the old, unwelcome, 'if it hurts it has to be good for you' mentality. Still trying to believe that what feels bad must be bad for us and that what feels good, is good. But the truth is, we're lazy. The moment we get satisfied, we get sluggish. Then we get bored, then depressed. Affluenza generates depression; it's simple cause and effect.

In a recent *Sydney Morning Herald* article, Adele Horin argued that residents of the inner-Sydney neighbourhood of Leichhardt, catalogued by social analyst Richard Florida under 'creative classes', are the most 'disgruntled' in Sydney. So, it was suggested, they should abandon Leichhardt and move out to new US-style 'latte towns', which are a kind of Crown Street-on-sea. But perhaps the truth is the other way around: that to be creative is to be disgruntled; the moment you get gruntled, your creativity is over.

Envy

If no other characteristic defined us as hierarchical primates, the dominance of envy in our emotional spectrum would do it. As Miranda Priestly smiles farewell from her *Devil Wears Prada* limo, her parting shot is: 'Everyone wants to be us.' Envy, at once an accusation and an expectation, is now a standard weapon in the class war that we pretend is dead. Right-wing commentators regularly accuse social-justice activists of indulging in 'the politics of envy'. Our desire for the envy of others derives from our gregarious and hierarchical animal nature. Being envious makes us insecure, inclining us to see ourselves, at least partly, through other people's eyes. This need for peer-affirmation becomes both a civilising force and a social glue. Without it, we would be less lovable – and less successful – creatures. So this, too, has evolutionary purpose.

You may *think* you want the Seychelles holiday, the harbour view, the 20-metre yacht for its own sake. But in fact, as Irvine notes, 'if our neighbours ridiculed rather than admired the owners of SUVs, expensive wristwatches and 15,000 square foot mansions, it is unlikely we would put ourselves out trying to acquire these things'. Having something someone else wants, even if it's only a supermarket car-space, gives you a warm affirmative glow at the same time as making that thing suddenly more valuable. Many people are driven almost exclusively by the desire for envy. Studies repeatedly show that, faced with a choice between a salary significantly higher than our peers', and a much higher amount where everyone else is earning still more, people will consistently choose the former.

HL Mencken defined wealth as 'any income that is at least one hundred dollars more a year than the income of one's wife's sister's husband', and Gore Vidal was even more succinct: 'It is not enough to succeed. Others must fail.' These days, however, we positively encourage envy. Revel in it.

Canadian philosopher Mark Kingwell reflected during a recent talk in Sydney that:

> the facilitation of envy is the aim of all advertising and much of the lifestyle pornography that passes for design theory in the magazines and trade shows of our slick privileged world. We speak of house-envy, that particular form of inadequacy that comes upon people who cross the thresholds of others, like visiting vampires invited inside, and find themselves feeling drained and wan, unable to see anything but what they don't have: those window treatments, that tchotchke, that granite counter or stainless steel fridge.

Status, in other words, matters more to us than money; money, beyond the basic needs, is desirable only for its purchase-power in the status store. Status makes us feel superior, and underpinning status is envy – or at least our presumption of it in others. As developer James O'Neill told the *Sydney Morning Herald* recently, people who are anti-development are simply 'a case of envy, and a chip on their shoulder'. This makes the near-universal desire for fame and fortune (including professional success and recognition of all kinds) really one desire – for the regard of others. The test is this: On a desert island, would we bother?

Civilising as it is in small doses, the craving for envy, taken to extremes, can be destructive, manifesting as insatiable greed, neediness or narcissism. Those who climb to the top of corporate and political hierarchies, for instance, often depend on adoration like a drug. Edmundo Chirinos, the psychiatrist attending Venezuelan president Hugo Chavez, reportedly told *Atlantic Monthly* correspondent Franklin Foer, for example, 'The love of the people is a narcotic to him. He needs it, the same way he needs his coffee.' (Chavez famously consumes up to thirty demitasses a day.)

What do we use to generate the envy-drug? Our means are few in type, since anything that is not universally valued immediately loses currency as an envy-generator. Envy-generators need, further, to be demonstrable, in-yer-face obvious, visible like a billboard at 60 kilometres an hour. They include fame and fortune, stuff and territory, bodily perfection and beauty.

Safety and fear

Fear is another defining characteristic of our times. Helicopter-parenting and offshore processing, childhood obesity, nanny-statism, gated communities, SUVs and political conservatism – all are based on fear. Fear is shaping our culture and, just as surely, shaping our environment. Never mind that we're safer now than ever. As our world gets statistically more secure, our sense of threat grows steadily more intense. The safer we are, the less safe we feel.

And yet safety, we presume, is the very opposite of fear. Safety is supposed to kill fear. Says British sociologist Frank Furedi:

Safety has become the fundamental value of our times. Passions that were once devoted to a struggle to change the world (or to keep it the same) are now invested in trying to ensure that we are safe. The label 'safe' gives new meaning to a wide range of human activities, endowing them with unspoken qualities that are meant to merit our automatic approval. 'Safe sex', for example, is not just sex practised 'healthily' – it implies an entire attitude towards life.

Most governments, many institutions and pretty much all advertising would be lost without fear. They caress our hopes, but play to our fears. And fear is fertile ground – fear of old age, of sickness, of fat; of bad breath, bad teeth, bad jeans; of being left out or locked in or simply ignored. Human fears are limitless.

Fear is why we vote for safe, dull governments over adventurous, interesting ones. It's why we build gated communities, and also why residents of those communities sometimes get so fearful of what's beyond the wall that they're reluctant to venture out at all. So easily does the fort become the prison. Fear is why we over-eat, why we over-build and why we over-spend.

Psychologist Tim Kasser studies what he calls 'the chains of materialism'. He lists the ways in which materialistic values diminish our wellbeing – by sustaining our insecurity, keeping us on the treadmill, disrupting our relationships and infringing personal freedom. People with materialistic values, Kasser has found, are more prone to social conservatism, more inclined to debilitating self-consciousness, more likely to suffer from low self-esteem and more inclined to over-value the esteem of others. They are also more likely to watch a lot of television. Materialists are also more prone to death-dreams than others, and less able to overcome the fears manifest in and generated by those dreams.

At the far end of the spectrum, extreme fear of death, and the longing for it, are generally regarded as classic narcissistic traits. They reflect the narcissist's dearth of inner resources and constant need to reinforce exterior boundaries, fending off the ever-present death-wish with a permanent, on-tap supply of external regard: love, admiration, envy.

So the questions for us are: Can materialism signify a tacit self-hatred, even a death-wish? What might it mean for a society if such a syndrome became generalised? And is this what we're doing?

⊙ | Stuff

Materialism, originally a philosophical approach that equates the real with the tangible, is in large part the basis of what Alvin Toffler described in *Future Shock* as 'the man-thing nexus'. And while there is nothing inherently destructive in our natural affinity for things – indeed, quite the contrary – the essential survival skill of acquisition, overfed by surfeit as well as by the disposability revolution, and watered by our ongoing need for envy, generates a desire for stuff, stuff and more stuff.

Stuff is the most common, and perhaps the most straightforward of our envy-genic desires. Because stuff pushes the safety button. We desire stuff for the pretty lies it tells our troubled psyches. To own the perfect, shiny object, it whispers, is to become in some way perfect; to become, in a word, immortal. Which is why the mid-life crisis so often presents as an acquisition-explosion; we know it's stupid, but still we feel that the shine, the newness, the minted innocence of the freshly manufactured object will somehow rub off. And it does, for a while. Like a drug, the purchase act exchanges money, a form of embedded energy, for a brief surge of immortality-energy.

One of the ironies is that our increasing obsession with material wealth has coincided precisely with the so-called information revolution, predicted to detach us from the thing-ness of things and re-attach us to things virtual. The opposite has happened, suggesting that perhaps we feel a need to make up in quantity for what we have lost in the deteriorating quality of our relationship with the material world, which is why shopping, and the ubiquitous shopping mall, has become a defining feature of Western life. So much so, and so unabashedly, that the US State Department website notes: 'there are more shopping centers than movie theatres, school districts, hotels or hospitals. There are more malls than cities, colleges or television stations. The shopping center space has increased by a factor of 12 in the last 40 years'.

The first fully-enclosed shopping mall in America, and probably the world, was the Southdale Center in Edina, outside Minneapolis. Built in 1956, it is credited to Austrian immigrant architect Victor Gruen, who wanted to recreate the intimate scale and feel of the traditional Viennese plaza. Ironically, the opposite has happened. In this climate-controlled bubble, Gruen used an aviary, an orchestra, a hanging garden and artificial trees to entice people and keep them shopping. 'More people – for more hours,' he wrote in 1973, 'means cash registers ringing more often and for longer periods.' So successful was he in this that today's malls are bought and sold on the basis of their 'Gruen transfer' factor. This is a measure of the seconds or nanoseconds it takes, from the moment of entry, for the mall to slow a shopper's purposeful gait to the ambling stroll that signifies 'scripted disorientation'; for the hunter to become the gatherer, the wolf to become the sheep.

We all do it. It is impossible to imagine, as you wander the halls of the latest gargantuan Westfield or Wal-Mart, that all this stuff – endless supplies of wine thermometers and shower radios, in-car phone sets and TV screens wider than your bed – is necessary, or even genuinely desired. Who could possibly buy it all? And yet, somehow, mysteriously, it gets sold. It's not population-driven. Most Western populations are barely growing, scarcely replacing themselves without immigration. And yet each week we take home mountains and mountains of stuff. Like the gut flora of some poor, fixed creature, addicted to this bulimic cycle of buying, getting and getting-rid-of, we extract what we want, or think we might want some time, and excrete the excess – the packaging, the recycling, the half-digested junk.

Even in the throes of our addiction, however, we are increasingly aware that possession itself can become burdensome. Not-having can be stressful, but having can be more stressful still. The 'endowment effect' is what happens when the negative effect of loss, or of fear-of-loss, outweighs both the pleasure of having and the negative of not-having-had. Once you've climbed the peak, there's only one way to go. Down.

But that's not all. As psychologist William James noted, back in 1958, 'lives based on having are less free than lives based either on doing or on being'. This has been the essential message not just of Christianity, but of many of the world's major philosophies and religions for millennia. Now much contemporary study is devoted to finding scientific proof, or at least concurrence, for what we are no longer prepared, or able, to take on faith.

Perfection

Many of us in the middle-class West experience life as a relentless struggle for perfection. The right house, the right schools for the kids, the right facelift, the right sparkling view. Such luxuries have become, for many, necessities, whose absence is unthinkable since that very absence denotes failure. A house with no harbour view, unconcealed signs of age, children who are not musical geniuses; these are our failures.

But what will we do when, as may be inevitable, perfection becomes a real option? Assuming that the right drugs or the right genetic splicing will sooner or later come on stream, the question is this: In a world where we could have our heart's desire, what sort of world, what sort of lives, what sort of selves would we design? What sort of bodies, what sort of perceptual fields will we design ourselves to be? What would we – will we – design out? Pain? Ugliness? Suffering? Do we actually want to be perfect?

The Edge, a website devoted to the intellectual life of the 'third culture' – aka scientists who can actually write – includes a section called the 'World Question' which, each year, poses a question to a selection of the world's top thinkers, from scientists to writers. In 2006 the question was: 'What is your dangerous idea? An idea you think about (not necessarily one you originated) that is dangerous not because it is assumed to be false, but because it might be true?'

Correspondents offered a range of dangerous ideas, from the thought that 'souls do not exist [and] all human acts are just brain processes' (Yale psychologist Paul Bloom) to the idea that 'science will never silence god' (University of Arkansas psychologist Jesse Bering). The reason the question is interesting is, of course, that assessments of 'dangerous' are subjective, so each person has their own answer. For me, a truly dangerous idea, one that becomes more dangerous as it approaches truth, is the notion that humanity is perfectible.

Harvard psychologist Dr Robert Epstein recently described his date with the 'world's most attractive android', a silicone-skinned Eurasian robot called Repliee, created by Osaka University computer scientist Hiroshi Ishiguro. Repliee talks, blinks, smiles, moves her head and changes expression. With the help of room-sensors she even responds to sound and movement with subtle movements of her own. Epstein reports finding her not only beautiful but 'compellingly human' despite the cold skin and limited conversation. But she's not perfect. Repliee's face, modelled after a well-known TV personality, is, says Epstein, 'utterly realistic down to the smallest blemish'.

This is important; the blemish is no accident. Like the deliberate flaw in the exquisite Persian rug, it reassures the gods that we're not after their job. An enormous proportion of earthly activity is driven by the tantalising idea of human perfectibility. The fashion, health, automotive, housing, insurance and advertising industries, to name a few. But it's as though we intuit, at some deep level, that perfection is a sort of asymptote in the curve of our lives; an endless goal towards which we must strive – the Platonic ideals of perfect beauty, perfect justice, perfect happiness – but must, for our own sakes, never reach, since to achieve perfection is death.

As psychologist Viktor Frankl notes, 'if all men were perfect, then every individual would be replaceable by anyone else. From the very imperfection of men follows the indispensability and inexchangeability of each individual'. We forfeit our imperfections at our peril. All of which would be strictly academic were humanity not, as we speak, teetering on the brink of making such choices for real.

'When will we have the perfect android?' asks Epstein. Ishiguro's answer is maybe thirty years to sophistication; maybe a hundred until we have an android capable of, say, marriage – but, he cautions, 'I still believe that robots will never be completely human. They may want to be, like Mr Data in *Star Trek*, but they will always lack some humanness.' The important implication is that here perfection means realism; the closest possible approach to imperfect humanity, not to some sort of ideal.

In a truly designer world, then, a world that was all 'pull', no 'push', which way would we go? If we can have any kind of humans we want, how will we design them? Will we make them physically perfect? Mentally? Will we in fact even know what that means? Will a baby be blonde-and-blue-eyed, say, or slim and smooth, if such characteristics are no longer rare but can be simply spliced in? Or will designer babies be born with, say, zebra stripes or sequins?

Choice and overchoice

One of the things we want, or think we want, is freedom, specifically freedom of choice. Choice is the god of our times. Building-use studies repeatedly show that office workers want control over their environment: choice of furniture, carpet, air-conditioning, lighting and so on. The internet is typically presented as a soldier for democracy, and even for truth, because it offers a near-infinite choice of opinion and content. Free markets and deregulation have become sacred because of the freedom of choice they supposedly bring the consumer. We wage war on countries like Iraq in the name, at least, of imposing freedom of choice.

Almost forty years ago Alvin Toffler predicted that 'the people of the future may suffer not from an absence of choice, but from a paralysing surfeit of it. They may turn out to be victims of that peculiarly super-industrial dilemma: overchoice'. Now this has come to pass. Between 1950 and 1963, he noted, 'the number of different soaps and detergents on the American grocery shelf increased from sixty-five to 200 ...' Thirty-four years later, in *The Paradox of Choice*, US sociologist Barry Schwartz counts '80 different pain relievers, 40 toothpastes, 150 lipsticks ... 116 kinds of skin cream ... and 360 types of shampoo', all in one modest store. The same choice-explosion, he argues, has occurred in education, entertainment, insurance, healthcare, cosmetic procedures and even religion.

Consciousness, explains Schwartz, is a kind of filter. Too many choices, especially of the small, insignificant variety – what economist Fred Hirsch, writing in 1976, called the 'tyranny of small decisions' – clog the filter. The cumulative effect is stress. People faced with too many choices feel overcome by a kind of white noise, comparable to the sensory overload experienced by autistic people in places of high sensory input like busy streets and shopping centres.

Equally destructive is excessive choice in situations where the individual has no means of making a properly informed decision. Schwartz cites postmodern medical practice, where general practitioners, having resiled from the old, paternalistic model and come to see their patients as customers, will address no question and offer no services other than those requested by the patient. This no doubt well-meant idea ends up providing a much narrower kind of care and a lower level of responsibility, in the name of patient 'empowerment'.

Even in 1984, physician and ethicist Jay Katz suggested this power-shift had gone too far. 'Patients,' he said, 'frequently don't want the freedom we've given them.' Patient autonomy, he notes, can mean being able to relinquish that autonomy and hand control to someone else. Patients, especially when seriously ill or stressed, are generally in no position to make difficult or demanding judgements.

Forcing judgement back on the individual is clearly inappropriate in situations of professional expertise. But much the same goes for many so-called choices proffered by governments as the 'exercise of market freedom'. The choice of private medical insurance, or superannuation, or even telco, is just as impossible; the plethora of choice, of 'packages' with incomparable features, means that making a truly informed decision on any of these things would require weeks of full-time study.

Miswanting

To some extent, the failure of desire-gratification to bring us either the pleasure or the happiness we expect can be put down to the fact that we want the wrong stuff. At which point it is interesting to note the linguistic shift within a century or so: in Dickens' time, want meant need. Now want just means want, a whimsical and more or less arbitrary desire.

Psychologist Martin Seligman was one of the first to document, in the 1970s, the West's depression epidemic, stemming from the constant disappointment of increased, affluence-based expectations. Barry Schwartz notes that America's 'happiness quotient' has been dropping for more than a generation, and Oxford academic Avner Offer remarks the same phenomenon in Britain: 'since the Second World War, and especially since the 1970s, self-reported "happiness" has languished … or has even declined'. That is the paradox of happiness. The things we think will make us happy don't and yet, like teenager in love, that only makes us want them all the more.

This collection of paradoxes has a name. 'Paradise Syndrome', an idea first tested in a 1968 episode of *Star Trek*, is the severe depression caused by having it all. Martin Amis' novel *Night Train* (1998) is an exploration of Paradise Syndrome, focused on the suicide of the beautiful, brilliant and beloved Jennifer Rockwell, who bails out precisely because the perfection of her life has become intolerable.

It's an extreme example of what US psychologists Daniel Gilbert and Timothy Wilson call 'miswanting'. Miswanting is what it sounds like: our tendency to want all the wrong things, things that are wrong not just morally or environmentally but even in their capacity to deliver the satisfaction they promise. Based on a faulty theory of what will make us happy, miswanting occurs because we are hardwired to mispredict both the intensity and the duration of our emotional response to getting what we desire. We think things will make us happier than they do, for longer than they do.

Gilbert and Wilson's studies show that even when people accurately assess the kinds of things that make them happy (social rather than physical factors in housing, for example) they tend not to make decisions accordingly, focusing on factors that are more immediate or intense (more 'salient') rather than the ones that they know really matter. Miswanting combines with habituation or adaptation – our primate tendency to acclimatise readily to particular pleasures, or particular levels of pleasure – to keep us in a state of perpetual dissatisfaction.

This in turn locks us into what psychologists call the 'hedonic treadmill', a constant round of wanting and getting, fuelled by dissatisfaction and disappointment. Princeton psychologist and Nobel laureate Daniel Kahneman extends this idea to the 'satisfaction treadmill', which involves habituation not just to particular pleasures, but to particular levels of pleasure.

It's all down to a mismatch between our conscious and unconscious minds. In the Vedic scriptures, desire originates in the soul, thought in the mind (or 'subtle body') and action from sense organs in the 'gross body'. Desire is the father of thought and thought the father of action. Modern hedonics offer a similar notion, dividing desires into 'instrumental' (the new Beemer) and 'terminal' (the happiness we expect from it). Whereas our terminal desires are hardwired and largely involuntary, our instrumental desires are front-brain. So the BMWs and the Seychelles holidays are our conscious attempts to appease, like idiot villagers, the wrathful gods of our unconscious. Miswanting derives from our conscious mind's failure to predict accurately what will keep our unconscious satisfied.

This offers some hope, because consciousness is educable. So the question is: If what we want now is all wrong, can we learn not to want it, and to want what is right instead? We are living out King Lear's heart-breaking self-description of having 'loved not wisely but too well'. Can we learn to want more wisely? The answer is that there are indications both for and against. Against is the degree to which our pleasures are evolutionarily determined, and for is the degree to which they are, nonetheless, open to change. (We know, for example, that we can 'educate' our tastes, not just to tolerate but to like, even crave, things that we know to be good for us – green tea, say, or celery.)

● | Making us miswant: the BIS

If what we want is all wrong, what is it that makes us want it anyway? Part of it is simple imitation. From childhood, imitation is our main learning tool – not just the sincerest form of flattery, but our best means of cultural transmission and another essential social glue. So, like envy, it is hardwired into our brain structure.

Tucked into the ventral pre-motor cortex of the macaque monkey are certain neurons, known as 'mirror neurons,' that fire during hand actions. The same neurons fire when the monkey observes those hand actions in others, and even when the monkey, having watched the start of such an action, is prevented from watching the rest and therefore must infer it. Similar mirroring responses have been noted in human brains. As Harvard psychiatrist John Ratey notes, 'the same area of the brain that responds to offensive tastes – the anterior insula – is also activated when one person sees another making a face showing disgust'.

Mirror neurons are one of neurophysiology's latest toys. If (as some still doubt) they exist in humans as well as macaques, mirror neurons may help explain both our relentless urge to imitate and our rather less reliable capacity for empathy. Imitation, of course, is the basis of much learning, most shopping and all advertising: I see it, I want it – to have it, do it or be it. There's nothing like watching Bogart to make you crave a martini. Nothing like the picture of the young couple in the red sportscar to make us think, almost without thinking, *That could be me. I could be doing that*. Imitation – the capacity and the urge to copy – also produces envy, which brings us back to the seven deadly sins.

Advertising is persuasive, but where are the buttons that it so adroitly pushes? William Irvine postulates a biological incentive system, or BIS, responsible for making sex feel good and wounds feel bad; for making sweet or fatty high-kilojoule foods taste good, and for making rotten food and many poisons (such as hemlock) taste disgusting. According to Irvine, the BIS behaviours are in-between, in terms of their openness to conscious control; less involuntary than the black box of instinct, and less volitional than consciousness.

At instinct level, and in evolutionary terms, most things that feel good *are* good for us, and things that feel bad *are* bad for us. Raising babies feels good; chopping off a leg feels bad. Mostly, though, we operate in the in-between, the realm between the unconscious and the will, where behaviours are neither wholly involuntary nor wholly rational. Rather, they're behaviours we can choose either to enact or ignore, since our BIS does not decide for us, but simply prejudices our decision, using desire to incentivise but not enforce one outcome or another.

The BIS, in other words, is where morality enters the desire system. Morality, you might argue, is our way of putting pressure on ourselves to choose long-term and enlightened self-interest, including a more abstract or public good, rather than letting the lower chakras hold sway.

In helping us decide whether to eat the chocolate cake, for example, or whether to be seduced, the BIS may mete out punishment (hunger pangs, guilt, sexual frustration). Alternatively, it may dangle reward, such as anticipated pleasure. It may pull in both directions (the guilt versus the pleasure, for example) or it may be unequivocal, making one or other direction so compelling that we find it difficult to choose otherwise. Crucially, though, the BIS still leaves the final decision to our conscious and (more or less) rational will.

This in-between land is desire's home territory. We desire to have pleasure and avoid pain. Desire, in other words, makes the biological incentive system operable. And just as desire incentivises behaviour, pleasure incentivises desire. Without it, without the capacity for pleasure and pain that are the primary objects of our desire, we would be different creatures indeed; immune to incentive but also dead to most of the cues that tell us we're alive.

One of the troubles with the biological incentive system, and one of the reasons it makes us so susceptible to advertising and emulation, is the salience factor. Salience is the intensity or vividness of perception that makes us much more susceptible to the immediate objects of our senses – to what we see and feel – than things we abstractly know. Salience is what makes here and now so much more compelling than there and then. It's what makes real estate agents so keen to get you in the house, not on the lawn; it's what makes us believe that the white-coated man making the flyspray on the TV ad is a highly qualified chemist. We believe what we see, although we know it may well be false. As essayist and philosopher Francis Bacon noted, back in 1620, 'things that strike the sense have a greater influence than even powerful things which do not directly strike the sense'.

Salience, then, is what renders us so susceptible to seduction of various kinds, including advertising. It is also what makes us consistently prioritise present over future pleasure, and consistently prefer future pain to present pain.

And this, in turn, is what gives rise to morality. The middle ground of desire is the moral ground. Without volition, there can be no morality, and without temptation – without, that is, our recognition that needs and wants are not the same thing – morality would be superfluous. Morality may be no more than a herd survival code, but it exists in order to counteract our constant and reliable desire to do, to want, to pursue what we know, at some level, is contrary to our own long-term interests. We invented morality, one might argue, precisely in order to stiffen ourselves against our own miswanting. Morality incentivises wisdom.

◈ | The fourth hunger

Much recent psychology has been devoted to proving accumulated intuitions of philosophy and religion – such as 'money can't buy happiness'. But if money, pleasure and stuff won't make us happy, what will? The new science of hedonics has moved from what US psychologist Sonja Lyubomirsky describes as a 'fuzzy, unscientific topic' twenty years ago to a marginally less fuzzy and distinctly more respectable branch of the discipline. What has it found? Largely, what Christianity and other theologies already knew. Psychiatrist George Vaillant, for example, finds that humour and above all altruism are the characteristic of long-term 'successful' people. Lyubomirsky is still studying, but proposes to test 'kindness, gratitude and optimism' as obvious strategies to lasting happiness. In *Man's Search for Meaning*, psychologist Viktor Frankl puts it thus:

> Don't aim at success – the more you … make it a target, the more
> you are going to miss it. For success, like happiness, cannot be
> pursued; it must ensue, and it only does so as the unintended side-
> effect of one's personal dedication to a cause greater than oneself or
> as the by-product of one's surrender to a person other than oneself.

One of the most interesting and forward-looking constructions of the problem comes from British philosopher and medic Raymond Tallis. Tallis postulates what he calls the 'fourth hunger' (the other three being for survival, for pleasure and for recognition, respectively). The fourth hunger, generated by our nagging consciousness of the unbridgeable gap between our fantasy lives and reality, is that craving for connection, for seeing clearly, for touching it and *being there* that we notice most when our other immediate hungers have been satisfied. And yet the commonest response to the fourth hunger is 'increasingly frenzied activity, usually involving consumption of goods, substances, entertainment or one another. More cars, bargain breaks, Stella Artois, orgasms etc'.

This is classic miswanting, since none of these offerings can appease this particular god. Two things that can are art and creativity. The best treatment for this 'wound in human consciousness' lies in music, painting, literature and, at its finest, philosophy. 'Art,' Tallis notes, 'offers an intermission in the otherwise permanent condition of never having been quite there.'

Art, unlike 'the swooning egocentricity of closed-off uncaring hedonism ... from which we awake to bitter solitude', opens us to reality. This is promising ecologically, as well as spiritually, since it not only offers an alternative to our increasingly routine orgies of consumption, but encourages us to find, awaken and employ our latent creative powers to benefit both ourselves and the planet. As psychiatrist Irvin Yalom notes, 'death-anxiety is least where self-realisation is most'. So many of our desires, we will then start to see, are more enjoyable when unsatisfied. Maybe, we'll realise, Jagger's 'Satisfaction' was less a lament than a hymn to the limitless spring of creative hunger. *I cain't get no satisfaction. Thank god.*

2 | **Beauty and the struggle for power over death**

It is only shallow people who do not judge by appearances;
the mystery of the world is the visible, not the invisible.

Oscar Wilde

There is a moment in Hans Christian Andersen's *Thumbelina* when our tiny heroine is kidnapped for her beauty by a June beetle and proudly flown home to impress his lady friends. They, to his profound dismay, are underwhelmed. 'Oh, she has no feelers!' they sniff. 'And her waist is so slim! She looks just like a human being. How ugly she is!' Thumbelina, suddenly valueless, is peremptorily dropped by her suitor and left to live or die by her own devices. Andersen's point is not simply that beauty is subjective but also that it is a positional good, whose value lies partly or wholly in exciting the regard of our peers. Without the admiration or envy of others, he suggests, beauty, like so much of what we desire, is valueless. Thumbelina herself is unchanged but, unadmired, she is worthless.

Beauty, of course, is one of our main motivating desires; we crave it in ourselves, in others, in our lives and surroundings. But why 'of course'? Why, since we can never agree on a definition, or even whether such definition is possible, is beauty so obviously something we'd yearn to possess? This yearning for beauty, as we have seen, drives Raymond Tallis' relatively spiritual 'fourth hunger'; but it also drives a good deal of very unspiritual wanting and getting: generating wars, motivating feuds, impelling thievery, sustaining balance-of-payment deficits.

The truth is, beauty has become a problem. Behind us stretches a tradition that expected both beauty and moral instruction from both art and religion; a tradition in which the nexus between the beautiful and the good was clear and, broadly, consensual. For the future, meanwhile, as postmodernism morphs into whatever may follow, the theorists generally agree that beauty and truth are both making a comeback, as quasi-objective entities, and this return to solid values can perhaps be expected to trickle from the pointy-heads down. But for most of us, here and now, beauty remains largely personal, wholly subjective and entirely unrelated to anything we might call goodness. The more we crave beauty, indeed, the further it seems to drift from our grasp as the world slides further into trashy mall-sprawl and couch-potato land. Which makes it all the more timely to wonder why contemporary culture, privileged in ways other eras and cultures could only dream of, finds beauty so damnably difficult to achieve?

We have our beautiful moments. Architecture gives us Kazuyo Sejima and Ryue Nishizawa's translucent museum in Valencia; Tadao Ando's Chapel of Light in Osaka; Luigi Snozzi's houses in the Ticino and Peter Zumthor's St Benedict Chapel in Graubüngen. Such buildings seem effortlessly to prove Stendhal's intuition that 'beauty is the promise of happiness'. But these are the exceptions. And while beauty is always exceptional, by definition, it is much less common in our built urban lives than it was, say, in Ancient Athens, Renaissance Venice or Enlightenment Paris. Generally, for reliable beauty we look to the old: to the Taj Mahals and the Afghan Buddhas, to tenth century churches and sixteenth century plainsong, to Chaucer and Shakespeare. Why is this, and can it be changed?

We don't talk about beauty much; not outside of thigh boots, Brazilian waxes and the soft porn of what Stanford academic Terry Castle describes as shelter-lit. In serious debate the very word sounds geeky and uncool. A critic who calls for a return to beauty in art risks serious rejection as a philistine. Not only do we no longer expect art to be beautiful, we regard beauty in art as frankly suspect and more than a little, well, suburban. In intellectual circles beauty is barely even respectable. Barely meaningful. Almost a hundred years ago Dadaist Tristan Tzara expressed a 'mad and starry desire to assassinate beauty'; and perhaps this has finally happened. For most of us now, beauty is not just indefinable and incommunicable but really rather dowdy. Beauty is old-fashioned, not least because, in stripping it of objective or moral import, we have removed all but its most superficial meanings. We have made beauty banal.

Catholic theologian Hans Urs von Balthasar says something similar when he declares:

> We no longer dare to believe in beauty and we make of it a mere appearance in order the more easily to dispose of it. We can be sure that whoever sneers at [beauty] as if she were the ornament of a bourgeois past ... can no longer pray and soon will no longer be able to love.

This chimes with some recent post-postmodern thinking on the subject. Philosopher Alexander Nehamas, for example, argues that the twentieth century forgot the essence of beauty, namely, love; that in rejecting love it rejected beauty also, replacing it with frigid abstractions.

The banalisation of beauty, then, is relatively new. Historically, beauty was to die for, inspiring quite as much piracy, perjury and murder over the centuries as hosannas in paint or plainsong. Personal beauty was revered by bards and poets, while in religion, music and the arts beauty formed deep wells that were constantly replenished by humanity's tireless attempts to transcend the mundane. All the great traditions through recorded time – Middle Kingdom, Moorish, Classical, Gothic – had beauty at their core. Is our contemporary failure to make beauty either a core value or a daily goal, our refusal to install it in our streets or churches, our entertainment or our arts, a failure of desire, of the creative spirit? Or a simple failure of imagination?

Traditionally, beauty was an aspect of goodness, even equated with it, as in Keats' famous 'Beauty is truth, truth beauty'. Einstein too intuited a truth–beauty connection, seeing his theory of gravity – well before any sign of serious experimental back-up, much less peer support – as 'too beautiful to be wrong'. Such an equation depends, though, on broad consensus as to both our moral and aesthetic framework. Morality, as society's essential backbone, must be broadly shared and, to that extent at least, objective. So, for beauty to somehow equal truth, our aesthetic value must also be largely consensual. And this, history tells us, is true only in traditional, relatively homogeneous societies.

Modernism blew all that away. Notwithstanding its universalising aesthetic, modernism liked to separate things – disciplines, city precincts, art forms – enabling each to be defined, quantified and scientised. Valuing depth over breadth, and clarity over fuzz, modernism simply quarantined ethics from aesthetics, treating any attempt to re-link beauty with goodness as ridiculous and countrified. Thus did literature move from being the Victorian era's primary moral carrier to being, in the subsequent century, mere entertainment. As Oscar Wilde put it, 'There is no such thing as a moral or an immoral book. Books are well-written, or badly written. That is all.'

Modernism, wiping from its boots the existentialist despair of two world wars, quickly concluded not only that beauty was dead, but also that morality itself was no longer possible. In *Seek My Face*, John Updike's recent novel on the artist-as-archetype, the Barnett Newman character Bernie Nova caricatures the situation thus:

> Beauty is dead. Impressionism began to kill it, the rediscovery of primitive and archaic art finished it off. Beauty and comedy belong to the same Christian lie. Nietzsche said it: 'Truth is ugly.' He said, 'We possess art lest we perish of the truth.' The only virtue left in this day and age is courage before the hopeless. The only art is one whose symbols will catch the fundamental truth of life, its tragedy. Primitive art is magical because it is shaped by terror.

It is this terror, and its aftermath, that has forced our retreat from beauty. Philosopher John Armstrong likens the twentieth century to 'a traumatized child [for whom] going numb and pretending to be brainy might seem the only refuge'. For a while, the old reserves of beauty, the old habits of loving it, held up. But now, at modernism's fag-end, both art and religion, beauty's traditional reservoirs, are running on empty. Religion, once a perennial source of beauty, is now principally a bums-on-seats business, competing for market share with every other lifestyle choice, from scuba-diving to virtual reality games, and striving therefore to be groovy, unthreatening, accessible and, above all, popular. It's not just the Calvinists, either. Even many of the old, pre-Reformation churches have come to regard beauty as elitist and intimidating, bad for the numbers. Sydney's Cardinal George Pell, delivering his 2007 Easter sermon in the grand sandstone-and-incense bastion of St Mary's Cathedral, focused more on attendances and popularity politics than on any sense of the enduring mystery.

Art also strives for popularity. It wants to be bankable, provocative and, if it's still possible, shocking. But not beautiful. As Tom Stoppard's Tristan Tzara notes in *Travesties*: 'doing the things by which is meant art is no longer considered the proper concern of the artist. In fact it is frowned upon. These days … a man may be an artist by exhibiting his hindquarters'. Affecting Warholesque vacancy, an artist may drawl, 'Oh, I just do whatever looks good, darling.' But he must never confess to striving for actual beauty. No way. Performance artist Mike Parr exhibits his fifteen days of urine in as many plastic buckets in a Woolloomooloo gallery; in Berlin it's Gunther von Hagen's plastinated body-parts; in London it's Damien Hirst exhibiting a bisected cow-and-calf, a bovine pieta pickled in formaldehyde. Beautiful, you might say – but the very fact that we *might* say it shows just how far from traditional notions of beauty we have come.

Even the now widely predicted return of beauty brings no plausible idea of what such beauty might actually be, on the ground. In 1991 US art critic Dave Hickey wrote an essay called 'Enter the dragon' which, in positioning beauty as 'the issue of the decade', was hailed by many of his art-world confreres as having, in Ronal Jones' words, 'flipped the beauty switch back on'. Hickey himself called his idea that beauty had made a comeback an 'improvisatory goof … that rose unbidden to my lips from God knows where' but, since then, other critics have hopped aboard, declaring beauty to be the 'new Lazarus'. For many, like John Armstrong, this brings an immense relief, as though a return to beauty might at long last signal the end of postmodernism. On the other hand, that Hickey's examples of such beauty – evidence, even – were plucked from Robert Mapplethorpe's fist-fucking photos and similar, suggests there's still a deal of redefinition to be done.

But – and here's the thing – it's not just the artists. We too are implicated. We may reject modernity's puritanical separation of aesthetics and morality, but it has become, like the Westminster system of government, a basic Enlightenment tenet. The twentieth century changed how we see art, and what we expect from it, probably forever. After Marcel Duchamp's *Fountain* urinal of 1917, that was it. Suddenly anything was art – and by the same token nothing was. A Camel billboard, a tape-bound construction site, a rotting apple on a table. That art was all around also meant, in a sense, art ceased to be possible. Even the fabulous velvety rust of a huge, clanking Richard Serra sculpture gives you nothing you couldn't find more vividly in a working shipyard. Then came Warhol, whose flaky I'm-just-in-it-for-the-money vainglory made art that much simpler, and that much more complex.

So it isn't simply that modernism put an end to beauty in art – failing first to value it, then to teach it. It's also that we, the art public, are no longer satisfied with innocence. Here, you'd have to say, we're conflicted to the point of being seriously messed up. On the one hand, we still apply the criteria from the days of beauty-in-art, distinguishing 'fine' art from its merely 'applied' or 'decorative' cousins precisely by its disdain for utility (implying an outright pursuit of beauty for its own sake). Beauty is not only not-useful; uselessness is of the essence. So ruthless is this distinction, even now, that anything useful is immediately downgraded to mere craft, barely worth a serious review, much less any serious footing in the art market. This makes art, foot-bound and doll-faced, the original blonde.

On the other hand, we no longer want an artist who can simply paint like an angel. Chances are a Caravaggio working now would be hung in some third-rate suburban showroom. We expect message; need it even. Message is what we feel as depth in art. But at the same time, as conceptualists like Damien Hirst and Tracy Emin roundly show, message by itself is not enough. Message doesn't move us the way beauty does. We are torn – wanting beauty, needing its transcendent power, but at the same time despising it; like some bedridden neurotic determinedly refusing the one therapy she needs.

Still, while among the pointy-heads beauty may be making a 'comeback', out there in mass-cultureland it never died. Out here, where beauty is still relatively innocent of anything you might call meaning, it's bigger and hotter than ever. Girls (and boys) smoke, starve, and get lung cancer in its pursuit. Girls become amenorrheic. Boys fight and steal, die for it. Marketeers fake it, businessmen trophyise it, car-manufacturers vie for it, governments vainly legislate for it. So beauty must mean something; something that, if not real, is at least reasonably consensual. Part of this, of course, is that personal beauty has become more than ever commodified. It has always had currency – women, willingly or otherwise, have always sold their beauty to the highest bidder. Now, though, beauty is not only sellable but purchasable, through simple day-procedures that either add beauty to nature or subtract ugliness from her. 'Get me some new breasts for my birthday, honey.' For us, just as for poor Thumbelina, beauty's commodity value is fully official.

Still, there's a nagging sense – call it Tallis' fourth hunger, call it intimations of immortality – that beauty matters. That there's more to it than a bit of shoved-in collagen or silicone and that, in some serious way that places it above mere commodity, beauty signifies. That modernism, in depriving us of beauty's transcendent potential and dumping us in what psychologist Ken Wilber calls the positivist 'flatland', has betrayed us. At the same time, there's that thin utilitarian voice wheedling that the last thing we should waste time and energy on, especially in view of pending planetary crisis, is aesthetics. This is modernism's nastiest, most reductivist moment.

But beneath it lies a deeper and truer intuition: that planetary crisis is as much symptom as cause. That this largely self-inflicted mess reflects a deeper spiritual malaise and that *if* there is a solution – it's a big if – it will involve some species-wide raising of consciousness. We need somehow to transcend our primate selves and find some more altruistic mode or, it seems, we're doomed. And this, potentially, is the role of beauty. Beauty is no simple commodity. For us, as for most peoples through history, beauty can be a vital connector, a bellows with which to fan the spark of divinity in us all. Essayist Alain de Botton, wrestling with this question and wanting to reinstate beauty as a moral force, nevertheless concedes 'the moral ineffectiveness of a beautiful house'. And yet, we sense, beauty can not only make us feel better but tempt us into better selves and better lives. Beauty gives salience, the difference between the good idea and the craving; the vividness that generates desire. Beauty is our reward, the carrot with which we seduce ourselves into goodness. Magically, beauty not only promises happiness, it makes us want to be good. Beauty incentivises morality, and morality incentivises wisdom. We banish it at our peril.

Beauty, power, connectivity

Ask any man in the street and he'll tell you: 'Beauty, mate? It's in the eye of the beholder, innit?' This is the length and breadth of popular aesthetic debate. Beauty is not real, so what's to discuss? Then again, if it's not real, in any shared sense, and not useful, why do we still care?

'Power' is the short answer. As any 16-year-old knows, beauty confers power – both on its possessor and on its possessor's possessor. Beauty is power, and power is currency. Which is why, as art critic John Berger pointed out, advertising employs the norms and conventions of classical painting in order 'to sell the past to the future'. We talk of beauty's subjectivity but, in fact, without widespread consensus as to what it is and who has it, beauty-as-currency would cease to exist. Valueless, it would find itself also powerless, no longer a tradeable commodity. Picasso's *Boy with a Pipe*, which sold in 2004 for US$104 million, is worth all those millions only because it satisfies some unwritten but still largely consensual code of the beautiful. Otherwise it'd be trash; some obscure personal treasure of the artist's great-grand-nephew's daughter-in-law. And this, establishing consensus, is what fashion is for: the latest look in faces or bodies, paintings or video clips, is the agreed locus of power.

Beauty, in securing the desirability or otherwise of certain goods or people, is a key tool in the establishment of hierarchy, a key positional good. We are familiar with this dynamic in the devotedly superficial arenas of personal beauty, male and female; also with regard to cars, fridges and mobile phones. Much the same goes for the *power* of the beautiful object. (Again, witness *Boy*.) Indeed, the surprising thing is the degree to which this value underwriting consensus does exist, not just in fashion, screen idols and glamour autos but also in paintings, films, theories of the universe, architecture. Every time we give an architectural award we assume a broad consensus as to the building's meaning and its (predominantly visual) value. That is, its beauty.

It could be argued that the beauty consensus is entirely fabricated in obeisance to two of our most primal human instincts: the coherence of the herd, and the establishment of an envy hierarchy, a pecking order of the type to which humans are so relentlessly devoted. As philosopher Mark Kingwell says: 'positional goods … are designed to create deprivation, and corresponding feelings of enjoyment in those not deprived, what Veblen famously called "invidious distinction through conspicuous consumption"'. Even so, it's hard to accept that our concept of 'the beautiful' could be wholly artificial, wholly subjective. The beautiful object, after all, can't be just any old thing; there must, surely, be some quality inherent in the object that we value for its own sake, above and beyond its role as envy-generator or exclusionary device; some quality that offers something we crave. In other words, beauty is desirable because it brings power. Equally, beauty is powerful because it is desirable.

Underpinning this circularity is the simple fact that beauty makes us feel connected. Plugged in. From our small, imperfect lives, it lets us glimpse immortality. And in connecting us it makes us feel safe. In buildings, as in people, the qualities we prize as beautiful are those that promise, at some deep level, to palliate our rich array of all-too-human fears. We love big-roofed houses for the deep maternal protection they seem to offer. We love how the serene and abstract order of the Parthenon promises an answer to entropy and chaos. We admire designer interiors for the sweet-nothings they whisper about the flawless and godlike lives that might, just, be liveable within.

This gives beauty its own power, of which the possessor's power is a mere shadow. The power of connectivity. Connectivity with what? For philosopher and novelist Iris Murdoch, it is a sense of the Other. Of some greater existence, call it truth, call it reality, call it god. 'Art and morals are, with certain provisos ... one ... The essence of both of them is love ... Love is the extremely difficult realization that something other than oneself is real. Love, and so art and morals, is the discovery of reality.' For Plato, a longstanding subject of Murdoch's scholarship, humanity was trapped in a cave, from which we see not reality, only its flickering shadows on the wall. Beauty's power, says Murdoch, is 'the magnetism which draws us out of the cave'. As EM Forster so famously put it in *Howard's End* in 1910:

> Only connect! That was the whole of her sermon. Only
> connect the prose and the passion, and both will be exalted,
> and human love will be seen at its height. Live in fragments
> no longer. Only connect, and the beast and the monk,
> robbed of the isolation that is life to either, will die.

Beauty and the ancients

But step back a moment. A brief survey of how, over the ages, beauty has been seen makes one thing very clear. Beauty hasn't always been skin deep. This is a comparatively modern reduction: ancient thinkers enjoyed an understanding at once more holistic and more wholesome, eliding surface and inner beauty into one. Our forebears have generally worried less about beauty-as-status and more about beauty-as-purpose; less about whether beauty was objective or subjective (since for them it was obviously the former), and more about whether beauty was a completion of nature or a stripping-down to nature. Whether, as a life-procedure rather than day-procedure, beauty was additive or subtractive. This became an important spiritual and even political question: Is beauty revelation, or merely decoration? Does beauty involve giving nature a makeover, or a peel?

Neither Plato nor Aristotle distinguished between visual and moral beauty. For Plato it was all relatively simple. Beauty was a single, abstract, ideal Form, of which all earthly beauties – whether found in literature, in artefacts or in lovers – were flawed and temporal copies. So beauty's transcendent aspect arose from the striving for ever-closer copies of the Form. Plato saw himself, the philosopher or 'lover of wisdom', as enjoying privileged access not just to earthly beauty, but to the Form of the Beautiful, 'absolute, pure, unmixed'. This, he believed, helped him apprehend 'true virtue'. Aristotle, although always more worldly than Plato, also saw beauty bound to goodness, even goodness of an imperfect, earthly kind. Aristotle's term *arete* conflated the ideas of moral, scholarly, political, physical and visual excellence. He advised anyone wishing to acquire arete first to mimic its habits and behaviours – to adopt the mask of virtue on the basis that its characteristics would slowly 'wear in' and create the real thing, much as aspiring Rembrandts were later advised to begin by copying the master.

By Aquinas' time, a millennium later, philosophers were beginning to distinguish between visual and moral beauty, and to recognise beauty as being at once objective and subjective. Drawing on Aristotle as well as Plato, Aquinas saw beauty's objective part arising from the object's internal order or 'essence' – what we would call its nature – while its subjective aspect came with perception. This is not so different from a modern or even postmodern view. The order of the world, argued Aquinas in the thirteenth century, is given by God, a spark of the divine; but such order only becomes beautiful when 'it speaks clearly and with no uncertain voice [but] to a human intelligence'. Beauty then became 'that which, being perceived, pleases'. This made human perception an active and essential part of the beauty experience. Subjectivity had arrived.

Nevertheless, the idea that physical attributes naturally denoted, and even generated, spiritual ones lived on through medieval times. The Middle English *vertu*, in Chaucer's Prologue, for example, sustains Aristotle's combined human excellences but adds a further meaning, often translated as 'power'; the perennial, irresistible life-force in nature. A century on again, fifteenth century theorist Leon

Battista Alberti set out to help drag culture from the squalor and superstition of the Middle Ages by setting a conceptual agenda for renaissance architecture. Alberti supported Aristotle on the unity of physical beauty, *concinnitas*, and nobility, *virtue*. *Concinnitas*, he argued, was architecture's reason for being, its essential concept. Alberti was careful to distinguish this, however, from mere ornament. Ornament, he argued, in his famous treatise on the art of building, could help reveal *concinnitas* in a building, but could never replace it: 'Ornament may be defined as a form of auxiliary light and complement to beauty … Beauty is some inherent property, to be found suffused all through the body of that which may be called beautiful; whereas ornament, rather than being inherent, has the character of something attached or additional.' In other words, beauty is deep; decoration is surface.

This was the inner-outer dualism that Shakespeare would dramatise and redramatise tirelessly. The dyspeptic adolescent Hamlet, for instance, fresh from his modernising, Protestant university at Wittenberg, warns Gertrude that his appearance belies reality: 'I have that within which passeth show – these but the trappings and the suits of woe.' Later, exasperated, Hamlet lapses into old-fashioned Aristotelian scholasticism, telling his mother to 'assume a virtue, if you have it not. That monster custom … is angel yet in this, that to the use of actions fair and good he likewise gives a frock or livery that is aptly put on'.

Eighteenth century philosophy sustained this idea of beauty as an amalgam of subjective 'taste' and objective 'disinterest.' Gradually, the interaction between the two came to be seen as the business of perfecting nature. This, it was thought, was the role of art: using the human element, taste, to complete, as it were, God's handiwork. The Abbé Batteux, for example, writing in 1746, defined the fine arts as 'choosing among the most beautiful parts of nature, to make of them a beautiful whole, which is more perfect than nature herself, without, however, ceasing to be natural'.

Still, this goal of perfection was seen as a given; the classical ideal, or Platonic Form. Neo-classicist Johann Winckelmann, for example, writing in 1764, saw beauty as a gradual approach to divinity: 'our idea of beauty advances towards perfection in proportion as it can be imagined in conformity and harmony with that highest Existence ... This idea of beauty is like an essence extracted from matter by fire'. Beauty, he argued, is therefore elusive. The moment we try to grasp it, it disappears 'like the best kind of water, drawn from the spring itself; the less taste it has the more healthful it is considered'.

At the same time, Enlightenment thinkers were exploring and developing this dualism, dwelling on the idea of beauty as 'taste'. Immanuel Kant, for whom the intent to give visual pleasure was the essence of art, argued both that 'the beautiful is the symbol of the morally good' — that beauty is, as it were, manifest goodness — and that perceptions of beauty are subjective and personal, or 'judgments of taste'. Kant's idea of 'subjective universality' has confused scholars for generations, but it may suggest no more than his concurrence with the ancients' desire to see beauty as something both objective and subjective. Kant's famous example starts with the beauty of the nightingale's summer evensong, where the discovery of a mischievous boy, rather than a nightingale, as the melody's source would rob it of its charm. (Some, of course, admiring the boy's imitative skill, might enjoy his version more.) The brilliant Scottish philosopher David Hume argued similarly that 'beauty in things exists in the mind which contemplates them'.

This eighteenth century idea of taste was, admittedly, rather more received and less subjective than ours, which implies near-total relativism. Many still clung to a universal idea of beauty, tied as it was to a universal morality. Even the nineteenth century poet and educator Matthew Arnold was happy discussing universal standards of beauty, and recommending people's education in these for their moral improvement. Arnold wrote in 1869: 'Culture indefatigably tries, not to make what each raw person may like ... but to draw ever nearer to a sense of what is indeed beautiful ... and to get the raw person to like that.'

Nevertheless, subjectivity was spreading. Andersen's Thumbelina story, written in 1835, predated postmodernism by 150 years, yet both Andersen and his audience were clearly comfortable with the beholder's active role in beauty-creation.

Beauty and the moderns

Modernism's commitment to strip beauty of its moral content was little short of revolutionary. This, certainly, was its intention. Deriding both decoration and morality in art, modernism strove to transcend the entire form-versus-content argument, but the struggle was riddled with irony and contradiction. Adolf Loos, for example, argued in his famous 1908 lecture 'Ornament and Crime' that the urge to ornament was a primitive one, which sophisticated modern people should be capable of resisting, that 'what is natural in the Papuan or the child is a sign of degeneracy in a modern adult [and] the evolution of culture is synonymous with the removal of ornamentation from objects of everyday use'. Loos' wording may have been a little extreme but his no-lipstick Puritanism was a stance with which the entire modern movement was broadly in sympathy. Beauty was legitimate insofar as it arose directly, without guile or forethought, from content. Form, in Louis Sullivan's famous words, should follow function.

But this was itself a moral stance, revealing a Calvinistic tendency to see physical gorgeousness as proof of inner corruption that sat oddly with the movement's avowed humanism. The truth is, modernism was conflicted on beauty: wanting it and not wanting it; seeing it as the authentic face of virtue and at the same time rejecting it as phoney, a mask. Some even went so far as to elevate ugliness. 'All deeply original art,' critic Clement Greenberg declared, 'is initially perceived as ugly.' Adolf Loos himself, postscripting 'Ornament and Crime' in 1929, insisted that his bare, undecorated houses (one of them, appropriately, for would-be beauty-assassin Tristan Tzara), which had caused a storm of indignation at the time, were 'now accepted as expressions of pure, functional form'. For John Cage, 'hiding beauty' was the artist's highest duty. Marcel Duchamp wanted a strictly intellectual art, all idea and no thing-ness, no sensual qualities at all. Roger Fry, building relativism into this anti-aesthetic stance, insisted that things were ugly until they were perceived as beautiful. Paul Cézanne and Paul Klee, both accomplished draftsmen, famously tried to strip drawing back to some supposedly innocent truth. Walter Gropius wanted architecture bare of all decoration or pretence.

So arose the idea of abstraction; of art not as a perfecting of nature, but as a stripping-back to some sort of essence, some deep, hidden truth that was beauty's real core. That was the idea. But what happened was pretty much the opposite, with art becoming so remote and inaccessible that most people saw nothing in it at all – no beauty, no threat, no subversion. Nothing. By the 1960s, as critic Harold Rosenberg put it, art had become so abstract and self-serving that 'instead of being an act of rebellion [it] is being normalised as a professional activity within society'. Pop art, especially as personified by Warhol, became the apotheosis of this view, living out Rosenberg's later quip that 'the artist's first creation is himself.' Shocking by refusing to shock, Warhol used relentless repetition to generate a reputation for originality and strove overtly, in Robert Hughes' words, 'to turn the art world into art business' – being all the while exalted for disdaining the very market to which it played. Nice work.

Plus, it looked good. Pop art had a profound effect on the beauty thing. Pop art made it okay, even among intellectuals, to be vacant, popular and venal – as long as you looked good. Subversion had nowhere to go. In architecture, the stripping-back produced abstraction, transparency, 'truth-to-materials' and functionalism, where function was expected not only to shape a building but be evident in its form and detail. Of course, this in itself was clearly contradictory, since abstraction tended to produce houses that looked like factories and schools that looked like warehouses. All of which made postmodernism, when it came, feel like an immense sigh of relief. In an atmosphere flavoured by Ed Ruscha's glorified gas stations and strip-development, by Reyner Banham's LA-inspired love of billboards, silos and road-culture, and by Robert 'architecture-as-decorated-shed' Venturi, Charles Jencks, Philip Johnson, Robert Stern, Charles Moore, Frank Gehry and the rest cut their variegated postmodern teeth. Beauty, by the eighties, was skin deep at most.

And now? Now we mark time, wondering what will come when postmodernism really does shuffle off. Even now, despite the much-vaunted 'return to beauty', art continues to reiterate conceptual moves that stopped being shocking decades back, and artists who show any serious beauty-leanings are politely shown the door to Hockney-land.

We no longer even crave a Caravaggio. Postmodernism has had its way. Art, like almost everything else, has become text. But perhaps it should count itself lucky. Architecture isn't even text. Gehry, now architecture's most luminous star, made a name in the 1970s manipulating ordinary, off-the-peg elements in strange and remarkable ways. In the eighties and nineties he played the same form-game in a different, more bankable way. Turning architecture into sculpture, he showed that form without content is not only possible but immensely, globally marketable.

Human beauty

Human beauty has probably always been prized – certainly since Agamemnon fought the 10-year Trojan War to retrieve his brother's wife, Helen, the world's most beautiful woman, around 1200 BCE. Ideas of exactly what is beautiful, however, have changed dramatically, with time, cultural norm and circumstance. Rarity can be a powerful determining factor – making cultures in regions and eras of scarcity prize plumpness, for example – although the line between prized rarity and ostracised abnormality can be narrow. Health is also a factor, often evoked by those wishing to explain beauty in Darwinian terms as a reproduction-enhancer for the selfish gene. Our attraction to beauty, the argument goes, is really an instinctual response to health indicators – shiny hair, good teeth, good muscle tone – which promise more and stronger offspring. An intriguing counter-suggestion springs from recent work by US biologist Dr Kristen Navara and her associates, whose study of house finches suggests that nature actively compensates the offspring of ugly fathers, in a manner that might be regarded as directly counter-evolutionary. The male house finch's beauty derives from nutritionally-related red-and-yellow plumage. Navara shows that in the yolks of eggs fertilised by unattractive fathers, mother birds deposit more embryo-enhancing antioxidants (including up to 2.5 times the vitamin levels) than in eggs fertilised by fathers with more colour-saturated plumage. The mother birds, it seems, are unconsciously compensating for suboptimal pairing. House finches live for only two mating seasons, so 'they're trying to make the most of the reproductive event', says Navara. Either way, though, biogenic arguments for beauty are finally unsatisfying.

Beauty's legendary and at times frightening power derives less from its reproductive promise than from its symbolic qualities. The Athenian siege of Troy wasn't about Paris or Menelaus' need for Helen's babies; rather, the intensity of Helen's beauty gave her a symbolic role in the lives of entire nations. Beauty's magnetism is generated by our belief, right or wrong, that beauty signifies nobility. As *Spectator* columnist Paul Johnson noted in 2003:

> prescriptive societies associated gifts of beauty with leadership. Handsome princes could breed best from flawless belles. That was why they were awarded the golden apple, and why Paris stole Helen. The good looks of the gods and goddesses reflected their membership of the pantheon – 'effortless superiority', to borrow an old Balliol accolade. Apotheosis demanded glamour, as well as conveying it.

It's not just the ancients. Hollywood too is addicted to the beauty-equals-virtue convention, appealing so habitually to our deep intuition of beauty as a portal into a person's inner moral universe that we barely notice it. It's basic marketing. If the good guys aren't good-looking, the movie will flop; not just because we don't like to watch ugly people, but because suspension of disbelief must work in tandem with our hardwired hunch, however suspect, that beauty symbolises virtue. There are exceptions to this. *Little Miss Sunshine* works precisely because the actors look like real, ordinary people. But, especially where there's a strongly moral storyline – in a James Bond movie, say, or *Star Wars* – we rely on goodness to look good. In much the same way, Miss Universe and Miss World 'beauty' contests are always at pains to prove their winners are law students with strong inclinations to charity work, this inner nobility being taken as the difference between beauty and mere sex-appeal. Our hardwired hunch, however regularly disproved, is that beauty not only symbolises but, in some mysterious way, *is* virtue.

We know this is nonsense. We know that the beautiful face may not represent any sort of inner beauty. We know about evil queens. And yet we go along with it. The huge uproar that surrounded the exhibition of Édouard Manet's *Olympia* at the Salon de Paris in 1863 – to the point where armed guards had to be stationed next to the painting – wasn't about any perceived physical ugliness. Far from it. The fuss was about perceived spiritual or moral ugliness in the muse's professional status as courtesan, her casual, confronting nakedness and her undeniable beauty. She was shocking *because* she was beautiful, and employed all the contemporary conventions of beauty, but with absolutely no pretence at virtue. Form, as it were, without content – at least, without the right content.

That was 150 years ago. And yet we find the idea of a beauty–virtue link hard to shake. Cornell history professor Joan Jacobs Brumberg tells of a young Jewish girl growing up in 1920s Massachusetts, who felt the appearance of teenage pimples reflected badly not only on her family's newly-acquired social status but on her own moral qualities. 'How terrible I am,' she wrote after a fight with her sister. 'For that I get another pimple.' And as the *Spectator*'s unregenerate columnist Taki lamented of his friend Charles Glass (famous for stepping out with both Goldie Hawn and her daughter), 'Charlie has the terrible habit … of seeing carnal beauty as physical evidence of spiritual beauty.' Or, as John Armstrong wrote recently in the *Sydney Morning Herald*, beauty includes 'touches of grace, in whose face are traces of kindness, nobility and wisdom. Physical and psychological beauties melt into and enhance one another'.

Or is this just what we want to think? Certainly it's what we expect – and exceptions surprise us: the familiar disappointment we feel when a beautiful person destroys the entire image the moment they open their mouth to speak; our delighted astonishment at the ungainly or unattractive person with elegant manners and angelic eloquence. Beautiful-but-evil characters, like Snow White's jealous stepmother or the malicious Cruella deVille, thrill us almost more than the beautiful-and-good; but they thrill us precisely because they flout our expectations that beauty signifies goodness. They break the golden rule.

And yet for many of us, the recognition that outward beauty is taken for inner purity, far from impelling us to reveal all, makes us all the more eager to buy it and stick it on. If the truth is not beautiful, then let's at least have the look. Hence the explosion in cosmetic surgery, always more valuable if it looks 'real'. K, who ran a Sydney make-up and deportment school in the 1970s, says: 'If I was going to a ball or somewhere special, I could spend an hour and a half doing my face. And when I was done, I looked like I was wearing no make-up at all. I looked as though I was just naturally beautiful.' This, of course, is the ideal to which many an art form aspires: contriving to look uncontrived. But when the artwork is oneself, or something like it, the moral issues become intriguingly twisted, partly because of our primitive and surprisingly persistent intuition that beauty is not just skin deep but represents a deeper spiritual or moral beauty. Or was Aristotle right? Might this external application of beauty actually wear in?

Beauty in architecture

Beauty, trashed by art, rejected by the church and traumatised by popular culture, is still, at some admittedly rather debased level, expected of architecture. Not that it's exactly delivered with the daily paper, and not that architects would mention the word in respectable (paying) company. But they still revere beauty. Most architects' idea of a good time is to get together and gawp at slides of breathtaking Mexican houses, Japanese temples or Spanish villages. No words needed. No explanation. Just the visuals. Twist and turn as one might, there's no way round the fact that architects, by and large, are the last remaining beauty professionals. Beauty is about the only territory that architecture hasn't already relinquished to other, more predatory professions. Beauty is the only thing no one else does.

More than that, though, beauty – or if you prefer it flavourless, aesthetics – is what makes architecture meaningful, what makes it architecture. Why, then, is so little of what we build visually tolerable, let alone beautiful? That architects still obsess so compulsively over the visuals only makes it the more mysterious that they produce so little of it. And the world gets uglier. Has architecture abandoned its core territory?

'When did architects stop wearing bow ties?' was the whispered question at Harry Seidler's Sydney wake in 2006. Well, when did they? In a dress circle replete with *eminences, grise* and otherwise, there were black shirts, corduroy jackets and collarless suits a-plenty, but not a bow tie to be seen. So the question, despite its wife-beating overtones, is apt, especially if taken metaphorically. When did architecture depart the gentlemanly mindset to become that saddened and compromised shadow of itself we see today? Could it have been the same moment that our excitement at a new development nearby turned to dread?

Certainly, the tie thing flags deeper changes. As Sydney sociologist 'Dr Garry' Stevens notes on his eccentric but entertaining website:

> architects always like to dress 'differently' … The bowtie, especially, has been the motif of the devil-may-care architect since the Modernists pioneered it almost a century ago … Architects like to project themselves as chic radical artists. The truth is that [architects] are the most slavish servants of those in power … No 'art' depends more for its existence on toadying to the good and the great than architecture. So how to project an air of dangerous radicalism, while in fact spending all your days doing the work of those with power and money? Simple: wear a bowtie …

In other words, the bow tie is camouflage, hiding the bruises of enslavement. Such an interpretation, though, ignores the bow tie's observed decline, neatly dovetailing with the rise of architectural enslavement. Even so, Stevens has fingered some part of the enduring mystery as to why built beauty is now so rare.

The answer to the core territory question is 'yes'. Architecture used to be about beauty. Now it's just about money. What has changed? Well, everything, really, in three revolutions: social, theoretical, cultural. The social revolution occurred when democratic capitalism took money from the hands of a cultivated aristocracy and gave it first to the mercantile classes and then to the plebs (us). This fitted architecture with an entirely new client-class, which is really two classes – the developers who build, and the people who buy. Neither of them especially interested in architecture, urbanism or the making of place. (In any case, the post-Thatcherite 'share-owning democracy' has made the notion of 'cultivated' itself pretty much irrelevant, since the developer-class now comprises almost entirely shareholder-companies for which motives other-than-profit are virtually inconceivable. The populace, meanwhile, is viewed as a bland consumer mass, all individual tastes subsumed beneath ever more conventional developer-wisdom as to 'what sells'. Even if an educated client-class did exist, there'd be nothing for it to buy, since the market works to a one-size-fits-all dollar value. And even if the developer were interested in a higher-value product, he'd be almost certainly overridden by the pension-fund board members, concerned only about dividend and profit.)

The second revolution was, if not theory-led, at least theory-coated. In the mid-twentieth century, design-meisters Le Corbusier and Walter Gropius jointly marched architecture towards an engineering aesthetic of bare functionalism. That they did not practise their creed made their preachings no less effective, and led, inevitably, to a wholesale burning of the books. Which was the third revolution. The people are not the only ones who know what they like but can't get there. In schools and academies across the planet, ignorance of the ancient (or indeed, modern) canons of beauty is profound. Which is not to argue beauty as a rule thing. It's more that old tenet that knowing the rules is especially essential for those who would break them.

The problem, therefore, is not just a lack of clients-with-taste-and-money, though this is real enough. It's that the knowledge itself is no longer in architecture's dilly-bag. Beauty has become an embarrassment, never to be discussed outside those inner-sanctum slide-nights where architects warm their hands against the tiny flame that flickers even now at the profession's core, blowing protectively on the coals lest the chill winds of commerce extinguish the flame forever.

In the British absurdist play *The Hanging Man*, architect Edward Braff hangs himself loud and long for fear his latest half-built work, a cathedral, will be mediocre. And perhaps that's what it'll take to soothe the tortured minds of the commentators – more of a life-and-death take on beauty. Perhaps, indeed, this is the bow tie's real significance: less sartorial pretence, more symbolic noose, proving just how deeply your architect cares.

Can beauty make us good?

Beauty in our built world is extraordinarily elusive. The more we want it, the less we seem able to make it happen. And the uglier things get, the more people automatically resist and resent any proposed development, and the more justified governments feel in sidelining communities to 'fast-track job creation'. Thus the people are left disempowered, wondering who gave the nod to each new monstrosity, and how such ugliness became so normal within a system where we all, theoretically, have a say. Why, despite our best efforts, immense wealth and near-limitless technical prowess, is environmental beauty, or even pleasingness, so extraordinarily difficult to achieve?

Alain de Botton puts a similar question in a different frame: Why is it we no longer trust our unbuilt future? Why do we automatically resist and resent the new house or town next door, rather than welcoming it? After all, he says, in 1770 or thereabouts, 'when bands of workmen arrived to sketch out the crescents of Bath or Edinburgh's New Town ... few tears would have been shed at the impending destruction'.

There is more to this habitual resentment of development than simple Luddite conservatism. A half century or so of bitter experience tells us that what comes is generally worse than what goes; new development is usually out of scale, out of character and almost always ugly. The reasons for this are mysterious and complex, and are explored further in chapter 8. Underlying this issue again, though, is the presumption that beautiful environments not only make us feel better but also, by extension, make us behave better.

Do they? De Botton presumes as much, writing of the 'theoretical affinities between beauty and goodness'. An ugly room, he reflects, 'can coagulate any loose suspicions as to the incompleteness of life, while a sun-lit one, set with honey-coloured limestone tiles, can lend support to whatever is most hopeful within us'. Indeed, he calls his book *The Architecture of Happiness*, and speaks of architecture's 'capacity to generate the happiness on which its claim to our attention is founded'.

The trouble, as de Botton is the first to admit, is that the evidence is largely against him. Even 'the noblest architecture can sometimes do less for us than a siesta or an aspirin'. And when it comes to generating goodness, fine architectural surroundings are even less effective, as the sheer splendour of the SS officers' mess, or of Nero's palace, shows. De Botton's characteristically charming answer is that while architecture may 'possess moral messages, it simply has no power to enforce them'. All care, no responsibility.

Modern attempts to produce moral benefit by applying visual pleasure have been notably unsuccessful. Take, for example, the attempts of the 1960s and 1970s to remedy social problems by providing cheap but attractive housing. In Britain, such thinking surfaced in the work of people like sociologist Alice Coleman, who squarely blamed the Brixton riots on the Brixton slums, and Prince Charles who, in a long and lachrymose fit of when-men-were-men-and-everyone-knew-their-place nostalgia, established a proselytising school of architecture and a thatch-and-picket model village that looked like an escapee from the set of *Wallace and Gromit*. But wanting architecture to be socially reformative did not make it so. In the end, most of those involved had to admit that social problems usually have social causes. People do not riot simply because they live five, or even twenty, storeys off the ground. Children do not turn delinquent because their mothers cannot call them from the kitchen window as they play. People do not stop rioting, wife-beating or shooting up because they suddenly have nice homes to go to. The Nazis were Nazis despite dining in beautiful rooms on fine china, and well-heeled doctors and lawyers live happily in Berlin in buildings that are physically indistinguishable from those thought to have 'caused' race riots in Brixton.

New Urbanism, as pushed by Andres Duany, Elizabeth Plater-Zyberk and the rest, is an update of this thinking. Cuter and more market-savvy, but no less naive. Duany and Plater-Zyberk's picturesque village of Seaside, Florida, actively encouraged the belief – or at least, the spin – that the enclave's low crime rate was causally linked to its architecture, rather than to its homogeneous WASP demographic. As *Village Voice* critic Michael Sorkin points out, the New Urbanism 'overestimates architecture's power to influence behaviour' even more dramatically, if anything, than the modernist tyranny it overthrew. Beneath a rhetoric of pluralism, tolerance and individual freedom,

New Urbanist towns, says Sorkin, depend on 'a labyrinth of restrictive covenants, building regulations ... codes of behaviour and engineered demographic sterility ... Dull as the suburbs but lacking their vivid underlying pathology, New Urbanism is becoming the acceptable face of sprawl'.

In truth, it takes less than a moment's thought to see there's no direct causal connection between environmental beauty and human virtue. From the Garden of Eden to the SS officers' mess, beauty has generated neither goodness nor truth in the human animal, and is entirely compatible with – perhaps even facilitates – evil. Equally, while crime may correlate statistically with environmental squalor, it is clear that the two are merely co-symptomatic of underlying social deprivation, rather than being causally linked. On the other hand, beauty clearly *is* good for us. Back in the 1880s, designer and social improver William Morris was widely ridiculed for insisting that a 'healthy and beautiful house' was a social improver as well as a human right. But there is growing evidence now that music and the visual arts can deliver physical as well as psychological benefits. A 2003 study conducted by Dr Rosalia Lelchuk Staricoff from London's Chelsea and Westminster Hospital examined physiological changes in response to music and the visual arts. Her findings showed that levels of the stress-hormone cortisol were 48 per cent lower after such exposure, while anxiety and depression fell more than 30 per cent, lending a whole new meaning to the words 'beauty therapy'.

How does it work? There's nothing especially new in the idea that the mind-body relationship is more intimate and more complicated than we thought. Even physical beauty may exercise power that is metaphysical or, for want of a better word, spiritual. For Stendhal, beauty was 'the promise of happiness'. Iris Murdoch, who as philosopher and novelist was much concerned with beauty's moral aspects, regarded beauty as a 'sacrament', capable of liberating the self from its ego-prison into the selflessness that is heaven. Beauty's power is 'the magnetism which draws us out of the cave'. This idea resonates with the mystic and Sufic traditions, where apprehension of beauty related to the achievement of ecstasy, *ex stasis* meaning 'to stand outside'. Murdoch and the ancients agree: to touch the beautiful is to stand, free from ego, outside oneself.

For theologian Hans Urs von Balthasar, beauty, truth and goodness – the three 'transcendental properties of being' – are mutually dependent, a triangular confluence whose intersection-point is what we call God. Murdoch, for whom these were lifelong obsessions, saw beauty as 'the visible and accessible aspect of the Good'. Poetics aside, though, the idea of beauty as therapy resonates with psychiatry's recognition of altruism as one of our healthiest, most mature and most long-term beneficial coping mechanisms. And while altruism has no necessary connection with beauty, the shared theme of disinterest lends weight to the possibility that beauty's therapeutic effects derive from its support of our puny efforts to transcend the confines of the self.

3 | Against beauty: the search for honesty through ugliness

This pleasure of being half-deceived ... makes [man] prefer truth disguised to truth naked ... man fears the truth as much as the lie.

QUATREMÈRE DE QUINCY (1788)

Truth may be seen as a bone that we, puppy-like, bury and re-bury in a thousand backyards and rubbish dumps – in poetry, painting and song – for the sheer, tail-wagging pleasure of finding it again. Even just for the joy of the hunt. Sometimes, of course, we forget where we hid our truth; sometimes we even forget there ever was a truth to find. Then we persist with the hunt for a while but soon, deprived of possibility, forget that there was any fun to be had and give up. That's when we settle down, head on paws, in front of the telly. That's when we slip into Blubberland.

• | Warts and all

Keats may be right. Truth may be beauty. But modernism's rejection of beauty made its search for truth no less intense; only diverted it neurotically through ugliness instead. Generally, according to classical art history, the onset of ugliness flags the onset of decadence. In Hellenistic Greek sculpture, for instance, and fourth century Roman art, the abandonment of the conventions of nature-perfecting 'beauty' for a warts-and-all naturalism is generally associated with those civilisations' decline. But decline wasn't the whole picture, even then. For first century Romans as much as for twentieth century moderns, naturalism – or a willingness to portray 'ugly' – was also a search for the particular. Beauty, in the classical canon, is generic; a question of rules and conventions, a search for essences. As Johann Winckelmann noted in 1764, 'another attribute of lofty beauty [is] the absence of individuality'. And where beauty is generic, ugliness individuates.

For modernist painters, the search for ugliness was a search for truth. After the fuss about Manet's *Olympia*, too beautiful to be a whore, Toulouse-Lautrec and Degas made headlines by painting prostitutes and ballerinas without trying to perfect them. A century later Picasso, who greatly admired Degas' 'pig-faced whores', developed his armpit-test for real painting. 'Is this woman real?' Picasso demanded of his friend Georges Braque. 'Could she go out into the street? Is she a woman or a picture? Do her armpits smell?' Paul Cézanne, a consummate draftsman, tried bitterly to *unlearn* beautiful drawing in order to smash cliché and reveal truth. That he never succeeded in this desperate attempt to touch reality did not prevent his being reviled for it. Nor did it stop Paul Klee similarly trying to forget his skills and draw again like a child, in order to re-learn innocence. This idea that cultivation itself had become a barrier to the search for truth became a prevailing *leitmotif* of the modern century. Think, for example, of Ivan Illich's *Deschooling Society*, and the whole back-to-nature movement that peaked, but did not end, in sixties hippiedom. This idea has become so pervasive that even confirmed aesthetes like former Australian Prime Minister Paul Keating believe 'that which is primitive is more pure'.

In the twentieth century's architecture, truth-ugliness was even more pitiless than in art. For Le Corbusier, the excavation of truth emerged as primitivist fundamentalism, in which everything from geometry to scale is justified by appeal to the primitive in all of us. This de-schooled version of Leonardo's Renaissance Man came with a full set of creative first principles to which latter-day humans had been blinded by generations of the acquired prejudice we call civilisation.

Bauhaus founder Walter Gropius, after an early foray into log-cabinism with the Sommerfeld House (Berlin, 1921), repudiated craft-primitivism for something much barer, more functional and more truthful. Much, in other words, uglier. Like Corbusier, Gropius saw the engineer as the ideal professional, unsullied by aesthetic education, driven only by objective reason. The architect had 'over-valued his usefulness ... the engineer, on the contrary, untrammelled by aesthetic and historical prejudice, has arrived at clear, organic forms'. This was architecture's 'take me' invitation to positivism. Positivism (with a little help from capitalism) obliged, and for forty years engineering and its anti-aesthetic ruled.

In architecture today the engineering look is unloved but, sadly, not departed. In the very serious world of contemporary art, on the other hand, not-being-beautiful is still a plus. Since the main function of contemporary art is to amuse or shock an audience that is routinely overstimulated and virtually unshockable, 'not being beautiful', as philosopher Paul Ziff has pointed out, 'needn't matter'. Ugliness, meanwhile, is actively sought. And not just on the fringe. Francis Bacon became world famous painting decayed, violated, blown-apart and putrefying bodies. Lucian Freud, who famously abhors glamour, became so glamorous that the likes of Jerry Hall and Kate Moss prostrated themselves on his battered studio couch. (Although even Freud has standards, reportedly refusing to paint Princess Diana before her death 'because, he said, he couldn't find the real character beneath the image'.) What makes Freud so sought after by the beauty-set? It's the quality proudly noted by Australian Federal Arts Minister Richard Alston in unveiling the National Gallery's new $7.4 m acquisition *After Cézanne* in 2001. Freud's forte, what he does really, outstandingly well, said the Minister, is 'maximising ugliness'. Well, natch.

Dave Hickey defended his declaration of beauty's rebirth through the unlikely midwifery of Mapplethorpe by insisting that such images, aggressive as they may be, exemplify 'transgressive beauty' pursuing truth through unflinching embrace of imperfect human life and unlovely human flesh. Bacon and Freud are other obvious instances. Critic Daniel

Kunitz notes that 'Freud attends to every lump and wrinkle with all the lingering care one would expect if he were painting an odalisque'. So is this our (perhaps decadent) society's groping towards its own take on beauty, a take sufficiently complex, edgy and contradictory for our times? Or is it just another denial strategy against the too-daunting fact that we can no longer make things, or places, we love?

Necessity, work and wabi sabi

But if beauty is truth, and ugliness is also truth, that puts beauty and ugliness dangerously close together. One response is a relapse into relativism, a kind of aesthetic despair. But there is another approach to the conundrum. It's called *wabi sabi*.

Wabi sabi? It may sound like some icy-looking green paste that shoots fire from your nostrils during ritual sushi, but it's actually a concept from sixteenth century Japanese aesthetics, loosely associated with Zen Buddhism, that some see as the next big thing in Western misappropriation of Eastern ideas. Next after yoga, kung fu, meditation and feng shui, that is. Wabi sabi is probably our best antidote to the reverse-entropy that is visibly affecting the textural life of contemporary cities; the relentless drift from authentic to synthetic, from down-and-dirty to schmick-and-span, from wholegrain to lip-gloss. From Paris to Singapore, Kings Cross to Green Square, from local to global. From wabi sabi, that is, to lifestyle, there is a push to model the city on the stainless steel, germ-free kitchen.

Wabi sabi counters this by celebrating the humble, the timeworn, the ambiguous, the shadowy and the derelict. Originally, *sabi* meant cold, or lean, or withered; *wabi* implied a socially isolated and cheerless state. Over the centuries, however, wabi came to imply a philosophical or spiritual way of life, while sabi refers to the aesthetic qualities of the object, including art or literature. To modernism's geometric obsession, wabi sabi answers organic form; to its universalising, mass-production approach, wabi sabi answers the particular, the personal and the idiosyncratic; to its emphasis on the slick and shiny, wabi sabi answers the crude, rough, the degradable and even the degraded. To modernism's crusading flaming-arrow of a time-line, wabi sabi answers with the dark, the cyclic, the mysterious and the seasonal; and to modernism's closed-box metaphor, wabi sabi's answer is the bowl.

Wabi sabi, in other words, puts time back into beauty; time as a friend, not an enemy; a piece of eternity, not a herald of death. This, the sense of eternity, is one of the qualities of which modern cities and lifestyles, in their desperate denial of time, deprive themselves. We build, and live, for the now, the moment; the short-term lease, the city of designed-in obsolescence. It is an attempt, perhaps, to see ourselves as the gods do: *sub specie aeternitas*. To see ourselves not subject to time, but somehow above it. This narrow hubris gives a shallowness to our lives and a tackiness to our built world that we feel without understanding it. Wabi sabi, by contrast, requires us to participate in time and space by being open to both. Hence the bowl.

In the shallow world of tourism, wabi sabi translates into something like 'authenticity' or 'local colour'. Wabi sabi is the natural ally of anything small, local, old or textural; all the dollar-valueless causes normally steamrolled by the capitalist juggernaut. Tourism, however shallow, is one of the few overtly commercial enterprises to recognise such values; we travel to see the real thing, not a plasticised, sanitised version. And yet, although we traverse the globe in search of genuine local colour, when it comes to our own city grunge, our kneejerk response is to reach for the bulldozer.

There's nothing new in the bulldozer mentality, of course. Modernism's attacks on inner-city 'slum' areas were driven by the same mix of motives the world over – expanding CBD, maximising yield and 'cleaning up' the poor. We're still doing it. Cleansing our red light districts, our drug districts, our bohemianism, out of existence. As if there's a refresh button somewhere to make it all innocent again. As if, in reborn houses with freshly-paved streets, people will drop all those bad habits and behave clean, like nice folks. As if you can solve social problems with bulldozers. And yet, we know it's not just doomed but dangerous. Just as we now know that you can over-sanitise childhood, expelling the very bacteria that give us resistance to ailments such as asthma and food allergies, we know, too, that you can over-cleanse cities. And that to do so is detrimental to the health of that city, deterring the very people – tourists and locals alike – that cities need.

In Sydney, the latest target is Redfern, the oldest urban Aboriginal community in Australia. Not community as in gated. Community as in real, living, breathing, historical community. But you know the signs. First there's talk of the place as an eyesore, then a 'running sore'. Then you know demolition will soon strike politicians as the only plausible solution.

And at first glance it's a tempting idea. A glance, though, is about the proper length of its shelf-life. Now, quite as much as a century ago, slum-clearance flags a deep misunderstanding. As Sydney historian Shirley Fitzgerald puts it:

> the idea that poor environments generated poverty, immorality
> and human misery justified the removal of housing which
> offended bourgeois notions of what a prosperous city should
> look like [while ignoring the fact] that poverty was endemic,
> and that demolishing substandard housing in one place
> would only encourage its emergence somewhere else.

The surprise is that we still need to say it. It's back to that old argument about whether ugly buildings beget ugly behaviour, and whether physical improvement is likely to have any social effect at all.

But surely, you argue, something needs to be done? Surely we can't just let the drug-taking and the violence continue unchecked? But the reality is, the difference between the slum and lifestyle is not hardware but wetware. You don't stop people peddling drugs, getting drunk or beating women by giving them smart houses to do it in. Redfern's tower-block slums are virtually identical to the white-collar yuppie towers of, say, Green Square. No, the causality runs, if anything, the other way around. Social problems have social causes; it's the behaviour that generates the slum. But cities have layers. And underlying the quasi-social fuss is a classic rich-against-poor big-city dynamic. The class war manifests also as an aesthetic war, a mission to rub out the city's last pockets of wabi sabi, to remove the eccentrics, bohemians, creatives and dysfunctionals who shelter in its folds.

For wabi sabi is dangerous. Always was. Sen No Rikyu, the subversive tea-master who took the idea to its sixteenth century apotheosis was, like Socrates, forced into ritual suicide at age seventy. It's hardly less dangerous now. To modernism's slick, synthetic monotheism, wabi sabi opposes the unpretentious, the overlooked, the contradictory. To modernism's unwavering forward faith, wabi sabi answers 'all progress is illusory'. Subversive? Sure. Then again, maybe, at a moment when everything we add seems to diminish rather than enhance Sydney's inherent beauty, it's time to wonder whether 'Onward Christian Soldiers' is the only tune possible. Time to nurture wabi sabi, learning to love the real, even in the very tyre-tracks of Mammon.

Authenticity and work

It was science fiction writer Philip K Dick who famously imagined a future in which sheep, real sheep, had become so scarce that only the very rich could afford them, so everyone else to make do with electric versions of the dopey woolbearing quadruped. Dick was fantasising, of course. Now, though, if you believe economist David Boyle, the fantasy has come to pass. Boyle's recent book *Authenticity* argues that we've all had such a gutful of virtual reality – of genetic modification, fast food, theme parks, e-dating, so-called 'reality' TV and phoniness generally – that we are gripped by a great primal yearning, a lust (his word) for real life. For real, honest-to-god, working reality. Hence slow food, geek-chic and a generalised desire for warts-and-all authenticity. This is what Boyle calls the New Realism.

Sure, it's a stretch to believe that authenticity will ever catch on in that bastion of the artificial – popular culture. But there is a craving for realness, all the same. Even in hedonistic Sydney, it seems, we've had enough. Enough of the hype, the gloss and the spin. In cities too, we intuitively equate work with the real. We know that real cities have never been just about having fun, or even watching other people have fun. Fun is absolutely a by-product of cities. They are, after all, fun to be in. But fun is not the driver.

We understand, for example, that in Sydney's Darling Harbour, that devotedly work-free precinct where you can't do anything *but* have fun, we were sold a pup. Such leisure-only zones have an irreducible flaccidness due largely to the simple absence of work. It's strictly tourists-only; Sydneysiders stay away in droves. The same is at the core of the working harbour debate, where the proposal to extract from the harbour all work other than cruise ships and cottage industry – anything big or clanking or salty or old-fashioned or *dirty* – will leave it loose and shapeless, a toothless mouth shaped solely by the random dentures of plastic leisurecraft.

We have watched with scepticism the sanitising push in Sydney. Cleaning up Kings Cross, expunging the grunge, filling every grubby warehouse and mossy cleft with polished floorboards, lifestyle canapés and Miele fridges. And we're wary, quite properly, of the same thing happening to the harbour. Cleaning up is one thing, but full-on napalming of history and culture is another. So we're torn: we want things safe and comfortable, but we've started to see that safety and comfort come at a cost. That reality is not actually like that, and that the cost of generalised comfort, even assuming it's achievable, is generalised denial. A kind of collective solipsism technically known as bullshit.

So suddenly we feel sickened by the sanitising itself. By the gloss, the hype and the spin. We don't want a city that is all wealth and white collars, all banks and boardrooms, all surface and no depth. We want to keep some realness in the city's central places; and we feel intuitively that this means keeping some work – some authentic dirty, smoky, grungy, old-fashioned work – around the place.

Or do we? Is this a genuine value or simple old-fashioned nostalgia? Is it *real* working reality we want, or just the look? This is important, since preserving the working harbour *for the way it looks* – for the tugs and trawlers, the Jeffrey Smart supergraphics of cranes and container ships, and the picturesque, seagull-trailed fishing fleet – to keep the working harbour for these, merely visual reasons would be to undermine the very realness we wish to preserve.

So what is work, exactly? What is the essential difference between work and play? Seriousness? Purposefulness? Not-being fun? Is work just whatever makes money? Could it be that the save-the-harbour mob is pro-commerce? Uh, no. Not so simple. The reason we equate work with realness – the reason we see a working harbour as a real harbour – is to do with necessity, the need thing. Work *has* to be done; pleasure is optional. So work brings with it a sense of useful necessity. And it is that, the sense of necessity, that we crave. The sense of unequivocal, undeniable importance.

And then there's the undiluted craziness of removing Sydney's central port facility, in order to truck everything back, making the big smoke even smokier. It's not as if it could ever be replaced. We should know this from the 1950s, when trams were removed from the city centre. The decision was taken by Minister Shoebridge who, within weeks of the last tram, took a job with the company that supplied rubber tyres for the buses. So it behoves us to examine our motives. To be aware that a working harbour must be a proper working harbour – not just a few little boatbuilders and sailmakers scattered around the shores, enticingly romantic as that image may be. To kill off the working harbour so that foreshore land can be flogged for fast-buck inner-city residential is both cynical and shortsighted. There will be no second chances. When the working harbour goes, it's gone for good.

A more fertile view springs from recognising the harbour as both nature and culture, inextricably combined. To restore it to nature would certainly end in tears; rather, we need to understand the harbour as a fabulous work of art. A work already of mythic proportions, but a work very much in progress, an ongoing collective masterpiece. Which means it's up to all of us to resist the sanitised, plastic version and keep working at keeping the harbour real, for everyone. No electric sheep.

◆ | Churches against beauty

It's not just our working lives. Churches too, for so long our main source of beauty, seem determined to snatch mediocrity from the jaws of transcendence. Everywhere, under every log and rock, nice old churches are being melted down into imitation dry-cleaning shops, nightclubs and ad agencies while the new, bursting-at-the-seams versions have the common-or-corporate look so down pat it's hard to pick them from the general high-street line-up.

And yet they're spreading like cane toads. The Real Life Christian Church on the road in from Melbourne's Tullamarine airport sits in a dry paddock, leaning-to against a discount Tupperware outlet with only a sign to distinguish it from a fibro shed. The Anglican Crossroads Church in Sydney's Redfern does a convincing imitation laundrette, while the Church of God of Prophecy in Darlington apes a 1950s haberdashery. Your average Hillsong Church looks about as spiritual as your average dentist's waiting room, distinguished from its office-park ambience only by the vigorous up-front merchandising; the Newcastle City Church, next but one to Fanny's Night Club, has the same low-rent crematorium-style aluminium-and-air-con look, complete with receptionists, blond timber and muzak – while the same franchise down the page a bit blends right in between a greasy spoon and a Noodle Boy. Paradise Church in South Australia was deliberately symbol-stripped so as not to signify 'church', while Chinatown's Central Baptist tags itself 'the original Star Trek'.

Nor is it just the out-there evangelicals. The dumbing-down is across the board. St Andrew's Anglican Cathedral now wheels in its altar as-and-if needed. The Church of St Peter Julien of the Blessed Sacrament in George Street dresses as a 1960s city bank. St Mark's Anglican, Malabar, could easily pass for pensioner housing. And the new St Patrick's in Parramatta uses a dog-leg axis, sideways entrance, central altar, too-flat-too-low ceiling and thoroughly horizontal aspect to provide the mystery level of a standard high school gym.

Why would it matter, especially to a pagan? A wilful dumping of eons of mystery and symbolism may be irritating, but it's their mystery, isn't it? Their symbolism, their right? Well, yes, but it's also cultural. The church of myth and memory is, as Rilke said of the tree, centre of all that surrounds it, focusing our aesthetic as well as spiritual hungers. And the tree, universal religious symbol, makes an apt simile since, from Buddhism to the esoteric *kabbalah*, the tree has for millennia signified centre, source and *axis mundi* (linking underworld, earth and heaven), as well as knowledge, fertility and life itself.

In ecclesiology the tree traditionally abstracts as both cross and steeple. These days, you're lucky to get either. These days, we turn trees into toilet-paper and churches into lowest-common demagoguery, pulping both through the relentless numbers game. Times when sacred music, liturgy and architecture were troves of transcendent beauty are long gone, good-riddanced by the ever-more-populist church herself.

It's not that church doesn't do Church any more – far from it. Hillsong, for example, promises its Yuletide customers 'awesome church' in the same cheesy tones with which Viagra retailers promise 'awesome sex'. It's more that church-as-activity has come to preclude church-as-artefact. So that now, although the corporate church is more publicly and politically apparent than for decades, the buildings themselves camouflage into the commonplace with an aesthetic language that is deliberately mundane. Not a steeple or stained glass window in sight.

But, you counter, isn't this Christianity's point? Isn't it good that the church should shrug off its material trappings and focus for once on content? Isn't this what that nice Mr Cromwell fought for? Well, yes and no. It may look like Reformation II, but the underlying theology is no New Puritanism, as you'll see from a ten-minute sampling of Hillsong's heady 'I believe!' group endorphins – complete with big band, stage lighting and dry ice. Or, indeed, from a glance at its shop, with Bobbie Houston's latest book, *I'll Have what She's Having*, titled for Nora Ephron's now-sanitised orgasm joke. No, the new church doesn't deny the senses. What it denies is the traditional role of abstraction and metaphor – beauty, in a word – in engaging those senses. Just as the Bible is increasingly literalised, so the material church is being systematically stripped of all penumbral and symbolic meaning. Why?

Populism, in a word. The contemporary church, without recourse to the stakes and thumbscrews of its bloodiest historic moments, is forced to pursue popularity. And popularity, it is assumed, demands ordinariness. As Brian Houston, Hillsong Sydney's head personality icon, says, 'We're not anti-Christian symbolism. But most people see church as cold and austere. We want it warm and embracing.' It's Mohammed's problem with the mountain: a problem to which the church's traditional answer has always been inclusion. Catholic *means* catholic, after all, because of the church's apparently limitless absorption coefficient, allowing it to envelop, over the centuries, a range of pagan ritual from Zoroastrianism to voodoo.

But this time is different. This time the core artefacts themselves are distorting under populism's gravitational pull. As South Sydney's Anglican Bishop Robert Forsythe puts it, 'function is creating form, and function is changing'. The church's centre, he says, is 'no longer the altar but the audiovisual suite'. Or in US commentator Leonard Sweet's words, 'Church architecture must [accommodate] screens ... The screen is the stained-glass window of the postmodern age.' Hence the easy alliance between the New Church and the McMansion: both centre on home-entertainment technology.

Such trends, needless to say, are American-led. As Ray Robinson, of American Church Builders, notes on the organisation's website:

> following typically American trends of one-stop shopping centers, the contemporary church often incorporates cafes, gymnasiums, computer centers and even rock-climbing walls and bowling alleys. These facilities are designed to increase religion's prominence in the activities of everyday life and develop a sense of community among congregations that can number well over 20,000.

Sounds harmless, if a little dull. Underpinning it, though, is a profound paradigm shift. Abandoning the mystery, axiality and otherness of the traditional Eucharistic church, the new church models itself on relationships. Human relationships. This changes everything.

The traditional, cruciform church plan can be read as a symbolic *corpus Christi*, making the altar rail, at the crossing or shoulders, a threshold not only between body and head but also between this world and the next; between humanity, if you like, and God. But the implied distancing and subordination (of humans to God) is no popularity cinch. So the new church exchanges vertical for horizontal, gloaming for daylight, otherworld for world; relationship with God, perhaps, for a 'community of relationships, where people feel at home and welcomed'. Church, it seems, may these days be awesome, but not awe-full. Monsignor Francis Mannion, president of the US Society for Catholic Liturgy, calls this phenomenon 'the cultural canonization of the intimate relationship'. Just as the workplace has been domesticated by the tyranny of intimacy (flatter structures, domestic feel, workplace childcare), so the church. Which explains why Sydney's St Andrew's Cathedral has no communion table any longer, no altar other than one on wheels, but an in-nave coffee table instead. Where to from here?

The two basic religious building types are usually seen as the temple, or house-of-god, and meeting house, or house-of-the-people. The Christian church generally locates itself somewhere between the two, a people's house with a god-valency at one end, where the material church and its artefacts are themselves sacramental objects. This falls foul, of course, of Cromwell's view, which saw any emphasis on the stuff of God rather than the Word as idolatry. And on the face of it, this seems right and proper. After all, as scholars like US sociologist Richard Sennett have noted, Judaeo-Christian culture is at root nomadic and unfurnished. Jesus was born in a stable, not a palace.

But it begs the beauty question. Is ecclesiastical beauty, so reviled by the Puritans – the carved angels, the wafting incense, the wondrous lilt of plainsong – icon or idol? Does it connect us to God? Or substitute for him? For St Augustine (and, for that matter, Plato) the physical beauty of sacred objects, far from being diversionary, actually conducts both the eye and the soul to God. Sennett calls this function of beauty the 'conscience of the eye', and it implies an important role for both beauty and distance in the theology of church design. This, however, is clearly not the mood of the moment.

For the record, I prefer Cistercian to Benedictine, Anglo-Saxon to Gothic, Gothic to Baroque, almost anything to the total, over-the-top barley-sugar Rococo of, for example, Fischer von Ehrlach's 1716 Karlskirche in Vienna. But even that to the high-street tax office model of church. Are these judgements aesthetic or moral? Is there in fact a clear distinction? Is the difference between icon and idol one of degree merely, or of kind? And where, in this urgent, moralistic stripping-down, do you stop? At what point does austerity itself become as much a mask as opulence?

Who the f... is Jackson Pollock?

It sounds trite. But how accurate is Keats' famous truth–beauty equation? Arthur Koestler recounts an anecdote of a woman who, finding her favourite Picasso print to be in fact an original, promotes it from staircase to drawing room. When queried, she insists that her judgement was revised on strictly aesthetic grounds, 'composition, colour, harmony, power, what have you'. The work was unchanged, but she saw it differently, because of what she now knew. A recent *New York Times* story, in similar vein, told of Teri Horton, a 74-year-old retired truck driver, who bought a $5 San Bernardino junk-store canvas. She and a friend would have used it as a dart board, only 'we never did get around to it', but the canvas turned out to be, probably, an original Jackson Pollock. 'Who the f... is Jackson Pollock?' responded Ms Horton. And yet who Pollock was, and the provenance of a single fingerprint, had the power to change her life, and her children's and grandchildren's lives, forever.

New York art eminence Arthur C Danto in 1981 put it like this: take three identical canvases, all square, all painted red. One is a famous minimalist painting, one a 'clever bit of Moscow landscape', and one a paint sample. The objects themselves are indistinguishable and yet the first is priceless, the last without value of any kind. This is not decreed by some oligarchy of art tzars but agreed to, without demur, by the entire art market: us. On what basis do we sustain this remarkable consensus?

Philosophers divide into two camps: the formalists and the contextualists, or modernists and postmodernists. The formalists, including early modern critics like Clive Bell and Roger Fry, held that a painting's aesthetic value inheres solely in its formal, visual qualities. So a molecule-perfect copy ought to be every bit as valuable as an original. But this is clearly not the case. The contextualists, on the other hand, emphasise the importance of external factors, including the work's history, theoretical framework and authorial intentions, in determining aesthetic value. What we know, in other words, is at least as important in determining our response as what we see.

As Harvard theorist Nan Stalnaker says in her essay 'Fakes and Forgeries':

> It may seem irrational that Etruscan statues long enjoyed for their beauty were removed from view at the Metropolitan Museum when they were discovered to be forgeries. But the contextualist insists that ... the forged Etruscan objects, because they are not genuine, may subtly reflect the culture and time in which they were copied in ways that misrepresent Etruscan culture.

So, is intention the essential difference between Danto's three red squares? Do the artist's purpose and beliefs imperceptibly inform our understanding of the work? And how are such intentions communicated? By tiny details of moulding or brushstroke? Or by the narrative tag on the wall? What if the paintings' likenesses were molecule-perfect and the *only* difference was in the blurb? In that case, and assuming the spectator still believed them genuine, could the forged Etruscans be shown without detriment? Why do we intuitively feel this exacerbates the fraud, rather than remedying it?

Clearly, there is validity in both camps. Logically, the formalists are right to argue that the artwork be valued for itself; equally, it is clear that perception is profoundly conditioned by knowledge. Appreciation of art – any kind of art – is impossible without an understanding of its place in culture and history. Seeing is a mental act, as much as, or more than, a physical one. What we see, and how we value it, is constantly shaped by what we know.

Postmodernism took this idea to the extreme, making all knowledge subjective and truth so relative as to be non-existent. This was clearly silly. But postmodernism's central question, which plagued all philosophy after Hume, remains intriguing. How much of what we see is conditioned by what we know? How far is 'beauty' generated by our readings or expectations of nobility, authenticity or truth?

The classical approach to the truth conundrum, as to the beauty conundrum, was to recognise both an objective and a subjective element in play. As essayist Francis Bacon noted in 1660, 'the human understanding is not composed of dry light, but is subject to influence from the will and the emotions, a fact that creates fanciful knowledge; man prefers to believe what he wants to be true'. But modernism, uncomfortable with such ambiguity, settled on a view of truth that was as reductivist and utilitarian as its take on beauty. Just as beauty became mere form, truth became 'a mere reporting of the facts' and modernism exhausted itself trying to make peace between its warring parents, form and content. Postmodernism, bored with the fight, took a 'what conflict?' stance, solving the problem by insisting that nothing is either true or beautiful, in any supra-individual way. That since all truths are contingent – on culture, context and perception – we all, in the end, make our own. For pomo, truth, like beauty, was a construct.

But this attack on fact, as modern philosophers like Simon Blackburn are at last pointing out, has had a corrosive effect on public culture, civic life and, perhaps more importantly, on our educational institutions. In Blackburn's words, it 'rots our precious civilization from within'. As GK Chesterton reportedly said, 'The problem with people who lose belief in God is not that they end up believing nothing, but that they will believe in anything.' Our loss of fact has been similar. Like children, we take refuge from factlessness in protective blubber. Which may help explain why now, perhaps more than ever, we are possessed by the authenticity bug.

Which may also be why truth and beauty are returning, not just separately, but jointly; and not through art but, curiously, through science. Science has sustained its idea of truth but jettisoned (or at least diluted) its positivism – the idea that only what is measurable exists – reinforcing its truth-search with a parallel pursuit of the beautiful. Following Einstein's insistence that his theory of gravity was 'too beautiful to be wrong', Nobel physicist Steven Weinberg similarly cites the beauty of string theory – the latest unifying theory of matter – as the most compelling evidence for its validity. And now, it seems, science has found, or at least intuited, the truth gene. Invited to nominate something he believes but cannot prove, Stanford neuroscientist Sam Harris writes that the neural processes by which we judge truth or falsity are also those by which we judge beauty or ugliness. Suddenly, our metaphorical intuitions of 'smelling a rat' or believing a politician to be 'a bit on the nose' may be, in theory, verifiable. 'Truth,' writes Harris on *The Edge* website, 'may be beauty, and beauty truth, in a more than metaphorical sense. False statements may quite literally disgust us.' Keats may have been right after all.

At an intuitive level too, realness seems to matter more, not less, as it becomes threatened. Imagine, for example, that you are entering the picturesque central square of a small French town. A carillon sounds. How beautiful, you think, remarking that way to your companion. 'Oh, it's not real,' responds your friend, who has read the Michelin guide. 'It's electronic.' Suddenly your bubble bursts. Not only is your delight in the sound destroyed but you find yourself looking around wondering what else might be fake – the gorgeously crumbling stone? The faded medieval flags? The very geraniums? Or take Phar Lap's heart, proudly pickled-in-a-jar in the National Museum of Australia. The fascination depends entirely on authenticity; some other horse's heart, or worse, some plastic replica, would, like the fake tool, exude no charisma at all.

Why does authenticity matter? If the work is good, or the carillon lovely, or the heart huge, why should we care about its origins? Why is realness so significant for us? Why is forgery such a problem? So long as the copy is sufficiently skilled and faithful, logically, it shouldn't matter. Logically, the pleasure should derive from the object, not its papers. But matter it certainly does.

Art: lying to tell the truth

Most conspicuously, and most ironically, truth matters in art. We no longer expect honesty from politicians. Even science is lengthening its leash. But of art, which never was supposed to 'tell the truth' in any linear or verifiable way, truth is increasingly required. Art, by definition, shapes, edits, invents, lifts, abstracts, colours, remixes, twists or embroiders fact to create something that is explicitly not fact, but imaginary. Truth is not the point; from performance peeing to online architecture, art is essentially make-believe. Making-believe is what it does. As André Malraux noted, 'the original work of genius, whether classical or not, is an invention'. And yet we continue to be scandalised by failures of authorial authenticity.

This hasn't always been the case. For classical artists from Phidias to Leonardo, copying was a way of life, as well as a teaching method, with masters signing works produced by assistants, and in-the-style-of or from-the-school-of copies often proving technically superior to the originals. Then there's the *nom de plume* tradition of George Sands, Henry Handel Richardson, John le Carré, Emily Rodda and Lemony Snickett, to name a few. And we're okay with all that. We've digested Warhol's triple-takes on mass-production and originality and we've survived, more or less, twenty-odd years of postmodernism's snipping at whatever meagre threads still tethered perception to truth – snuffing the author, blurring the fact-fiction line and denying the very existence of fact. So you could reasonably expect art, by now, to be well beyond mere veracity. And yet authenticity continues to make big-T trouble in the art world. It's not just that a genuine Rubens or Warhol or Whitely infinitely out-values a copy, fake or repro. More interesting are the ongoing controversies over transparency of authorship, background and material; as though fiction itself had some kind of responsibility to fact.

Clearly it's not about verisimilitude, the work's likeness to reality. That's not the kind of authenticity that matters in art. A horse painting – even a horse photograph – can depict its subject as a crested toucan, and all will still be well. No, our truth-concern is less with the object than with the belief structure that frames it; the authenticity at issue is authorial. A Whitely demonstrably by Whitely fetches thousands; a Whitely by professional faker Will Blundell is all but worthless, even if indistinguishable from the real thing. There is something crucial in the relationship between the author and the work.

The case of Helen Darville, for example, who as Helen Demidenko wrote *The Hand that Signed the Paper*, was complicated by charges of plagiarism and anti-Semitism. A large part of her sin, though, was pretending to be someone else. The book was a novel, and an award-winner at that, but this pretence, when revealed, was seen not as imaginative virtuosity but as a form of cultural snaffling that debased the work itself. A similar scandal erupted in 1997 around the novel *My Own Sweet Time*, written by white male Leon Carmen in the guise of Aboriginal female Wanda Koolmatrie. The book, published by Broome-based, Australia Council-funded indigenous publisher Magabala Books, won the 1995 Dobbie Award. Two years later, when its true author was uncloaked, the book was withdrawn from sale amid calls for the return of all moneys. When Aboriginal novelist Ruby Langford Ginibi accused Carmen of having 'ripped off' black heritage and culture, agents and publishers swore off him. James Fraser, Pan Macmillan's then director of publishing, said, 'We're blessed with genuine writers. Why would we bother with imposters?' But how can a writer be an imposter? Have we come to a point where only documentary, only lived experience is acceptable? Where imagination is immoral?

The art world is scarcely more forgiving. For years, painter Elizabeth Durack used her late-adopted, Aboriginal male alter ego Eddie Burrup as a liberative persona, enabling her to create an imaginative world quite unlike her own. This harmless imaginative feat produced a storm of accusations. For her sin, of alleged cultural theft, Durack was never really forgiven, either by the art world or by the indigenous community, despite choosing to reveal her own deception. Such hoaxes, said vocal Aboriginal magistrate Pat O'Shane, denote 'the depth and complexity of racism in Australia'. The work of Elizabeth Durack and Leon Carmen 'would never have received the acclaim it did were it not falsely presented as "Aboriginal"', says O'Shane, and to adopt a cross-cultural *nom de plume* in this way shows a dishonest desire cash in by 'becoming' the dispossessed.

But perhaps the real sickness is our obsession with authentication. Is it a moral concern? Or some undeclared urge to protect the market – as exemplified by artist Pro Hart's decision to foil forgers by micro stashing personal, database-linked DNA in each painting? It's like the drug debate. If authenticity had no snob value, there'd be no black market in fakes, and few such fakes to fall for. Is a fake Rolex less valuable than a real one, if it does the job as well? Is it, in that case, even fake? Is authenticity, then, just one more fiction sustained, like beauty, by a market determined to protect the scarcity upon which it depends? Or is it a queasy response to the remorseless removal from our lives of any fact-base on which we can reliably depend? Our sense of entrapment, like Hamlet's, in an unweeded garden that grows to seed.

We have always looked to art, from myth to music, as a reservoir of truth. This is what Frederich Schiller meant in 1794 when he said that 'truth lives on in the illusion of art'. And it's what contemporary British dramatist Sir David Hare calls the artistic paradox – that 'by telling lies we reach the truth'. But it's not ordinary truth of which Hare speaks. Not mere fact, but some 'higher truth [that] can only be reached by the curious stratagem of lying'. These days, though, we increasingly source common-or-garden fact, too, from fiction.

Film, as often noted, is the medium of our times. More than that, it has replaced fireside storytelling and the Bible as the principal wellspring of our collective mythology. And it's not just myth. Increasingly, as postmodernism blurs the genre-boundaries to produce docu-fiction, advertorial and heavily fabulated 'reality' TV, our understanding of what actually happened – in the Vietnam War or the making of hamburgers, the JFK assassination or the Holocaust – comes from fiction. Whether this is a reasonable or even fair burden to drop on fiction is a pointless enquiry. But how did this extraordinary, even dangerous situation arise? And why? Is it the result of modernism's century-long reduction of truth to fact, followed by postmodernism's reduction of everything we thought was fact to mere fiction?

Perhaps the last laugh rests with Hungary's Elmyr de Hory (1908–76), the celebrated subject of Orson Welles' 1975 *F for Fake*. De Hory, a professional forger, was such an accomplished producer of Monets, Matisses and Modiglianis that a genuine fake de Hory now sells for some US$30 000. Owners are now concerned about *fake* fake de Horys, of which a number are known to be in circulation. Who's kitsch?

4 | House as mask: only connect

Everything profound loves a mask.

FRIEDRICH NIETZSCHE, *Beyond Good and Evil* (1886)

Man is least himself when he talks in his own person.
Give him a mask and he will tell the truth.

OSCAR WILDE

In parts of Amsterdam the houses are so glassy that a casual walk in the street becomes an exercise in voyeurism. And sure, innocence has nothing to hide, but follow that string and you come to those mid-twentieth century sci-fi fantasies where naked humans commune inside transparent bubbles, permanently warm and well-fed, their every physical need met by one or other technological device. It's an appealing idea, the shelter that isn't – and not just for the bare flesh. Transparency appeals because of what you might call its presumption of innocence; its presumption that we can all achieve the kind of child-like, or saint-like innocence that is its own protection.

Then again, we've all felt the oppression of the fishbowl, where every movement and every flaw is ruthlessly exposed. We've all known the view so invasive you feel your eyelids have been surgically removed. Total transparency may be a modernist ideal, but it's also an established form of torture, from Bentham's nineteenth century panopticon onward. Humans crave interiority, not necessarily for mischief or even privacy, but for its own sake, the sake of in-ness. Perhaps it's a womb thing. After all, children especially love squeezing themselves into the cupboards and under-stair spaces, the nooks and crannies of the underworld dreaming. That the very word 'house' comes from the Indo-Germanic *keudh*, to hide, suggests there's something in it.

The obvious resolution to this yin-yangism is balance; we need both openness and enclosure. We need choice. But just how this balance should be struck depends on the psychology of that most basic human artefact, the house. On the self–house relationship and on what, beyond mere shelter, a house is actually *for*.

● | Pretty lies, buried treasure

Our word 'person' derives from the Latin *persona*, or mask. As contemporary Western culture becomes increasingly person-centred – prioritising the personal (over, say, the civic) throughout perception, thought, relationships and even religion – the idea of the masquerade settles into the very heart of things. As social critic Camille Paglia notes in the cancelled preface to *Sexual Personae*, 'Western personality thus originates in the idea of the mask. Society is the place of masks, a ritual theatre'.

Suddenly a range of familiar and even banal artefacts, from manners to make-up, to clothing to houses, appear as metaphorical masks: a series of layered, ritual disguises that we don and shed at our pleasure. The appeal of this metaphor lies partly in the pleasure of collective self-analysis, soothing as a mass nit-picking. And partly in the way the masking metaphor reinstates mystery at both the centre and the surface of a way of life that can seem relentlessly mundane.

But there's an implication, too, of fraudulence; of deceit. Masking is something we habitually see as a blind. Masking tape, for example, is opaque, designed specifically to prevent thoroughfare. 'Her make-up is so thick it's a mask,' we complain, meaning authentic connection has become impossible. So the mask-metaphor is generally taken to imply a view of personality as disguise, a polite-but-opaque facade designed to protect the inner or 'true' self from the outer world. Certainly, this idea of an outer armour protecting a buried and vulnerable truth is implicit in our normal talk of 'persona' as an adoptive self. It is implicit, too, in the Jungian psychology that has passed so strongly into popular consciousness, inclining us to see the dark within as 'truth' and the bright, outer, social face as a protective construct, a mask. A lie.

Such polarised thinking is a long-time Western habit. Dark-light, true-false, inner-outer, mental-physical, sensual-intellectual, Dionysian-Apollonian. It has the appeal of an order based on contrast. Which may be why modern psychology, from Freud and Jung to Adler, Laing and Fromm, has adopted the personality-as-mask metaphor as a standard. As Jung said, 'Fundamentally the persona is nothing real: it is a compromise between individual and society as to what a man should appear to be.' An acceptable front, nothing more. In such a regime the mask, on the face of it, becomes the very obverse of truth.

But the relationship between the hidden and the visible is not necessarily that of the iceberg. Traditional and tribal masking, from the Amerindian shaman to the Commedia dell'Arte and Japanese Noh theatre, has a more complex and more interesting phenomenology. There the mask is, simply, magic. Not pretence, not deceit, but real, transformative magic. For the lower Yukon shaman masked as the Great Grizzly, or the Zulu witchdoctor as a voodoo spirit, masking is not about resemblance but, in some magical way, 'becoming'. Here the masker acquires the power – be it for healing, exorcism or witchcraft – of whatever the mask represents. The mask, often representing the feared agents of death, also offers the potential to overcome those very agents and transcend death itself; to become, however briefly, immortal.

This transformative power persists in modern masks. The balaclava, for example, not only prevents identification but, in de-identifying, empowers. It is an invocation of the spirits; masked in reified darkness, his features obliterated, the terrorist feels himself transcend mundane morality, licensed to far greater dreadfulness than normal humanity would allow. In similar, although less sinister fashion, the masked balls of Renaissance Venice or modern Sydney free the dancers from their faces and, in so doing, free them also from their personae, bestowing the liberative anonymity usually reserved for foreigners. Someone 'off his face' on drugs is, similarly, outside the normal confines of the self. He could do anything. To be de-faced, even passingly, is to be, in some crucial way that can be either liberating or destructive, de-personalised.

So the mask, in its proper function, is less a barrier than a form of transformative, connective tissue. This connective power is what Arthur Koestler identified as the essence of the creative act: 'The shaman who danced the part of the rain god was the rain god, and yet remained the shaman at the same time'. The mask is therefore the Ur-artwork, paradoxically dividing in order to connect, lying in order to establish truth; designed less to hide the self than to merge with it, creating a new entity capable of establishing a new and transcendent connection. 'Art,' says Koestler, 'is an attempt to connect with the world. It springs from the urge to share ... and thus overcome the isolation of the self.' To achieve this, the mask must be not a simple barrier but a perforated barrier; a screen, that connects even as it divides. This returns us to art's essential paradox. Lying to tell the truth.

The same paradox nests within the words themselves. Latin *persona*, for example, comes from *per sonare*, 'to sound through'. Initially it applied only to the resonant clay mouthpiece with which the masks of classical and pre-classical tragedy were fitted. Tragedy, for the Greeks and Romans, was a catharsis, an exercise in self-transcendence. So the mask was named for its capacity not to hide an actor's identity but, rather, to create a new identity and a new, resonant inner-outer connection. Just as a small window in a solid stone wall dramatises the connection precisely by establishing separateness, the mask as mouthpiece was designed to let the player fuse with his adopted character and, transcendently, with his audience.

Mask also links to Old English *masc*, a mesh or sieve, emphasising flow and connectivity, the filtering and refining action of the mask, rather than its frontality; while a more tenuous connection to 'mash' suggests the gestalt idea of separate entities mixed into a new whole.

The mask, then, was less a deceit than a dwelling-place, an abode, a wrapping of the self. Perhaps in some way the mask stands for other wrappings we use to mediate the relationship between self and world; the body, clothes, houses and cities.

● ▎ Body as temple of the soul

The idea of the body as architecture, a kind of carapace for the soul, relies on the ancient but familiar belief that mind and body are separate. And not only separate, but of different stuff; the body material, the mind immaterial. Spirit, maybe. Many of us would take issue with this, pointing to recent science that seems to show all mental activity as electro-chemical. And yet, in our daily lives, we tend to presume that the mind is a kind of truck driver, sitting in its brain-cabin, directing the body through a number of mysterious buttons and levers although without physically engaging them.

Such an idea is immediately problematic. How can the mind have physical location if it does not physically exist? How, more importantly, can it direct physical events if it is not itself, at root, physical? This is one of philosophy's oldest conundrums, the so-called 'mind-body problem', in answer to which Descartes proposed his famous mind-body dualism. Dualism itself, of course, predates by millennia both Descartes and the Age of Reason. Being fundamental to most forms of belief in afterlife or reincarnation, dualism appears even in traditional Aboriginal culture, where visible spirit beings (like the evil Quinkins, or the Muramura of South Australia) have enough physical agency to steal children and create drought or general mischief. Underlying the world of action is the more abstract Dreaming from which these spirits arise. The Dreaming may be seen as broadly analogous to Jung's collective unconscious, a shared mythic reservoir, occasionally accessible to mortals, from which human souls come to embodiment and to which they return after death. In Rolf de Heer's award-winning film *Ten Canoes* (2006), the entire narrative of the Yolngu people of Ramingining originates within a mythic waterhole, where human souls wait as 'little fish' before birth and to which they return after death.

In pre-Socratic philosophy, dualism brought the idea of the soul, or psyche, imagined as a butterfly (the Greek *psyche* translates as 'butterfly') that flew from the mouth, liberated, with a person's final breath. For the Romans, too, the soul, or *anima*, was an immaterial animating force, a spark of the divine, in a physical world. A similar dualism infuses Christian theology, with its notion of an eternal, immaterial soul housed temporarily in a flawed material body – the body as temple of the soul. Some, like Aristotle, derided the whole question as superfluous – saying that to ask whether mind and body are one 'is as meaningless as to ask whether the wax and the shape given to it by the stamp are one', while modernist philosopher Gilbert Ryle has lampooned Cartesian dualism as 'the ghost in the machine'. But the idea of a mind or soul, that can exist and maintain identity separately from the body, persists.

Lately, the mind-body problem has been wrested from philosophy by the vast and tendrilled proliferation of neurosciences that have grown up around the nature of intelligence and consciousness. Most leaders in the field now agree that the brain and the mind are one; that thought and perception, and even laughter and love, can be explained in terms of chemistry, particles and electrical impulse. Neuro-geography has located many of our mental events on three-dimensional brain-maps, and researchers claim even to have found the god gene, responsible for humanity's persistent spiritual yearnings. The entire debate, though, is immensely complicated by Einstein's identity of energy and matter, which had meant that the distinction between the material and the non-material disappears and that energy, like light, can be seen as part wave, part particle, and even both at once. This brings science back to a perhaps surprising congruence with various strands of Eastern mysticism: the yogic view, for example, of 'mind' being capable of diffusion throughout the body, and the Sufic tradition of the single 'body-mind' entity.

For most of us, most of the time, the mind-body problem remains unresolved. For some, perhaps the majority, the middle decades of life involve a sense of fit between mind and body, but for anyone young, or old, frail or sick, the body as any kind of architecture for the self can seem a shoddy fit. And yet this reluctant and fallible instrument does become intensely personalised. You may curse physicality altogether. You may wish yourself disembodied, unencumbered by dull materiality – as if the thought of an immaterial 'self' even made sense – and at the same time put the finishing touches to your make-up, as though self and body were one.

Our emotions, further, not only have physical symptoms so familiar they have become clichés – stomach-churning anxiety, hot-headed anger, and so on – but there is ample evidence of causality working the other way as well. We know that physical exercise, posture and even facial expression can produce the endorphins that produce elation or the serotonins that make you depressed. We know that behaving energetically makes you *feel* positive; that the simple act of smiling helps generate the happiness that is generally thought to precede it. Indeed, entire therapeutic modalities are based on this behaviourist precept – that 'fixing' the behaviour will fix the problem. (In neuro-linguistic programming, for example, this translates into the tag-line 'motion produces emotion'.) It's an update of that old Aristotelian idea that imitating a virtue will engender the real thing.

More mysterious still are the legions of demonstrable and yet inexplicable physical symptoms of psychological causes. Psychosomatic and psychogenic illnesses, in which a childhood trauma, say, produces severe late-life stomach disorders, sound relatively straightforward when explained in terms of sustained fight-or-flight responses and adrenal overproduction. Even this, however, remains a mystery as to the actual moment of causality, the translation-point from emotional stimulus into chemistry. Stranger still are psychologists' reports of sympathetic symptomology, where the father of a boy burned to death in a car accident regularly develops extensive burn-like skin-blistering on the anniversary of his son's death, or the mother of a dead baby swells in a hollow but otherwise convincing replication of mid-term pregnancy on the anniversary of her miscarriage. It sounds like witchcraft. How, exactly, does it happen?

Documented cases like these lend genuine credibility to the tales of sympathetic stigmata opening in the hands and feet of the devout at Easter time. But the mechanism by which such 'miracles' are effected remains mysterious. Thankfully, we need not resolve this mystery here, but merely acknowledge that the mind-body relationship is more complex than that old default truck-driver analogy. The body is no simple vehicle, whether of a fluttering immaterial self or a complex electro-chemical brain. The relationship, one might argue, is more like that of mask and wearer, where the causality of the magic sieve works like a shimmering osmotic field, both inside-out and outside-in.

On the face of it

The point of closest approach between body and soul – the soul's most immediate *mise en scène* – is the face. Faces are the body-parts we scrutinise and remember; the face identifies and individuates. If personal identity resides anywhere in the body it is, we assume, here, in facial feature and expression. Faces are what we capture for driver's licences and passports. This is partly because, as cliché has it, the eyes are seen as the windows of the soul. But it's not just eyes that are important here. The world's first face transplant, performed in Amiens on Frenchwoman Isabelle Dinoire in November 2005, made world headlines, despite involving only the lower part of the face, because of the extraordinary contradiction that is implied in living behind someone else's visage. As the *Washington Post* noted at the time, such surgery is restricted to life-threatening cases; not because of the technical challenges, though these are real enough, but because of the 'potential psychological ramifications for patients in swapping one of the most personal and individual features of a body, which for many people is a reflection of persona'.

As primates, we cultivate facial recognition as a key survival skill; key not only in discerning friend from foe but, more crucially still, in maintaining the social relationships that frame the life of the herd. Within moments of birth, babies show a marked visual preference for human facial features over random patterns. We are hardwired to respond to certain stimuli and to read human facial expression instantly and minutely. Our brains also deal with face-recognition in a special way. Unlike most visual recognition, which the brain undertakes symmetrically, with faces we rely predominantly on the right brain hemisphere and the left half of the face in question. Damage to the amygdala, which is crucial to this process, results in a syndrome known as prosopagnosia, in which people still see and recognise the face but cannot associate it with the person 'behind' it.

So while the face may 'mask' the soul, it is no simple shield, since it must not just allow but encourage flow in both directions. Certainly the face has a protective role. It may dissemble and cloak; smile and smile and be a villain. More important by far is its role in facilitating thoroughfare; both expressing the inner world, and admitting the outer. To what extent does this thoroughfare wear its own facial grooves? Some suggest that the progress through life is one from the lucent transparency of childhood, through increasing opacity to old age, when the story of a person's life is graphically etched on their face. 'Through the years,' said Argentinian poet Jorge Luis Borges, 'a man peoples a space with images of provinces, kingdoms, mountains, bays, ships, islands, fishes, rooms, tools, stars, horses and people. Shortly before his death, he discovers that the patient labyrinth of lines traces the image of his own face.'

So we should feel little surprise at the human animal's long devotion to decorating face and head, elaborating their role, emphasising their significance. 'Economy in the matter of headgear,' wrote an anonymous Edwardian, 'is the last folly of the pauper.' This, though, was a precept rejected by modernism, with Adolf ('Ornament and Crime') Loos likening self-decoration to 'the childish babble of painting'. Loos offered pictures of 'savages' with facial tattoos and bone nose-rings but, crime or not, we're still very much at it, devoting ever-increasing money and time to elaborations of the face: make-up, sunglasses, haircuts, scarves, earrings and tattoos, and headwear of all kinds, including the religious kind. As American shopping guru Paco Underhill remarks, 'nose and toes ... are the area that matter most. The extremes – the face and hair and the feet'.

Thinking on decoration is surprisingly thin. In architectural theory, the most interesting contributors are still from nineteenth century theory, before decoration lost its moral and political significance – indeed, its right to exist at all. For the immensely influential John Ruskin, and those who followed him like Geoffrey Scott, decoration had a real role in architecture but should – and he meant this morally –

work to reveal structure rather than hide it. This was important, in that it gave decoration a role in truthfulness, convincing Ruskin, at least, of Gothic architecture's natural superiority over the classical.

Applied to facial decoration, Ruskin's idea goes to June Dally Watkins' point, in the 1969 *Book of Manners for Moderns*, that 'it isn't so long ago, since the use of make-up was considered immoral. No self-respecting girl in 1910 would have dared to appear in public with so much as a trace of lipstick'. This moralising was partly about authenticity, the rights and wrongs of interfering with God's handiwork. And partly about sex. *Manners* continues, 'it was the fathers and brothers who opposed [the use of make-up] in polite circles with such vehemence, while expecting and anticipating its use in naughty saloons'. Of course, such a Talibanesque arrangement had not always held, as the use of make-up by women from Cleopatra to Queen Elizabeth I to eighteenth century courtesans demonstrates. In America, and by extension the American empire, the change came about through the influence of Hollywood, as girls of the 1920s strove to emulate the glamorous faces they saw on screen. It was that mirror neuron again, and it meant that the same modern century that prohibited decoration in architecture, and made abstraction mandatory in painting and sculpture, also demanded less and less abstraction – more and more re-presentation – in feminine beauty.

So whereas in 1910 looking sexy was not respectable, nowadays not to look sexy is considered a sign of abject failure. For many women, and a few men, it is impossible to go beyond the front gate unpainted. Make-up becomes a kind of war-paint; empowering the wearer for the social and sexual battlefield. But for make-up to work its mask-magic it must enhance and intensify rather than obliterate the face beneath, emphasising structure, function and particularities. Special attention, as any women's magazine will advise, must be paid to eyes and mouth, those all-important perforations, in order to enhance connectivity, rather than substitute a simulacrum.

This distinction recalls the theological notion, central to the Reformation, that beauty can act either as a conduit to truth or as a barrier to it; icon or painted idol. But British writer Geoffrey Scott's nineteenth century advice is also pertinent; that what matters is not being honest, but looking it. This is the ideal of many an art form – contriving to look uncontrived.

◦ | Clothed and in his right mind

Once it was jeans and miniskirts; now it's veils and headscarves. We think we've become so clothing-tolerant and yet the post-9/11 Battle of the Burqa, waged throughout Western culture, shoved the old sixties issue right back onto the political stage. This time, though, it was back-to-front. Instead of rigid-orthodoxy-resists-wild-youth, it's become a story of orthodoxy wanting to embrace difference and reject repression but finding itself trapped between opposing hypocrisies, between repressing repression and tolerating intolerance. In Sydney, the unease was whipped to a frenzy in 2006 by Sheik Taj el-Din al-Hilaly's infamous 'uncovered meat' comment, suggesting that female rape victims should themselves be jailed for life for inviting the crime through their manner of dress. It was intemperate and inflammatory – but it also made obvious something we have been trying to deny. Clothing signifies.

It signifies in three ways; symbolic, behavioural and connective. That is, expressive, formative and masked. The symbolic function of clothing is probably the most obvious. From the Bondi lifesaver to the Ku Klux Klanner, the symbolic or expressive value of clothes is universal. All clothes, not just formal or religious regalia, have social, sexual and political significance which we manipulate with extraordinary subtlety and to remarkable effect. Much of this is in the relationship with the wearer, and our perception of that relationship, so that the same drip-dry shirt can look sad and ignorant on a decrepit old man or like clever ironic commentary on a young one.

Behaviourally, though – which is to say, with the causality turned inwards – the effect of clothing is every bit as marked. As the *Spectator*'s Petronella Wyatt observes:

> I live my clothes. When I bought a designer dress last summer
> I did so because its forties style made me think of women like
> Rita Hayworth and Dorothy Parker or heroines out of Raymond

Chandler, who spent their lives in semi-misery. As soon as I put on this dress I felt sad and wronged for two days...an outfit to drink gin in and then throw oneself over the nearest bridge ... In Italy I bought a genuine Borsalino ... as soon as I touch this hat I start talking slang out of the corner of my mouth, smoking cigarettes and turning up the collar of my coat. ... Clothes are made to create a new identity.

And they do. For women in particular, perhaps, but to some extent for pretty much everyone, clothes are fundamental to the fantasy life, or interior narrative, with which we sustain the necessary illusion of immortality.

This is why we love them; clothes renew and remake us. When Lear's mad rage has passed his servants 'put fresh garments on him', in order not just to signal recovery but to generate it. In dressing up, or dressing down, we acquire new selves and liberate old ones. These alternative selves can be opaque and fraudulent but more often, and more usefully, the second skin expresses an alternative truth, freeing the vulnerable self within to connect in new ways. And this is clothing's connective role, at once expressive and formative. Clothing is the ancient art of concealing and revealing the body in a single gesture. This paradox is crucial. Clothes, like masks, protect *in order* to help us connect.

In my father's house

The house, too, can be seen as a mask, a surrogate self, a marker of one's place in the ordered world. The identification of house and self goes way back. In part, this is gender-specific. The house as lover and mother – dark, receptive interior, a protective, warm and shadowy environment in which a man may sleep, may remove his mask and be vulnerable, runs throughout myth and literature. Czech poet OV de Milosz captures this sentiment: 'I say, mother. My thoughts are of you, oh, House. House of the lovely dark summers of my childhood'.

Japanese writer Jun'ichiro Tanizaki speaks similarly of the bodily identification of woman and house. For Japanese women, he says, life outside the house was barely conceivable. In traditional Bunraku puppet theatre, therefore, the female

> consists only of a head and a pair of hands [since] a woman of the past did indeed exist only from the collar up and the sleeves out; the rest of her remained hidden in darkness. A woman ... of society seldom left her house, and when she did she shielded herself from the gaze of the public in the dark recesses of her palanquin. Most of her life was spent in the twilight of a single house, shrouded day and night in gloom.

Sociologist Richard Sennett points our that in Ancient Greek cities, although male nakedness was commonplace and admired, women 'did not show themselves naked in the city; more, they were usually confined to the interiors of house, as though the lightless interior more suited their physiology than did the open spaces of the sun'. For DH Lawrence, deeply influenced by Nietzche, women 'be' while men 'do'; women represent a centred stillness, belonging to men's night-time, wherein they await the man's return from the day. Jung, similarly, saw the house as a nest, with woman sitting inside while man 'perches on the edge and looks about and attends to all outside business'.

The association here is not just with the interiority of the house, but with its role as a centre of fecundity; house as womb. Theorists point to the roundness and interiority of many traditional dwelling-types, from the teepee to the conical stone 'beehive huts' of ancient Scotland and to the etymological link with the hide. The Latin word for 'hearth', notes critic Margaret Visser, is *focus*; and the centrality of the cooking hearth to the house arises not just from woman's traditional role as cook, but also from a natural association of food and fecundity.

The image of woman closeted in domesticity is, of course, something that feminism roundly rejects. But even when we jettison gender bias, the association of house and self is undeniable. Not only are we hardwired, it seems, to respond intuitively (if at a relatively primitive level) to buildings with anthropomorphic appeal – instinctively liking symmetrical facades with two windows and door, or two eyes and a mouth, much like a child's drawing of 'house'.

As Alain de Botton notes, many of the world's most famous houses, like Palladio's Villa Rotonda near Vicenza, were conceived as idealised self-portraits which act as a suit of armour (or mask), an idealised, inspirational self into and through which the original or 'real' self can grow. The eighteenth century philosopher Giambattista Vico extended this idea, saying of the Romans, 'under the person or mask of the father of the family were concealed all his children and servants'. It's not just the house, either. Traditionally, office buildings have had a similar function, providing a permanent public face or façade that represents the 'wearer' in a way that is not just vainglory but also a kind of generosity towards the public realm and the joint project we call culture. The façade informs internal behaviour even as it offers 'readings' to the outside world. We shape our buildings, said Churchill, and they shape us.

Contemporary buildings, like contemporary clothes, bother less and less with this public-face role. This is partly a result of speculative culture, where buildings are made deliberately anonymous so they can be bought or sold at will. Partly an acquired track-suit mindset that bespeaks the invasion of the personal, mentioned earlier. And partly a product of our modernist addiction to low-rent building techniques. But if a building embodies no value other than dollar-value, what is its subliminal message, either to the public realm or to its inhabitants?

Then again, any message is better than no message, and any connection better than none. Ideally, the house offers a protective arena, a refuge within which we can safely be unmasked and private. These days, as the world becomes more bewildering, there is an understandable temptation to withdraw entirely into the refuge and stay there. As women's sense of entrapment shows, however, the moment the flow stops, the refuge becomes the prison. Which is why the fully-shrouded burqa-clad blankness of buildings like supermarkets and telephone exchanges is so offensive. Maskless, featureless, these are buildings of total erasure. This facelessness offends on three counts: behaviourally, connectively and symbolically. In prohibiting public engagement it is a behaviour modifier equal to footbinding. In all but prohibiting flow it breaks the life-giving connectivity rule. And in obliterating the expressive persona it implies not only the chattelisation of the wearer but a contempt for public culture that seems to deny humanity itself.

If architecture, then, is a mask, and the house is a hide, what are we to make of modernism's all-out push towards transparency?

Modernist architecture was consciously rational, geometric and masculine; in Nietzchean terms, consciously Apollonian. It was also explicitly revolutionary; committed to overturning the entire apparatus of history in pursuit of the godlike 'truth'. And it was in this pursuit that transparency became architecture's favourite device. They were all at it. In 1914 Paul Scheerbart wrote *Glasarchitektur*, describing the horrors of poor, cold, masonry Europe and the *Backsteinbazillus*, the brick-bug, that he believed inhabited the very fabric of the place. 'If we wish to raise our culture to a higher plane,' argued Scheerbart, '[we must] remove the sense of enclosure from the spaces where we live … not through a couple of windows but … through whole walls of coloured glass.'

Walter Gropius, writing the first Bauhaus Proclamation of 1919, described architecture as 'rising to heaven … the crystal symbol of the new faith in the future'. In 1923 Le Corbusier defined architecture as 'the masterly, correct and magnificent play of volumes brought together in light', and in 1927 Bruno Taut argued, 'glass brings us the New Age; brick-culture does us nothing but harm'. Even crusty old Frank Lloyd Wright argued in 1931 that 'in true modern architecture, the sense of surface and mass disappears in light'. When, in 1929, Hungarian theorist Lazlo Maholy-Nagy finally dragooned the term 'transparency' to describe the transcendent and dreamlike visions that were starting to colonise architectural discourse, clarity, light and movement became adopted as the currency of the century.

Transparency permeated modern architecture at every level, and glass was its obvious medium. At a practical level, in line with the health and hygiene push of the time, glass welcomed light, air, and a sense of spaciousness. Constructionally, it enabled the clear separation of cladding and structure – of bones, if you will, and skin – facilitating the 'honesty of expression' so prized by modern architects. Spatially, glass supported a cubist treatment, allowing the flow and interpenetration essential to the cubist illusion of multiple viewpoints. Socially, the open plan became a metaphor for democratic and egalitarian ideals. Visually it brought an exciting kineticism. Intellectually it promised all the Enlightenment goods – rationality, clarity, objective evidentiary practice. And spiritually it promised nothing less than truth and beauty.

It was intoxicating stuff, so ground-shifting it's hard to imagine what drove architecture before transparency became the grail. So habitually do we, even now, expect a house to be filled with sun and air – maximising flow, exploiting view and engaging nature – that it is easy to forget that the entire transparency-dreaming was not only unheard of but unthought of by architects little more than a century ago. Even for proto-moderns such as Edwin Lutyens and Louis Sullivan, for example, architecture pursued a whole different set of (essentially static) precepts; composition, graciousness, grandeur. Not openness, not flow, certainly not transparency.

The dream itself, though, is far from new. Humanity has probably always yearned for a transparent realm, a realm where there is no need of protection, since there is no source of fear; where lives are pure, clean, germless and filled with light. Indeed, transparency may be one of the oldest future-dreamings we have.

The Book of Revelations, for example, describes the ideal city, Jerusalem, as a prescient modernist heaven:

> The city lieth foursquare ... the length and the breadth and the height of it are equal. And ... the city was pure gold, like unto clear glass ... *And the street of the city was pure gold, as it were transparent glass ...* And the city had no need of the sun, neither of the moon, to shine in it, for the glory of God did lighten it ... And the gates of it shall not be shut at all by day: for there shall be no night there. (21:16–25)

Glass is automatically the medium of the future. For us, as much as the prophets, the house of the future (such an old-fashioned idea) was always glassy, spacey and open. We think of the past as shadowy and mysterious, although we've been there, while the future, however unknown, we picture as open, light-filled and diaphanous. Glass symbolises our mute anticipation of radiance to come. It offers, or seems to offer, the kind of ideal existence that, without glass, would be inconceivable: an existence based on the paradoxical (and deeply counter-intuitive) capacity to see and be seen, while staying warm, safe and inside.

This is the promise. What transparency really banishes, however, is not fear, but interiority. Not danger, but depth. Not mess, but mystery. It banishes, in other words, precisely those spatial qualities traditionally associated with femaleness, especially maternal femaleness.

Even now, architecture strives for openness and transparency, but the history of architecture is studded with glass houses that either end in tears, like Mies van der Rohe's house for Dr Edith Farnsworth (Farnsworth, a successful physician, commissioned the house at a dinner party, lived in it for two years, sold up and sued Mies for producing a house that was uninhabitable), or are designed strictly for the architect's own use, like the famous Philip Johnson house in New Canaan, Connecticut, and the Bill Lucas 'tree house' in the bush at Castlecrag, Sydney. Even then, of course, trouble can arise. Architects have wives, lives, lovers, children. The 2000 ABC documentary *In the Mind of the Architect* had Sean Godsell's wife, after living several years in their award-winning glass house in Melbourne, sweetly recalling:

> The first night we stayed here I became incredibly aware of the fact that there are no blinds in the front bedroom, and that I'd have to change, get into the cupboard and change, which I did. And after a short space of time *I got very used to changing in the cupboard.*

Architecture, the art of cladding the human spirit, is essentially about a balance between prospect and refuge. The all-glass house, that grail of modern architecture, destroys not only the house's protective instincts but also, in dissolving the mask itself, its capacity for connective magic.

5 | **Fat and the family home**

The devil has put a penalty on all things we enjoy in life.
Either we suffer in health or we suffer in soul or we get fat.

ALBERT EINSTEIN

There are terrible aesthetic consequences for any nation that heeds
the siren song of America: would you like fries with that?

MARK STEYN

Kellyville, two hours north-west of the harbour, is Sydney's latest greenfield land-grab. Kellyville is also home to Homeworld, the current new-houses hypermart, where houses can be mixed and matched, bought and stuffed, like at Build-a-Bear. For some, this is an experience close to heaven. But for your standard sensitive architect-type a half-day in Kellyville can cause deep existential despair. Not just depression. Despair. Despair of the go-on-without-me type. It's not just the vast McPalaces themselves, set bloatedly cheap-by-jowl along what passes for street. It's the heartbreakingly, wrist-slittingly obvious fact that this – this – is what people like.

None of this is sayable, of course. You can't say, my god it's ugly out here, without being reviled as a snob, an elitist or, worst of all, an intellectual. The word 'ugly' is both unacceptably negative and unacceptably judgemental. And partly because, even in Australia's supposedly classless society, any criticism across class divides is seen as class-based. Now, as political correctness works its way through academia, and 'post-suburbanism' provides ivory-tower academics with modish egalitarian garb, the criticisms have become all but unvoiceable in polite circles.

McMansionland

The truth is, though, that Kellyville's ugliness has nothing to do with class, and very little to do with culture, wealth or ethnicity. Robin Boyd, writing in 1960, saw this Dame Edna ugliness – for which he coined the term 'featurism' – as a uniquely Australian affliction. Australia's 'devastating combination of unconcern with essential form and over-concern with features', and our 'engrossing desire for conspicuous wealth', were, for Boyd, direct outgrowths of our convict origins – reinforced by each subsequent social wave and architectural look.

Federation, Queen Anne, Californian, moderne. The common thread is denial. 'Well-adjusted people,' writes Boyd, 'whether peasants or princes, who are content to appear what they are, scorn display and are not tempted by featurism.' Australians, he continues, being neither well-adjusted nor visually alert, and suffering 'a slightly neurotic condition brought about by loneliness', scarcely register the extent and frequency of their featurism.

In fact, a casual glance is enough to reveal both that rich suburbs are often every bit as ugly as the aspirationals – only more graciously hidden, at times, by those trees yet un-poisoned by view-nazis – and that Western cities the world over, from Moscow to Lyon to Denver, are increasingly marooned inside spreading seas of McMansionism. The style – which is to say, the particular self-talk fantasy being conducted – differs. From country to country, style varies according to dominant cultural myths; more pointy-roofed Germanic styles in the US, more mini-Ceaucescu's palaces in Russia; more quasi-Mediterranean mush in Sydney. But the ugliness itself is pretty much a constant. Why?

Between 1990 and 2003 the average NSW house grew by a terrifying 60 per cent, even as family size shrank by 40 per cent and plot size roughly halved. This put the average house in the state at a moderately hefty 270 square metres, but in Baulkham Hills Shire, in Sydney's north-west, the average new house was 64 per cent bigger again, weighing in at a massive 419 square metres. They're not just bigger, either, but glitzier, with all the glam extras now fully expected; the marble bathroom and gilt spa taps, the home-theatre, the dressing-rooms, the games rooms, the ensuites and the quadruple garages. Fat, fatter, fattest. In architecture, as in bodies, we may admire minimalism, but what we do – for the kids, the parking, the size, the garden, the extras – what we do, increasingly, is the bloated project home, swollen with as many extras as possible.

Gone are the days when pretence was vulgar and taste, not to say courtesy, required a degree of understatement or even tact. Gone are the modest materials, the fibro, corrugated iron and weatherboard of gentler times. Even the humble beach-shack is all but extinct, aggressively out-manoeuvred along our coastlines by vast, budget-bloated, glass-eyed dune-toppers, dimpled elbows jostling for the view.

Muses Sydney builder Sam Kassis on 'The Castle', a *60 Minutes* report from 2006:

> People love big. At the end of the day, big is beautiful ... Now
> [the market is] expecting five bedrooms at least. They're expecting
> the home theatre, most definitely the four car garage. I remember
> it used to be just double, then it moved up to triple, and now
> everybody wants four. And, yep, an ensuite for every bedroom.

It's as though our childhood yearnings to play kings and queens, to wear ermine and live forever in vast palaces, still haunt us; as though personal opulence is still the biggest and brightest outpost of our imagining. More educated than any previous generation, more travelled and (by our own reckoning) more sophisticated, and yet all we can think of to do, when we grow up and get money, is to acquire more, bigger houses.

We presume – call it the castle-premise – that democracy has made the rights of kings available to us all, and that some kind of fairy-dust has costlessly converted the undreamable dream into sustainable reality. This is why we love democracy, why we fight and kill for it. 'Our first home,' says Michelle from the Gold Coast, in the same *60 Minutes* report, 'was 12 squares. This one is 260.' When it's finished, this house she shares with husband Chris will have seven bedrooms, nine bathrooms and a fridge in every walk-in wardrobe. It'll cost $16.5 million. 'So we've come a fair way.'

Indulgent? Sure. But governments and markets alike smile on this behaviour, since it keeps us fat and infantile, keeps the dummy firmly stuck in our collective mouth. For Gold Coast builder Melanie Stott, this simply shows that god is in his heaven. 'We're just doing better than we ever have before,' she says. 'We're more successful as a country and many of us are not afraid to show it.' Fat houses are the built version of big hair. And they're popular alright. As Michael Stanbridge chastised the *Sydney Morning Herald* recently, 'People don't want to live in rabbit hutches. They want to be rich and successful … This is a big, rich country and people have the right to buy what they can pay for.' Which is a lot, since we are, on average, six times wealthier than we were 50 years ago. Even in the last ten years, the average Australian's wealth has more than doubled.

No law is being broken. It's our money to spend. But there is something obscene here, for all that, and not only because of the 100 000 Australians now living on the streets. Not only because entire families are regularly turned away from hostels and refuges that are full-to-bursting. And not only because, even as we roll our growing-fields under concrete and asphalt, we complain of an 'affordability crisis' that will prevent young people ever entering the property market (which in contemporary Australia is seen as some kind of death sentence).

Beneath all this are the 'why' questions. Why our vast wealth doesn't satisfy us but leads instead to still vaster expectations, why we demand a built lifestyle whose habitual over-indulgence is, by even the standards of our parents' generation, extraordinary? Why we continue to demand the fulfilment of these 'rights', despite the obvious cost to the planet? Why these houses, and the suburbs full of them, are so ugly? Is it an aesthetic or a moral repugnance? Is there a difference? Is it to do with sameness or, on the contrary, with the cacophony of individual egos, each shouting to be heard?

● | Phat

'Phat', as you know, is hip-hop for cool, or hot; fly or intelligent or otherwise admirable. There are a number of spurious etymologies for phat – including some trashy acronyms – but the truth is probably a simple, deliberate misspelling. The significant thing, though, is that while phat equals cool, fat equals distinctly uncool. This plays on one of the deep hypocrisies of our culture. We worship thin but, increasingly, do fat. Indeed, the more desperately we crave thinness, the more elusively it seems to float from our grasp and the fatter our bodies, our culture and our lives become. Thin has scarcity status. To quote US comic Sarah Silverman, 'I don't care if you think I'm racist. I just want you to think I'm thin.'

Sometimes it seems the entire world is competing for the title of world's fattest country. In undernourished societies, or those with a vivid cultural memory of scarcity, body-fat is understandably a status symbol. (In cultures that have moved rapidly from poverty to affluence this can cause the interesting situation where parents still deliberately over-feed their children, even when fat has already reversed its social meaning to become stigmatised. Thus the 'fat farms' of Mauritania, where girls are fattened like *foie gras* geese, sometimes to the point of immobility, to make them attractive trophy brides, despite the knowledge that such obesity is a health liability, not an asset.)

Meanwhile, in the overfed West, thinness, being difficult, has the cachet. But fat, being easy, has the numbers. Models may die of anorexia, making body-image politics into a major issue, but clothes sizes have ballooned. In the 1950s the average waist size of British women was 27 inches: now it is 34. Statistics from 2006 show that 22 per cent of British adults are obese and 50 per cent overweight, with childhood obesity running at 17 per cent. In 2002 writer Greg Critser titled his book *How Americans Became the Fattest People in the World*. Canadian columnist Mark Steyn says his Parisian friends won't visit the United States any more because they can't stand the fat on the streets:

> In America, you can be an obese child at 45. In Paris a couple of years ago, my French dinner companions harangued me at length about how they could no longer bear to walk down American Main Streets, filled as they are with 300lb middle-aged toddlers waddling along the sidewalk in Xtra-large Disney T-shirts and slurping super-sized sodas from plastic bottles with giant nipples. 'It is a culture of arrested development,' one disdainful Parisian sniffed wearily, 'of perpetual childhood.'

And in Australia, with 66 per cent of men and 50 per cent of women and children reportedly overweight or obese in 2003, the overall cost of obesity came, in 2006, to $10.8 billion; more than the entire NSW health budget. As Steyn scathingly notes, 'the coalition of the willing is also the coalition of the swilling'.

The blame is laid variously on food (too much, too fast), sitting (too much, too slow), genetics (body shape is hereditary and anyway fat people are more fertile), trans-fats, advertising, stress, complacency, climate control, government and city planning. What we are very, very, very reluctant to do is blame ourselves. This is part of the refusal to grow up.

Fat-city

In September 2006 Professor Paul Zimmet, director of Monash University's International Diabetes Institute, told the International Congress on Obesity that 'the insidious, creeping pandemic of obesity is now engulfing the entire world, led by affluent Western nations, whose physical activity and dietary habits are regrettably being adopted by developing nations'. What was to blame? 'In particular, our ... governments ... contributed to this epidemic by permitting ... the ubiquitous McMansion', with no attention to bike tracks, playing fields or exercise areas.

Zimmet may have been gilding the lily, just a little. And admittedly there are still those who deny the entire sprawl–obesity correlation. But increasing numbers of public health professionals agree. These include heavyweights like professors Tony McMichael (Director of the National Centre of Epidemiology and Population Health at ANU), Howard Frumkin (Director, National Center for Environmental Health, Agency for Toxic Substances and Disease Registry, and Centers for Disease Control and Prevention, Atlanta) and Anthony Capon (from the Australian Health Policy Institute), who point to statistics that clearly show obesity, diabetes and asthma all increasing with distance from the city centre, and see these unequivocally as the health issues of our era.

The emphasis varies slightly. For some, like Capon, there is a direct causal link between obesity and under-active suburban car-based lifestyles. Deakin University's Professor Boyd Swinburne, President of the Australian Society for the Study of Obesity, agrees, arguing that our built environment, pushing as it does a lifestyle-mix of fast food, inactivity and advertising, is simply obesogenic. Others, like McMichael, stand slightly further back, pointing out that 'the rise of overweight is not confined to big cities'. In Australia, says McMichael, although 'the recent rise in the proportion of fat people appears to have been a little bigger in country towns and rural populations than in the big-city population' the combined effect of urbanism, wealth, mass consumerism and labour-saving technologies is a way of living that is 'no longer attuned to our basic biology'.

The extraordinary international spread of the obesity pandemic positions it as our equivalent of nineteenth century public health epidemics like rickets, diphtheria and typhoid; the very issues that resulted, ironically, in the wholesale adoption of suburbia as preferred city form. Perhaps, this suggests, we'll re-shape our cities once again – only to discover, belatedly, the medication that could have obviated the need for such change in the first place? Already there is talk of a painless fat cure; something that takes the blame out of the disease and the hard work out of the treatment.

In the meantime, it's an issue of moment. As Professor Paul Knox, Dean of Architecture and Planning at Virginia Tech, points out, sprawl and obesity sit third on the angst-list of American planning professionals

– after 'big box retail' and 'ghost malls' but before traffic congestion, environmental pussyfooting and 'boomburgs'. It's more than metaphor. The link between sprawl and obesity has all the hallmarks of causality. 'The potential health and social consequences of our current pattern of urban development,' says Capon, 'provide a compelling rationale for a re-think of the way we are developing our cities.' House sizes may have doubled but the average block has roughly halved. So has the average family. This makes the amount of indoor space per person around four times what it was in the 1950s, while the back yard has shrunk to almost nothing. At the same time, paranoid parenting stops our children walking or biking to school or roaming the neighbourhood after. So, what do they do? Stay in, eat chips, play Xbox.

The US State Department says 67 per cent of American children watch at least two hours of TV a day. If you include internet and video games, they're spending four hours daily in front of a screen. That's America, but in screen addiction, as in holy wars, the rest tag along. In New South Wales (and it's likely a similar figure holds for the rest of the country), reporter Julie Robotham has discovered that 11- to 15-year-olds also spend four hours a day, average, on the small screen, more than half their waking hours outside school, and are more likely to be overweight.

Studies repeatedly show, further, that kids who spend more time watching television and playing video games are at higher risk of becoming overweight. While some studies ascribe this to fast-food advertising, others, including the Third National Health and Nutrition Examination Survey in the USA, have shown that watching television can use even *less* energy than resting, since its soothing effect can actually lower metabolic rate. Another study, of 5380 five- and six-year-olds in America, reported in the *Daily Telegraph*, showed that weight gain over the summer holidays, when the children's TV-time increased, was three times that during the school term.

It's easy to feel defensive of fat, and to look back at the jolly Friar Tucks and Santa Clauses of literature with nostalgic affection. As tenor Luciano Pavarotti quipped, 'the reason fat people are happy is that the nerves are well protected'. Is it fair or even desirable for fat to become a thing of the past? On the other hand, fat is no longer a minority interest, a charming eccentricity. And it costs. Not only in disease terms, either. Recent studies, possibly exaggerative, reported in the *New York Times*, suggest an extra billion gallons of gasoline and 350 million gallons of airline fuel are used each year now, compared with the 1990s, to transport fat Americans. Not to mention the extra food-miles.

To fight the fat, and stop it bubbling over into even more expensive hobbies like diabetes, we encourage sport. Which makes driving the people-mover between home, school, piano, dance and soccer someone's full-time occupation. Tax systems, designed to drive a home-ownership agenda, encourage bloat of this kind. Hence the four-car garages, the 24/7 citywide traffic jam, the skyward rocketing of the global CO_2 graph.

Fat living

Sprawl or no, there is a clear relationship between fat and affluence. Rich countries are fat countries. The IFOCE (International Federation of Competitive Eating) may be international, but its inventor, and its spiritual home, is America. Only in America could the Virgin Mary, who in 1996 appeared on a grilled-cheese sandwich to Florida jewellery designer Diana Duyser, be expected to preside, demurely from within a plastic box, over the $3500 World Grilled Cheese Eating Championship.

And yet, within Western countries, obesity's social patterning has reversed. Fat is still a socio-economic indicator, but now it points the other way. Throughout contemporary America, Europe and Australia, it's the rich who are thin and the strugglers who are fat. Rich people still live fat – if all people in the world had a footprint the size of the average denizen of Sydney's Mosman (or London's Chelsea or Westchester County NY), we'd need seven extra Earths to accommodate them, as the *Sydney Morning Herald* recently reported. They'll jet around the world for a conference on global warming, dine twice-daily at expensive restaurants, then pay again to look like they haven't eaten properly in months. To look fat is to look poor and uneducated. And yet we are hardwired not only to eat but, say some scientists, to overeat, which is why the weight-loss industry searches unstintingly for something – a pill, an injection, a gene-splice, anything – that would allow us to beat nature: to overeat *and* be thin.

Of course body fat is not the same as fat living. Indeed, the body fat thing stands to become something of a witch-hunt. As Mark Steyn puts it, 'the war on blubber seems to be the war on terror by other means'. And yet the connections are there, both at an ecological level, and symbolically. The ecological implications of (especially) meat-based over-eating include huge water and energy usage, significant greenhouse impacts from methane as well as CO_2 and, in Australia, soil damage. For most consumers, experts calculate, a switch to vegetarianism would cut GHGs three times further than an 80 per cent cut in petrol use.

But the symbolic implications of the war on fat are, if anything, more important. We're primates. Even as we think we've risen above our monkey cousins, science puts us ever closer to them. (Take, for instance, recent discoveries that we share 99 per cent of our DNA with chimps, and that capuchin monkeys regularly exchange sexual favours for profit.) And just as money is a convenient indicator of power, fat is a simple indicator of over-fulfilled primal needs. If body fat represents the over-consumption of food, fatburbia represents the gorging of those other primal appetites – shelter, clothing, comfort and tools.

This primate thing is a big plus, and a potentially bigger problem – for us, and for the planet. Scientist Edward O Wilson notes that he and most of his colleagues regard it as 'a misfortune for the living world in particular … that a carnivorous primate and not some more benign form of animal made the breakthrough into wholesale planetary dominance'. Why? Because even now, when our survival instincts have largely outlived their usefulness, that primate voice goes on insisting, deep down in the palaeocortex, 'if some is good, more is certainly better'. That if there is to be a last gasp of fresh air on the planet, I want it to be *my* last gasp. I want this so much, in fact, I'll die fighting for it rather than restrict my pleasures in order to increase the air supply, long term, for everyone.

These are our instincts, and they are voices we cannot ignore – despite, it seems, our dim cerebral recognition that we don't actually need more and more and more; that we're at our best, as individuals and as a species, when we're somewhat challenged. Stress – aka desire –

keeps us interested. Yet still our primitive ape-brains continue to chant, 'More is good, more is good.' Which is why, of course, all economies are based on the inviolable principle of growth. 'More is good, more is good.'

It was Andy Warhol who pointed out that 'buying is much more American than thinking'. (That was back when 'American' meant something good.) Warhol devoted a whole page of his treatise to the important subject of where to shop for underwear. When he died he left vast drifts of stuff, rooms and rooms full of boxes he had never bothered to open. Is such acquisitiveness just sublimated hunter-gathering, driven not by need but by the short, primal pleasure of the act itself? Acquisition soothes the troubled psyche, which is why shopaholism is a disease-of-the-moment. Feel upset? Buy something. And the amazing, disturbing thing is, it works. For a while.

The hidden assumptions that need equals want, and that satisfying wants equals happiness, are now widely questioned. But as Australia Institute director Clive Hamilton points out, although we're wealthier than ever, almost half of Australia's richest 20 per cent believe they cannot afford everything they really need. This is the real reason our children are fat. As Tony Capon notes, 'obesity results from an energy imbalance, where energy intake (diet) exceeds energy expenditure (physical activity)'. Too much in, too little out.

It's the same with our lives; too much get, too little give. And our hyper-lipid living patterns are rebounding on us in the same way as our bodies, with one in five Australians now suffering from depression or anxiety. The affluenza epidemic is (first-)world wide and worsening. It needn't be this way. Times of hardship and deprivation, as we know, are often remembered as the best times, and making do is often what makes us happy. Harvard professor of psychiatry George Vaillant has shown that by far the best cure for depression is altruism. And yet our devotion to consumption has become almost the new morality in itself; communities who opt out of materialism, be they New Age or Aboriginal or Amish, are seen as subversive, while the rest of us feed our addiction as though it's a cure, not a symptom.

Architecture, at its best, offers the optimal balance of prospect and refuge. A house, said WH Auden, is a 'toft-and-croft where I needn't, ever, be at home to those I am not at home with'.

But if, as suggested in the previous chapter, the house is not simply a protective device, but has also an expressive and connective function – if it is an adopted persona or mask – what does it say about us that we crave ever bigger, costlier and more flamboyant forms of mask? If Alain de Botton is right to see the house as an idealised self-portrait, does the advent of the McMansion indicate an ever-greater and ever-more widespread confidence in the universe and our place within it? Or is it the reverse? Is the McMansion simply part of an increasingly elaborate denial strategy? A wild over-compensation for our ever-present terror regarding the universe and our place within it?

In houses, unlike bodies, bigger is always better. Even downshifters, wanting a simpler life, seldom aspire to a smaller house. Simpler lifestyle, prettier surroundings, cleaner nature, sure. But smaller? Not likely. And even in body fat, the rewards of downsizing are not always as anticipated. The enormous determination required usually impels slimmers to nurture happy-ever-after-type expectations. Psychiatrists report that a common response to significant weight loss among the long-term obese is a sense of terror, of unwonted vulnerability; as if the hated kilos were themselves protective bulwarks. This exchange of physical excess for emotional depletion seems especially cruel in view of the sheer difficulty and endurance involved.

But could something similar happen with houses? Is it possible that in houses, as in hair, bodies and cars, bigness will simply slide out of fashion? McMansionism itself is a trickle-down thing, spreading by emulation from the wealthy postcodes to the aspirational boomburgs, where the newly-moneyed are determined to wear the mask, at least, of wealth. Perhaps the trend can invert itself? Perhaps big houses – land-hungry, greenhouse-dirty, energy-inefficient – will come to be seen as so ecologically greedy and so physically unhealthy that the taste-leaders will start to go for leaner, greener dwellings, the smart cars of the housing world. Could the big house, acquired largely for envy-generation, become fashion-death?

It sounds unlikely. But it has happened with cars (briefly, during the 1970s petrol crises), with bodies, with hair. So perhaps, with houses. In Los Angeles, the McMansion's spiritual home, the City Council recently made headlines by considering – just considering – imposing house-size maxima in areas like Bel Air and Beverley Hills, where 25,000 square feet is not uncommon. Most cities, including Sydney, have long limited the height and bulk of suburban houses, but such limits are usually based on site area. If the land is vast – and the sprawl loose – there is effectively no control.

Still, there are signs. Most Australian and many US cities show recent slowing or marginal reversal of the so-called 'white-flight syndrome' that produced all those hollowed-out edge-cities in the late twentieth century. Some, like Sydney and Melbourne, have undergone huge inner-city residential booms, mostly in new apartment buildings. In Sydney, although the proportion of first-home buyers purchasing inner-city apartments and other high-density dwellings is still under 20 per cent, the proportion is steadily increasing. The city's overall number of inner-city residents is also increasing steadily, at around 3.3 per cent per year, along with the rising proportion. While the upsurge has been recently encouraged by a slight fall in prices, the trend extends over at least 15 years and surveys suggest that it is based largely on a desire for amenity, proximity and inner-city 'buzz'.

Kitsch and the beach-shack

As telecommuting and downshifting gradually merge our working selves into our holiday selves, work-sprawl melds indistinguishably into leisure-sprawl; lazier and less controlled than ever. Pretty soon Australia's entire eastern seaboard – famed for its barefoot, sand-between-the-toes charm – will be lined, three streets deep, in the marble-veneer and smoked-glass balconies, the roundabouts and air-conditioned malls that have come to spell civilisation.

Gone is the classic beach-shack. The Aussie shack *du jour*, says a new book by Stephen Crafti, 'starts at 300 square metres' and is emphatically *not* 'designed to be filled with muddy dogs and sandy kids trailing wet, salty towels.' No modest fibro here, with its worn furniture, its found flotsam and its unmatching crockery. No way. That's no longer acceptable dune-top kit. 'The new beach house is a masterpiece of design and architecture,' says Crafti, complete with ensuites, air-con and guest wings, using sophisticated materials that reflect 'a new aesthetic and lifestyle – a world of luxury and design, glamour and desire'.

The tragedy is not that Crafti is wrong, but the extent to which he's right. Not just about the shack, either, but about architecture in general. It's as if, in rejecting modernism's commitment to truth, the entire architecture-game, as hurrahed along by architectural publishing, has become a flat-out race for pretentiousness *max*.

The beach-house argument, as Crafti puts it, is an economic one. Having paid through the nose for that piece of cliff or dune, the last thing you're going to do is put a shack on it. Which is to say, we've built a society where education and wealth have become so estranged that those who can afford either beachfronts or architects, and especially both at once, are unlikely to show serious signs of cultivation.

This shouldn't matter. After all, we chose democracy and the booming beachburb is its direct consequence. But matter it does. Not only because of the mad hypocrisy of replicating at the beach the very same array of nature-repudiating devices you left home to escape, like the archetypal American globetrotters with suitcases full of Mars bars and hamburger mix. Not only because of the environmental waste of such duplication, and not only because of its flab and ostentation.

Full membership of Blubberland requires a highly-developed tolerance of the inauthentic, and a number of equally sophistic denial strategies: denial that truth was ever accessible, or ever existed, or was ever worth pursuing in the first place. The whole of postmodern relativism is, arguably, such a strategy; evidence perhaps that pomo is less anti-modern than hyper-modern. Another, developed since the middle of the modern century and later subsumed into postmodernism, is kitsch. Kitsch is not just bad taste. Bad taste, as has become adored by the ironic pomo set, is fine. Kitsch proper, so to speak, is based on a deep deceit. It is, in a word, bullshit.

What is bullshit, exactly? It is not, as defined by Princeton philosopher Harry G Frankfurt, in his famous little book *On Bullshit*, the same as lying. And certainly it's not truthfulness. Rather, bullshit implies a total disregard for truth; a sort of a-truthfulness. The bullshitter, while not necessarily lying, wishes to get away with something, something not 'for real'. 'The essence of bullshit,' says Frankfurt, 'is not that it is false but that it is phoney.' Bullshit, of course, is everywhere, from politics to 'reality' TV. Work may be a kind of touchstone of authenticity but holidays, one can't but feel, need their own kind of realness. The holiday should be time-out from blubber, as much as time-out from work.

But no. As leisure has come to occupy more of our lives it has itself become increasingly occupied by kitsch. A nineteenth century German term of uncertain etymology, kitsch was widely discussed in the 1930s by modernist critics like Theodor Adorno and Clement Greenberg, who regarded it as a kind of false consciousness, the polar opposite of the avant-garde and of the authenticity that was, it was thought, art. Kitsch was sententious, pretentious, meretricious and vulgar. Kitsch is, said Greenberg, 'the epitome of all that is spurious in the life of our times'. Gillo Dorfles, writing the definitive text on the subject in 1968, defined kitsch as phoniness: the clock that looks like a spaceship, or the spaceship that looks like a tomato. He even – perhaps unpardonably – included in *Kitsch: An Anthology of Bad Taste* the proud sand-parade of Sydney's standard-bearing Coogee lifesavers.

Then came Warhol, who made 'kitschy' a compliment, giving it the ironic appeal that allowed his kitsch and Susan Sontag's idea of 'camp' to intersect. Suddenly anything exaggerated, caricatured, folkloric or mass-produced could be an icon of intellectual avant-gardism and – this is crucial – *no one would know the difference.* From the garish garden gnome to the Aphrodite-shaped pepper grinder, from the rubber Virgin Mary mask to the outsize Hitler Youth hologram; anything could be embraced as kitsch as long as it was sufficiently tasteless and sufficiently popular. And how like our self-regarding, over-complicated times that kitsch itself should become a beauty-substitute, both cause and commodity, ironic favourite of the very avant-garde it was invented to oppose.

And it's not going away. 'Like processed food,' observes UK critic Roger Scruton, 'kitsch ... passes from junk to crap without an intervening spell of nourishment.' Kitsch is art on holiday, art with no need for taste or morality. So maybe holiday is where our marble-and-glass beachside ostentations belong? Perhaps, who knows, they'll become the kitsch of the future, bad taste beloved of some self-appointed avant garde – ironically, of course – just as mid-century modern is now?

Perhaps, but it's difficult to imagine. A clue may lie in Milan Kundera's definition of kitsch as 'the absolute denial of shit'. This may sound like a jolly good thing – but what Kundera meant was not innocent vulgarity, but the sanitised, genteel self-parody into which we so easily slip in the headlong flight from death. Dame Edna is kitsch; Sir Les is simply bad taste. Kitsch is manifest euphemism.

And this is the contemporary coastal castle's least endearing aspect. Not its ugliness, its greed or its enviro-crimes but its relentless, vicar's-wife euphemism. Dutch intellectual Rob Riemen, leader of Holland's Nexus Instituut, spoke on 'Kitsch and the Crisis of the West' at the 2006 Aspen Festival of Ideas. Western cultural crisis is like mid-life crisis; perpetual, over-reported and often mildly enjoyable, but Riemen made some useful points.

Kitsch is the meeting point of ethics and aesthetics. Not the boisterously vulgar – the golliwog ashtray or the fur bikini – and not just fun, or cheek, or fantasy. True kitsch, so to speak, involves a deliberate cleansing of the truth. It is what impels us to pursue the comfortable rather than the genuine, and to make this pursuit socially required. Kitsch is the collective pretence that a second plasma-screen television is a genuine spending priority; it's the conformism that demands this pretence even from those who cannot afford and do not want it.

That's what makes these epidemic beach-mansions both rude and dangerous. With their glam and polish, their air-con and their mod-cons, they whisper the same false promise that high office whispers to politicians – exemption from nature and necessity. They lie, and we love them for it. As Scruton notes, 'the world of kitsch is the world of make-believe, of permanent childhood, in which every day is Christmas ... kitsch is an attempt to have the life of the spirit on the cheap'. Kitsch is nature parboiled, reconstituted, stacked with sugar and preservatives.

The charm of the endangered Aussie shack, by contrast, was its bare acknowledgement, even for a few weeks a year, that for all our aspirations and inspirations, we're still barefoot bipeds, still subject to the grandeur and wrath of sand, sea and bluebottles. The beach-shack tells us the humble truth. We extinguish it at our peril.

Kitsch and the humble boat

A similar dismay applies even to the modern boating holiday. Tooling about the succulent sandstone-and-angophora fiords of Sydney's venerable Hawkesbury River, for example, the gorgeous authenticity of nature merely throws the ugliness of contemporary leisure into even harsher relief. True, ugly isn't a word you can use these days, any more than beauty, now that postmodernism's trickledown has made every aesthetic opinion equally valid. But you go to the Hawkesbury expecting the famous houseboats: deep-shaded, verandah-fringed, elegantly drifting, iced-tea, *African Queen*-type houseboats. That was the mental image; part Yangtze junk, part Herrengracht barge, part UK narrowboat, with perhaps a hint of Mississippi paddlesteamer, Cornish trawler and Sydney Harbour tugboat thrown in.

In fact what passes for 'houseboat' on the venerable Hawkesbury is a graceless, shadeless, eaveless, godless tin box whose closest approach to aesthetic purpose is to ferry bucks' parties of bare-chested suburban blokes from one public mooring to another without actually tipping them in the drink (this in itself is a mistake) and whose finest aesthetic features are counted in numbers of plastic wood-veneer kitchens and on-board walk-in dunnies. And it's not limited to houseboats. The ubiquitous plastic stinkboat rising two or three storeys from the water and topped by faux-punk fishing paraphernalia is, if anything, a worse offence, having no higher goal than to tear up the quiet bays by day and pump the still evening air full of the cicada-deafening buzz needed to run the fridge, TV and air-con.

Why? What possesses so diverse and (occasionally) sophisticated a culture as Sydney's to declare itself satisfied with such third-rate holiday-ware? Australia, after all, has a fine array of noble and picturesque maritime traditions. From the cutters and schooners of old Sydney

Harbour to the broad-beamed paddlesteamers that used to choke the Murray at Echuca, from the low-slung, long-snouted Victorian couta boats to the chunky south coast fishing trawlers, we have the goods in the heritage boat department. And even modern tugs, trawlers and container ships have a rusted-on, Annie Proulx-type appeal. But the contemporary leisurecraft is not a lovable creature. Not now; not ever.

You scratch around for explanations. Is it temporal? Will today's moulded plastic leisurecraft, a century or so hence, have acquired their own improbable aura of romance – just as last week's fashion disaster is tomorrow's design classic? Somehow, I can't see it. Finally it comes back to this. Ugliness is not a strictly aesthetic quality. It's about authenticity and its opposite, kitsch. Kundera, writing in 1981, gave kitsch an existential edge when he defined it as the 'absolute denial of shit' – a genteel, sanitising totalitarianism in which grubby truths are blanketed by shiny denial. And certainly there's denial here. Denial, in those high plastic walls and after-deck barbecues, in the shipboard TVs and walk-in dunnies, of the entire experience of being at sea. The materials themselves – plastic, aluminium, fibreglass, Laminex, all selected for cheapness, lightness and convenience – reinforce this dissociative effect.

Since the 1980s, kitsch may have become required reading among the avant-garde, especially as camp affectation. (Note to self; market the bumper-sticker that reads 'It's OK, I'm being ironic'.) But truth, like beauty, is making a comeback, and with them comes authenticity. As Frankfurt notes, bullshit is especially prevalent when, as in public life, people are required to hold forth on subjects of which they are largely or wholly ignorant. In this way, argues Frankfurt, fact comes to be replaced by 'sincerity'; the look, rather than the fact, of honesty. And so sincerity itself becomes bullshit.

It's the same with boats. What we warm to in traditional boats is their *working*-ness. Work, rooted in necessity, has a cleansing and grounding effect – on the human spirit generally, and on aesthetics in particular. Work, being necessary, feels like a kind of truth, and truth is the medium in which we as humans dwell. It is tempting to suggest here the converse, that leisure is simply unattractive by nature. But counter-examples like the Baths of Caracalla, the Viennese *Kaffeehaus* and those fabulous flying fish, the Balmain eighteen-footers traditional to Sydney Harbour, suggest that no, the kitsch of leisure is a strictly modern, mass-culture phenomenon, straight from the freezer into the microwave.

In many traditions, as we have seen, beauty depends on uselessness; on inability to work. But there is another tradition, not dissimilar to wabi sabi, in which deep aesthetic satisfaction derives from things that are designed minutely to a purpose, from Chinese abacuses to Persian weighing machines and Portuguese sextants. Such objects are beautiful precisely for the finesse with which form follows function. A non-working copy of such a tool would be a worthless, charisma-less fake, all the more offensive for imitating truth. For being, in Frankfurt's sense, 'sincere'.

Some dim recognition of this drives the peculiarly decadent aesthetic in which leisure apes work: tracksuits with no intended use other than television-watching; utes with trays so high they cannot function except as status symbols; wealthy women who struggle for the starvation look; interior design in the pseudo-grunge 'industrial chic' mode. The same mindset, in the marine industry, has produced 'trawler-style' leisure boats, their plastic hulls moulded to imitate the caulked timber planking of the working boat. That's icky.

Bullshit, then, is not just a moral issue. Bullshit is everywhere, in everything. Just as long-chain plastic polymers have been discovered in breastmilk, so bullshit can be found up any muddy creek, resting gently on every mudflat, ready to plant in your head the long-chain carcinogen that makes bullshit groovy.

McMansionism, community and fear

It's ironic, perhaps, that the society of surfeit, with its special emphasis on surfeit at home, has sprung from Judaeo-Christian tradition; a tradition that not only aspires to non-materialism but is at root a wandering, unrooted tradition of nomadism and homelessness. The Old Testament's Yahweh was a wandering god, and his people, as theologian Harvey Cox has pointed out, were a wandering people. Christianity too is traditionally a religion of pilgrimage and dislocation. Have we lost our way? Have our houses become closed temples to worldliness, rather than celebrations of life-giving flow?

In *The Conscience of the Eye*, Richard Sennett argues that contemporary Western culture suffers from a divide between interiority and exteriority, a divide 'between subjective experience and worldly experience, self and city'. This divide expresses our fear of self-exposure and results in 'neutralized' cities whose spaces are limited to orchestrating consumption on the one hand, or tourism on the other, and are uniformly characterised by blandness. The public spaces of the modern city have become an exercise in 'sensory deprivation', in the denial of touch and texture. This, Sennett notes in *Flesh and Stone*, has arisen from the pursuit of comfort but, like so many other comfort-pursuits (such as watching TV) has the unintended side-effect of reducing our engagement to pathological levels. We watch, and 'watching pacifies'. And the McMansion is a primary instance: sealed and air-conditioned, cul-de-saced and pest-proofed, security-equipped and, as often as not, gated. For Sennett, this closing-off is about fear; fear of exposure, fear of engagement. Fear, in fact, of truth.

How does it work? Fear makes us turn things like beauty, materiality and architecture – gifts, if you will, of transcendence – into weapons of exclusion. Exclusion, of course, is the essence of tribal lore; we are us by virtue of being not-them. It's like the schoolgirl club whose only common ground is not-Mary. We are the not-Mary club. Or take material possessions. Stuff. We all have more stuff than we need, but our credit card balance is ballooning faster than our obesity levels because of the Alfa Spiders, Miele kitchens and French wrinkle-creams we simply have to have. Stuff, stuff, more stuff, to paraphrase *American Beauty*'s Lester Burnham.

But stuff, like beauty, also has a crucial exclusionary role. How, after all – without these costly, planet-crippling lapel-badges – how else can we know, and know *they* know, we're not them?

Architecture is a basic tool of community. And yet it, too, is inherently exclusionary since, at its most basic, architecture is the line. The line in the sand, the line on the drawing board, the line as-built. And the line is fundamentally an exclusionary device. Perhaps it's our nine in-utero months that generate our endless yearning for protective in-ness. Perhaps not. But yearn we do. And in-ness requires the line. The line divides here from there, in from out, us from them. The line creates in-ness by generating out-ness. What's out is other, them. What's in is us. We are us by virtue of being not-out, not-them. Not-Mary.

So today's developers flog not houses but homes; not estates but *community*. Community, though – real community – is not about rules, exclusion and conformism. It can't be made overnight, and it can't be sold. It requires common goals, civility and above all that most precious of commodities, time. In a pluralist democracy this kind of cohesion can be hard to come by, but one principle should be non-negotiable: if community means sacrificing pluralism, open-heartedness or democracy – in other words, if it enforces conformism, prohibits dissent, or declines to be inclusive – it's a fake.

The McMansion, then, is really an elaborate protection and diversion mechanism, one of the human animal's many denial strategies against death. But it is deeply counter-productive, no longer a working mask engendering creative transformation, but sealed and hardened into a death-mask.

6 | **Nature and culture**

Nature, Mr Allnutt, is what we are put into this world to rise above.

ROSE SAYER TO CHARLIE ALLNUT, *The African Queen* (1951)

Humans have always tried to dominate nature. Indeed, we take it as a primary reason for our success. It's no accident that Christianity elected to symbolise its struggle with an image of man crucified on the tree of nature. Nature, for most of human history, has been our enemy as well as our womb. And now, as we stand victorious astride Gaia's limp and bloodied form, feeling absently for a pulse, it seems we may yet prove victims of our own success.

● | **Nature and culture: the city**

Many people, asked for the cause of such planetary destruction, think first of the smoke and dirt, the crowding and pollution of the so-called concrete jungle. As this term implies, cities are usually seen as the very antithesis of nature. Ever since nineteenth century romanticism demonised the 'dark satanic mills' of the new industrial metropolis from which it grew, we have tended to see cities as regrettable and un-natural necessities, rather than the centres of culture, commerce and learning that they were for the ancients. Troy, Alexandria, Carthage, Athens, Rome, Venice: the cities of antiquity, built when humans were still largely at nature's mercy, were prized not just as artefacts but as intensive cultural generators. We, by contrast, even as we head for nature's jugular, habitually polarise the picture; nature good, city bad.

A more useful view is to see the city as a tool, or a form of mask. All culture, arguably, can be seen thus, as a more or less carefully-contrived interface in our perennial struggle to engage nature and survive her. And the city is our paramount cultural artefact. Like that first bone in the hand of the ape, the city is perhaps the essential tool in shaping our engagement with nature.

To see the city as a tool in this way forces us to recognise it as made, not given, and capable therefore of change. It also helps to break down the artificial nature-culture polarity, letting us see ourselves, and our cities, as creatures of nature. Cities, as localised modifications of the earth's crust, are designed not just around individuals but around the extraordinary social and material complexities of the hive. Using culture as termites use saliva, cities shape and civilise place in order to accommodate, shape and civilise the complicated human animal. Good cities are therefore richly textured, intensely energised and minutely explorable. Designed to engage our imaginations as well as our feet and our wallets, they offer secrets and surprises, dungeons and attics, mystery and risk. Good cities give shelter to eccentricities of all kinds, cloaking difference in anonymity; they offer the magic of unimagined worlds and the adventure of unpredictable discovery.

Cities represent immense investments of human energy. Energy is all. Pretty much everything we value can be seen as a form of embedded energy. This, arguably, is what value is. Which is why a cheap-and-cheerful approach to building, however functional or convenient, always ends up feeling like some tacky extra-urban office park, never generating that real city vibe. People respond intuitively to a sense of the energy – especially the human energy – embedded in a place. Think of the Pyramids, Stonehenge, or the Taj Mahal. Our awe is inspired as much by the immensity of human investment as by the breathtaking visuals.

This fine-grained, highly-textured, intensely energised quality, combined with the sheer intensity of human activity, is what gives cities their vividness. People love cities they can imagine. Call this quality imageability or energy or romance. Whatever you call it, Rome and Paris and Barcelona and Sydney have it. Baghdad and Trieste and Parramatta, at the moment, do not.

But it's not just charisma. Density also gives cities their creative edge. Density-based friction, which we so easily resent, is what generates the cultural spark, which is why artists and writers traditionally cluster in city centres. And, as it happens, density is also the key to sustainability. If we were, just say, to design a green settlement-pattern from scratch, the product would not be suburbia, or urban villages, or Greek fishing towns or even, say, Barcelona. It would be Manhattan. Manhattan – or something like it – is the greenest city on earth. As David Owen wrote recently in the *New Yorker*:

> The average Manhattanite consumes petrol at a rate that the country as a whole hasn't matched since the 1920s, when the most widely owned car in the US was a Ford Model T.

> Eighty-two percent of Manhattan residents travel to work by public transit, by bicycle or on foot. [In Sydney it's around 10–15 per cent.] That's ten times the rate for Americans in general, and eight times the rate for residents of Los Angeles County. New York is more populous than all but 11 states; [and yet] if it were granted statehood, it would rank 51st in per-capita energy use.

A New Yorker averages 7.1 tonnes of carbon dioxide production a year, compared with the America-wide average of 24.5 tonnes per person, reported the *Sydney Morning Herald* recently. This is all self-evident, when you think about it. And yet it is not widely understood, much less embraced. Mainly because we don't think about it, on the whole. And because it's counter-intuitive. We tend to think of hippies as the green types, living in mud-brick and growing their own, well, medications. And we tend in the same breath to characterise cities as environmental disaster areas – presuming, with Thomas Jefferson, that cities are 'pestilential to the morals, the health and the liberties of man'. But this is nothing more than habit. Straight old cultural kneejerk. The truth is vice versa. People living in the country *have* to get around by private vehicle. They travel long distances, they heat and cool one dwelling at a time, with all the energy loss which that implies. They occupy land that might otherwise be forest. It's expensive in terms of energy, and it's expensive in terms of space.

Then again, at least country living is (broadly speaking) productive. The suburbs, which look green and were sold to us, back in the 1920s, as the nature-lover's picnic moment, are in fact the worst offenders. And the wealthier the suburb, the more 4WDs and international holidays it supports, the bigger the eco-footprint per head, so to speak. And yet commentators persist in defending suburbia as the great Australian dream. In fact, there's nothing Australian about it. The 'garden suburb', as it was called, as formulated by Anglo-American Ebenezer Howard in 1898, began as a British dream (Hampstead Garden Suburb and the like) and spread from there to become, post-World War II, the American dream, the New Zealand dream, the South African dream and, by the late twentieth century, the virtually universal dream. Now, as postmodern populism has infected the academy, it has become fashionable, even among intellectuals who should know better, to defend sprawl simply for its popularity and to deride its critics as arrogant and elitist. It's like arguing that children should watch television and eat junk because they like it.

Some, like Australian commentator Bernard Salt, argue that the eco-imperative towards density doesn't apply in Australia because our cities are small by American standards. They're smaller, it's true, but Salt entirely misses the point. The point is that size isn't the point. In eco-terms it's not the size of a city that matters, but its growth-model – its DNA, if you like. And in this, sprawl sits at one end of the gene pool, tight-knit urbanism at the other.

Sprawl means people have to travel more for almost everything – to work or shop or play or educate or bushwalk. They have to travel further as well as more often, since low densities can support only a light smattering of retail and other services, *and* they have to travel by car, since low densities make public transport unviable. This, in turn, gives the roads lobby immense power, since it makes roads fundamental to existence. And this, from the politician's point of view, means there is no incentive to subsidise or even prioritise public transport – because no one uses it, there are no votes in it. Thus the incentive to build roads – more, bigger, faster roads – increases. But, as is regularly demonstrated, the more roads you build, the more people drive. Supply can never keep up with demand, because demand is essentially limitless.

We grizzle about traffic congestion but refuse to recognise that congestion is self-limiting. Building more roads doesn't work, because more people make more trips. Making the roads faster or more efficient, ditto. Road-pricing can work, as it has in central London, but it works at the cost of tipping the equity-balance even further against those who, already exiled by poverty to the city fringes where public transport is out of the question, are already more than usually dependent on, and less than usually able to afford, road transport. Limiting car-parking can work, but prices soar (also disadvantaging the poor) and the circling hunters of scarce parking spaces can significantly worsen both congestion and pollution. And improving public transport doesn't work unless it's accompanied by truly intolerable congestion – because if people can drive, they will. Congestion is an inevitable by-product of sprawl, which is why low-density, motorway-rich cities like Los Angeles and Auckland have the worst congestion, not the least.

People planning, building and living in leafy suburbia do so because they love nature. No question. They love the birds in the trees, the sun through greenery, the idea of innocence. Not real innocence, just the look. Not real nature, either, but nature de-fanged. Nature without tooth or claw. Which means the very essence of suburbia is a kind of kitsch; a denial, in Kundera's term, of shit. And the love? The nature-love that drives sprawl? The love may be real, but it's the kind that kills. Sprawlers are loving nature to death.

People living in a dense urban huddle, on the other hand, cannot help but share energy, share transport and share space to a degree that is inconceivable in any other situation. People who live in inner cities use about half the electricity of people who do not. Green architecture, therefore, is not made of mud-brick or adobe. Nor is it Federation bungalows surrounded by trees and birds and gardens – much as this might look nature-friendly. Green architecture is made of concrete and glass and high-speed lifts (which, by the way, are among the most energy-efficient passenger vehicles in the world). This is the crucial point, and it is hard to accept because we are such literal creatures. Green living doesn't look green. Green cities look more like *Bladerunner* than *Lassie*; more like Surry Hills than Mosman; more like Greenwich Village than Long Island. Green living depends on a highly artificial, heavily modified, densely urban environment.

Which is not to say that such a sustainable city environment can't be clean or healthy or even enchanting and romantic and picturesque. It can – although in most cities this, as they say, needs work. And it's not to say we can't have street trees or watercourses or luscious parks or densely planted garden courts or rooftop orchards and bowers. We can. Indeed, I believe, we must. The spin-off is palpable. Green cities are intensely cultural and the nature within them is, on the whole, cultivated, with no pretence at wilderness. The green city's greatest benefit, though, operates outside its boundaries – the release of nature from the taming, polluting, plasticising grip of sprawl. From the mowing and pruning, the kerbing and channelling, the asphalt-spreading, land-eating, water-guzzling, wilderness-destroying mass solipsism that the suburban dream has become.

Cities benefit nature by keeping us out of it. And the key to the green city, the essence of it, is density. Thus density becomes a point of convergence: a point at which cultural and environmental imperatives, so often seen as polar opposites, merge. Not only does the vital, intensive city increase our chances of avoiding environmental and cultural catastrophe. It also, as humanity's powerhouse of ideas, increases our chances of ducking that catastrophe, if and when.

◆ | Nature deficit disorder

The law of unintended consequences holds that every human action has at least one unforeseen result. Sometimes, as with the modern city, it's a big one. Really big. Sprawl was supposed to bring nature to everyman. But sprawl is a down-the-line modernist phenomenon. Modernism approached cities as a three-year-old approaches dinner, wanting all flavours and colours clearly separated and all texture reduced to a smooth, grainless pulp. The modern city paradigm came to resemble a poached egg, with an intense central business monoculture surrounded by flavourless, colourless sprawl. And this has produced almost the opposite of its intended effect. Rather than making nature available to everyone, it has made nature all but inaccessible to almost everyone – to the point of threatening nature's very existence.

It was the industrial revolution that, in generating a new class of urban poor, brought slums to cities in serious quantities, and it was as a reaction against these slums that suburbia appeared in the dreams of nineteenth century reformists such as Henrietta Barnett and Ebenezer Howard. Inner-city living was blamed not only for physical ills like rickets, diphtheria and even plague but also, and even more tenuously, for social and moral degradation. 'Without cleanliness there is no pure religion,' wrote Sydney reformist George Taylor in 1914. 'Crime is mostly a matter of environment. Give a man healthy conditions and faith in himself and you reform him.'

Wholesale slum clearance followed, but good intentions did not stop it being seen, then and now, as class warfare by bulldozer. As commentators noted in the hubbub surrounding demolition of New Orleans' mainly black Ninth Ward after Hurricane Katrina, it is a short mental leap from getting rid of the houses of the poor to getting rid of the poor. Same in pre-Olympics Beijing and in post-Olympics Sydney, where the immediate political response to a so-called riot in inner-city Redfern was to reach for the bulldozer.

Modernism may have believed in the great slum clearances that ushered in the twentieth century but, equally, it needed them. Then as now, the city fathers had a double agenda running. In Sydney, shooing the disease-ridden poor out to greener fields had the singular upside of liberating vast tracts of land for 'comprehensive redevelopment' on the scale that would facilitate the construction of the Central Business District. (The Sydney Harbour Bridge would never have been built had not the plague that swept through The Rocks in 1901 provided the perfect excuse for wholesale resumption and demolition.) Empowered first by the train and then by the car, reformists turned diverse, if chaotic, mixed-use downtowns into monocultural CBDs and outlying farmlands into dormitory sprawl; all for the very best of reasons.

In the British colonies, based as they were on a tradition of rural rather than urban wealth, people needed little enough persuasion to believe that a personal country seat was suddenly available for everyman. To inner-city slum dwellers and the middle class alike, the garden suburb seemed a way of being both in and not-in the city, at the one time. *Rus in urbe.* Have your cake, eat it.

And for a while the promise seemed real. Suburbia's salad days were the days of post-war optimism, when free education, free health care, free school milk seemed permanently and universally sustainable. Advertisements from the 1940s and 1950s show happy families at sunny gingham-topped breakfast tables, with greenery visible at the window and a car in the drive. In some ways, for some people, in some (usually older, inner, wealthier) suburbs, that dream still holds. But for the vast mass of suburbanites, and for society as a whole, the suburban dream is starting to look like an own goal. Far from combining the best points of town and country, the suburb, it now appears, simply combines their downsides; isolation and car-dependency *as well as* traffic jams and pollution and inter-neighbour warfare. Even now, with heavy industry largely gone from cities, it's the yuppie apartment-dwellers – the people who might actually be capable of the much-vaunted e-commute – who have moved downtown, while the poor and very poor remain mired in far-flung ex-urbia. Far from providing community and nature, sprawl has generally provided neither.

Could it have worked? Could we have had the pleasures of suburban living without its devastating long-term side-effects: pollution and congestion, obesity and depression, materialism, self-absorption and cultural stagnation? Could we perhaps, even now, 'fix' suburbia, making it sustainable, beautiful and welcoming? Certainly, evidence confirms what we already intuitively knew: people are happier and healthier when in contact with 'nature'. A 2003 study from the Netherlands found that, on three general health indicators – number of recent symptoms, perceived general health and psychiatric morbidity – people score better with more greenery around them.

On the other hand, such studies tend to deal with inner-urban areas that are heavily noise and traffic polluted, not recognising that most traffic is generated by the suburban sprawl around the cities rather than by the dense city centres themselves; that in this sense sprawl sends its unhappiness to the city. In pedestrian- or cycle-dominated cities such effects would likely be less or even negligible. Studies of this kind tend, further, to rely on the finding that while *general* health and longevity is actually higher in inner cities, city people tend to score lower on the mental health indicator. Put beside studies on creativity and psychopathology, however, this may simply indicate another thing we already knew, namely, that creative types gather in cities. This is not about happiness, not contentment-type happiness, but about stimulus.

Richard Florida, well-known proponent of creative cities, mapped college graduate concentrations across America to show that the concentration of the 'creative classes' in high-density areas is, if anything, increasing. It's a phenomenon Florida calls 'means migration'. Whereas in 1970, he says, human capital was reasonably evenly spread, now more than ever 'young graduates are flocking in ever-greater numbers to the "means metros" where they often live in penury until either making it or being forced out by the high cost of living'. Meanwhile, 'most rural and many urban areas are ... being left behind.' The reason, he says, ranges from aesthetics to economics but, essentially, it's about proximity: 'The physical proximity of talented, highly educated people has a powerful effect on innovation and economic growth.' Indeed, talent-clustering may be the primary determinant of growth. In Australia, whose cities are less afflicted by the centre-emptying 'donut syndrome' than their US counterparts, the trend back to the city core is visible everywhere. In Sydney alone, though, and for the first time, the Australian Productivity Commission reported that multi-unit brownfield building approvals in 2004 outnumbered approvals in greenfield sites, and first-home buyers are now more likely to buy an apartment than a house.

Perhaps it is no surprise that contemporary public health gradients directly contradict those nineteenth century ones that helped generate sprawl in the first place. In Australia, for example, recent figures from the 2006 State of the Environment Report show not only that life expectancy is greatest in the cities and decreases steadily with distance from the city centre but also that, of the 'excess' deaths outside city centres, half are due to heart, lung and cardiovascular diseases (excluding lung cancer) and a further 12 per cent to suicide and diabetes. Again, it's that old mind-body thing; the way physical activity levels reflect mental activity. Fulbright Scholar Professor Billie Giles-Corti from the School of Population Health at the University of Western Australia has observed:

> Many major diseases of the 21st century are associated with physical
> inactivity [which is] second only to tobacco as the leading cause
> of death and disability ... Never before in human history have so
> many people been so sedentary in the course of their daily lives.
> It has been suggested that trends in inactivity and weight status
> are partly due to the creation of obesogenic environments.

Further, according to the World Health Organisation and others, growing evidence implies that the increased social capital and sense of community in tight, pedestrian-friendly environments are important factors also in maintaining mental health.

Australia, like most Western countries, is more suburbanised than ever, as well as fatter and more depressed than ever. Over the 100 years from 1901 to 2001, as reported in a paper by TF Smith and M Doherty, the proportion of the population living in suburbia rose from 15 per cent to 58 per cent, with a further 20 per cent now living in non-metropolitan coastal sprawl.

Why? Precisely because suburbia is 'comfortable'. Far from promoting authentic contact with either nature or community, suburbia offers a cocoon, a safety bubble, where the great outdoors is only what can be crammed into the few minutes between the car and the front door, and 'public' is only what survives the censor of distance. As David Nicholson-Lord notes in an article entitled 'Drink Fresh Snow':

> No other society has lived so cocooned from the vagaries of
> climate and weather ... Up to 93 percent of Westerners' lives
> are now lived indoors. Research suggests that 99 percent of
> Americans spend less than one day in a lifetime in conscious
> sensory contact with nature. Out of 1,440 minutes a day, Britons
> average just one minute in the countryside or seaside.

Far from connecting us with nature, suburbia deprives us of it, and with this cocooning goes sensory deprivation – textureless city centres, colourless, tasteless sprawl. It's back to needs and wants; the suburb may be comfortable, but that's the problem. By distracting us with what we want – namely comfort – suburbia provides precisely the kind of cushiony environment that lets us overlook its obliteration of what we need. It may have promised to re-connect us with nature, but suburbia-as-she-is-done merely deepens the nature-culture chasm.

The bubble, the car, the *Umwelt*

Suburbia's happy oblivion bounces along on that other, ultimate bubble, the car. Most of the car's effects on our built world are familiar enough; the ten-lane highways, the billboards, the fumes, the drive-in lifestyle, the road rage, the sprawl. But we seldom question its effect on our mind-body relationship; the speed, the illusion of immortality, the way a car sucks space into a nutshell and makes 'me' it. And this is the conflicted nub of it. Just as we love food but hate fat, we love our cars even as we hate what they do to our bodies, our neighbourhoods, our planet. Why? And is there an answer to this conundrum?

Iambic metre, the West's most basic rhythm of rhyme and song, arose, it's said, from thousands of years of shared existence with the lop-sided *clip-CLOP, clip-CLOP* of the horse's walking hoof-beats. As our bodies moved, our minds were moved to create. This suggests that momentum, and the movement that produces it, matters; not just physically but emotionally, intellectually, spiritually. Musically, even. Many writers must walk to compose. We know, for example, that Wordsworth walked straight and unveering, while Coleridge zigged and zagged wildly. So what happens now that we can generate momentum *without* bodily movement, without so much as a hoof-beat? Now that the velocity-drug is ours at push-of-button, or turn-of-key, with little or no work required? What might be the effect on our minds and on our poetics when, millennia hence, we've internalised the rhythms of the humming, or maybe silent, cyber-engine? Will our lives still show a pulse?

You've heard the stories of nuns doing cryptic crosswords to stave off Alzheimers, and of Einstein learning the violin for the new neuronal pathways the unfamiliar finger-movements formed in his brain. The ultimate in this use-it-or-lose-it genre is the tale of the sea squirt. The sea squirt is a small marine invertebrate that swims like a tadpole for its first few hours or days (depending on subspecies), then spends its entire adulthood – years, maybe – stuck, nose-first, to a rock. In its larval form the sea squirt has a rudimentary brain which, linked by a primitive spinal cord to its tail, enables it to swim. Within seconds of embarking on its sessile stage, however, the sea squirt, having no further need for motion, crushes and digests its own brain. Known colloquially as 'dead man's fingers', the sea squirt sits out its remaining months or years with a mere dorsal ganglion for intellectual equipment.

Wags offer the sea squirt as a parable of university tenure. But its real lesson is that bodily motion feeds intellect, as well as vice versa. 'Movement,' notes Harvard clinical psychiatrist John Ratey, 'is fundamental to the very existence of a brain.' The inverse of Einstein's violin playing also holds; movement deprivation, like sensory deprivation, destroys neural pathways.

So perhaps we're headed in the right direction. After all, movement – more, bigger, faster movement – is the founding principle of the entire modern world. As Antonio Sant'Elia and Filippo Tommaso Marinetti proclaimed, in their 1919 *Futurist Manifesto*, 'we are no longer the men of cathedrals, the palaces, the assembly halls; but of big hotels, railway stations, immense roads, colossal ports, covered markets, brilliantly-lit galleries, freeways, demolitions and rebuilding schemes'. Alvin Toffler, writing *Future Shock* in 1970, noted that the average American would cover, during their lifetime, around 650 times as many non-walking miles as they had travelled in 1914. No doubt the figure has multiplied as many times again since. And while some of this travel is necessary for work, much of it – by car, plane or boat – is simply fun. It is as though humanity itself has changed. As Le Corbusier, a self-proclaimed speed-freak who happily modelled architecture on cars and planes, declared, 'generations are being born who will learn to live in my radiant city'.

Probably the will-to-speed was always with us; only the means is new. Think of spider monkeys swinging through branches, of kids swinging on long ropes over rivers, of the way both children and monkeys will suddenly run, flat out, for the sheer joy of it. Acceleration-exhilaration may well be hardwired. Certainly Canadian philosopher

Mark Kingwell argues that 'the human race has always been going as fast as it can'. Indeed, our very desire-vocabulary brims with words like 'drive' and 'gusto' that imply as much.

And that's fine. But perhaps acceleration is like food; perhaps, now that we can have it, at will and in almost unlimited quantities, our more-is-better impulses are outmoded. Even dangerous. Perhaps speed without movement, the thrill without the effort, is in fact destructive. This sounds like a moral pointer but could be simply practical. In speed, perhaps, as in calories; when necessity no longer disciplines us, self-discipline must step in. For although we tend to equate movement with velocity – much as we tend to equate pleasure with happiness – they're not the same thing. And just as pleasure can actually undo happiness, velocity can militate against just the kind of movement, and the kind of brain-stimulus, that we need.

Cars are an obvious example. In 1909, a full decade before the *Futurist Manifesto* appeared, *Le Figaro* published one of the earliest literary paeans to the automobile, Marinetti's loving account of an impromptu early-morning car race around the outer suburbs of Milan. Since then, cars have become fundamental to our lives, and Marinetti's fanciful prediction of cities shaped by speed seems no more than a description of normality. A recent Australian Bureau of Statistics survey showed that although almost all Australians are now engaged in recycling, 'concern for the environment stops at the garage door, with four out of five shunning public transport' in favour of the car.

First and foremost, of course, the car is a speed machine, as revolutionary in human living patterns as was that first domesticated horse on the Central Asian steppes, maybe 5000 years ago. As well, cars are fun. Especially in a voluptuous town like Sydney, where tearing across the Harbour Bridge in a Mini-Moke on a salty, sultry night can feel like the quintessential city experience. As Anthony Hopkins' endearing Burt Munro says in *The World's Fastest Indian*, 'you live more in five minutes on a bike like this going flat out than some people live in a lifetime'. Generally, though, cars enclose space. This is the second ingredient of our addiction. The car is personal, mobile architecture, a public mask for a private bubble. It is, in short, an *Umwelt*.

The car as *Umwelt*

Umwelt (literally, 'around-world') is a term coined by Estonian bio-semiotician Jakob von Uexküll (1864–1944), whose work lay untranslated and out of print until rediscovered by the postmodern cognitive science and cyberphilosophy sets. Von Uexküll, seeing mind, body and context as inseparable, for all animals, coined the word to cover an organism's physical life-support system and the subjective network of relationships and interpretations that give its world meaning. Umwelt is the world-bubble that makes meaning possible, for *you*.

Umwelten are therefore personal, varying from organism to organism. Compare, said von Uexküll, a meadow seen through the compound eyes and feeding priorities of a fly with the same meadow seen through the black-and-white but smell-laden senses of a dog. An individual Umwelt forms and is formed by its organism and, together with that organism, becomes what philosopher Elizabeth Grosz (a von Uexküll fan) calls 'an organ of survival'.

A car, then, is an Umwelt; a personal milieu that offers both physical support and mental interaction and which, as second skin, extends the essential boundary between us and chaos. This is under-recognised. Surprisingly, since most surveys agree that over 50 per cent of cars are now bought by women, most car-talk is conducted exclusively in terms of form and function: speed, gear-ratios; boy stuff. Critics and marketers tend to forget that the car is also, essentially, an interior. Not just any interior, either. Although usually underwhelming in design terms, the car-as-interior is perhaps the most compelling source of our emotional entrapment in the age, and cage, of the automobile.

Von Uexküll took the Umwelt idea from his close observation of the life, in particular the mental life, of the humble tick. The female tick, having mated, hangs on a branch until a mammal passes beneath; triggered by the smell of the butyric acid in the mammal's sweat, to which she is sensitive, she falls onto the mammal, and runs around on its skin until her thermoreceptors detect blood directly beneath the skin. She burrows in, sucks herself stupid, falls off, lays her eggs and dies. The tick's Umwelt comprises three essential cues, no more: sweat, warmth and blood. Wrote von Uexküll in *A Stroll Through the Worlds of*

Animals and Men, 'The whole rich world around the tick shrinks and changes into a scanty framework consisting, in essence, of three receptor cues and three effector cues – her Umwelt. But the very poverty of this world guarantees the unfailing certainty of her actions, and security is more important than wealth.'

The car enables us to act like the tick; entirely absorbed in and driven by our own immediate desires. We control our aural, temperature, smell and sound environments, reducing the world's chaos to some manageable order. In a car we can sing or phone, quarrel or fart to our heart's content; windows open or closed, roof up or down, exhibiting as much or as little of our self as we please. Mothers will do the school-run in bare feet and lingerie, providing they needn't emerge from the car. Couples save their long heart-to-hearts for the car; fathers their son-talks. In a car you needn't confront each other but can look, together, out the window. The car is a comfort zone, a suit of armour, an expandable, swollen ego.

As *Boston Globe* columnist Sam Allis notes:

> Car time is the last, best, private time left to us. Anyone with the intelligence of a yak knows this. Car time is defined as an extended period spent by two people in a moving vehicle. One person is a wake and three is a crowd. So two. There is no algorithm to car time. It is, like jazz, played a million different ways. Some car people top out at monosyllabic. Others sing like jay birds across state lines.

Allis talks as if 'car time' is some sort of ancient right, or rite, being slowly whittled away by modern philistinism. In fact it is brand new in historical terms and, far from being endangered, car time is running the show. One-fifth of all American meals, says US writer Michael Pollan, are now eaten in cars. There are drive-in banks, funeral homes, even (the mind boggles) drive-in toilets. The car is a shiny personal bubble that gives the illusion of vast personal control while in many ways controlling us. That gives the sense of authentic movement, while substituting the addictive drug of speed. That dangles the suggestion of 'auto-mobility' while, in reality, it moves, we don't. What does this mean, for our lives, our psyches, and our cities?

One of the car's most pervasive, most addictive and least recognised effects, however, is anaesthetic. Forget yoga. Forget acupuncture, hypnosis and mindfulness therapy. Bested only by television and alcohol, the car is one of the most effective anaesthetics ever discovered.

The car's overwhelming prophylactic efficacy relies in part on its even-handed appeal to both sexes. Basic gender-biology drives men towards projectile recreation (like football, guns and rockets) while women are drawn to reception and containment activities (feeding, shopping, socialising, handbags, house-making). The car meets both gender needs to perfection. Projectile container or pocket rocket, it receives and shoots at once. No wonder our addiction seems unbreakable. And both of these aspects – speed and the bubble – offer anaesthetic properties. Speed offers both the thrill of velocity and the action-addiction that allows us to stay busy by seeming to save time. And the bubble, the Umwelt, enhances these delights. Life, as the ageing mayor in the film *Shortbus* observes, demands porosity. But because this constant exchange also brings vulnerability, one of the Umwelt's functions is to provide a safe bubble from which porosity can operate: an injecting room, so to speak. From city-wall to cell-wall, this is the architecture of life. The car makes it portable.

And that's the problem. Cars are swollen selves, appealing directly to our lowest chakra, what Buddhism calls the 'self or own abode' chakra, the *swadhisthana*. And as Siddhartha reputedly said beneath the bodhi tree, 'selfhood blinds them … They crave pleasure for themselves and they cause pain to others … and how empty are their pleasures … without contents like the bubble'. So our motorways swarm-to-bursting with fat little *swadhisthanas*, swollen and bubble-wrapped like well-fed ticks, dodgeming about in a mayhem of road-rage and speed-addiction. Which is how our cars, for all their transparency, blind us to so many evident truths. This combined bubble-appeal to two hardwired urges – for speed and for safety – is what makes the car both so sexy, and so dangerous.

Decades back, Toffler argued that the new transience – lubricated by disposability, mobility, rental, contraception and divorce – was dramatically diminishing the vigour of our relationship with the material world, what he called the 'man-thing nexus'. This might sound like a good thing, like greed reduction. In fact, it's vice versa.

Our failure to connect properly with our material world is precisely what allows us to trash it with so little compunction. As with pens and shavers, so with architecture. Churches, post offices and banks – the institutions that once established the very eye-teeth of our cities – now lease space in speculative towers, shopping centres and office parks. We build for the disposable short term. As Marinetti predicted a century ago: 'Each generation will have to build its own city'.

Slippery cities

It's as though we deliberately conceive our shared world as a glass mountain, a surface designed specifically to repudiate all attempts at purchase, including our own. To Toffler's list of lubricant devices we could add all the various bubbles we blow to isolate ourselves from anything too closely resembling reality. These devices include not only the fully-home-theatre-and-pool-equipped McMansion, from which the dedicated telecommuter need scarcely ever emerge, but iPods, email, in-car television (aka backseat Supernanny), virtual reality and computer dating; portable devices designed to accompany us on those forays into the public realm that prove unavoidable. On a slightly more abstract level there's hot-desking, e-commuting, enterprise bargaining and outsourcing, all designed to exclude the other and increase the priority of the private over the public; to reduce the porosity of the mask. So marked are these bubbles, and so effective their isolationism, that the hunt is on for a term to describe the phenomenon. The *Atlantic Monthly*'s columnist Barbara Wallraff, answering a reader's query as to a name for the barrier erected by headphones, invited suggestions 'either for the barrier or for the "country" that a headphone wearer inhabits'.

Refuge and sanctuary are things that we need, certainly, and as we find less and less sense of refuge in the public realm of the city we seek it, increasingly, in our own, ever more self-sufficient suburban mask or castle. The trouble is that retreat, like so many of our instinctual drives, has largely outlived its usefulness and, over-satisfied, itself becomes a threat. Psychologist Toru Sato uses the shell-metaphor, arguing that we build shells around our 'self-system' and that the more damaged or traumatised the self, the thicker the shell into which the self withdraws like *Pithecanthropus* into a cave. The trouble is the shell, like the cave, is as much trap as shield. The thicker the shell, the mask, the more it encloses us, inhibiting the very interaction we need to heal the trauma. The suburban castle operates similarly, trapping us in a comfortable prison. The coincidence of McMansionism with postmodernism's culture of fear is no coincidence. But the withdrawal impulse is directly counter-productive. 'The thinner our shells are,' notes Sato, 'the more efficiently we adjust and develop and learn from our experience ... and remain in unity with other people/things.'

This slow thickening of the wall between our inner and outer lives, between self and city, as Richard Sennett puts it, is a triumph of the private and personal over the public and shared, and it results inevitably in distrust and impoverishment of the public realm. This inner-outer distinction, analogous to the mind-body distinction touched on in chapter 4, is one of Christian theology's great strengths since, in establishing the self as a separate, objective entity it encourages both individual conscience and abstract moral thought. But a great strength so easily becomes a great weakness. When the wall becomes too solid, its 'shadows ... continue to darken secular society' and the self is trapped, incarcerated, within.

In our city fabric, the casualties of this disconnect include texture and detail. Just as the internal combustion engine removes rhythm from our rhyme and song, it dulls our senses and blunts our brains by taking texture and detail from our material lives. And this smoothing over of the cracks and crevices in the city, combined with the loss of the sense of old-time or eternity, drives us, ironically, yet further into the bubble, sending the feedback loop spiralling in on itself. And just as car culture turns the small, local sign into the out-scale billboard – a high-impact low-nutrition device that is the visual equivalent of fast food – it applies the same coarsening effect across the rest of our urban geography, outsizing roads, degrading and fragmenting landscapes and reducing cities to slippery, non-grip surfaces across which we slide in our personal Umwelten, spectators in our own place. The result is what Sennett sees as the 'sensory deprivation that seems to curse most modern buildings ... and the tactile sterility that afflicts the urban environment'. Our determined and increasingly effective flight from discomfort, and our addiction to various forms of anaesthesia, has made 'the massive outer world [lose] its weight'. But we, too, lose, since 'watching pacifies'. Spectating renders us passive; as car drivers, television watchers, fast food consumers, we are deprived of authentic stimulus, our bodies dulled by comfort and speed. Thus does the kinaesthetic become the anaesthetic.

As the body, so the mind. The car, having sprung from our innate urge to lubricate our lives, is humanity's most widespread and successful friction-reducer to date. But, like so many of our successful lubricant devices, it is rebounding on us; its double anaesthesia of speed-without-movement and control-without-connection puts us in danger of destroying our minds, our bodies, our cities and our one, irreducible Umwelt, the planet. Unless we can learn more quickly, outsmarting even the smart-car, we may find out the hard way that, contrary to instinct, our much-craved comfort is really the enemy in disguise.

Porosity

Apart from the political and environmental aspects noted above, sprawl has a strong aesthetic component. And it's not just about the ugliness of the McMansion – the phoniness, the visual illiteracy, the pomp – either singly or en masse. Indeed some suburbia is very pretty, at the trees-and-streets level, but there is another aesthetic aspect, which relates to the explorability idea from the beginning of this chapter.

Explorability is not even a word – at least not according to Spellcheck – and yet it is, one might argue, the essential difference between a city that is engaging to inhabit and one that is not. Think of us as some sort of mobile marine creature – not a sea squirt but some equally vulnerable species doomed to eke out a living from the great, semi-hospitable rock on which it finds itself. Purchase is of the essence and for us, a primary means of establishing purchase on the rock – of scratching our lives into its surface – is urbanism. The city is a foothold in nature, not its enemy.

More than that, though, explorability allows play. We are, after all, not sessile marine creatures but free-moving primates – endlessly curious, endlessly inventive, happiest when our imaginations are fully engaged.

Play, argued Dutch theorist Johan Huizinga in his 1955 classic *Homo Ludens*, precedes culture: play is the primeval soil from which grow myth and ritual and, through them, 'all the great instinctive forces of civilized life'. These days, of course, we see play in more narcissistic terms – play enhances our mental and physical wellbeing, play promotes success. Nobel laureates play, psychopaths don't, and so on. Either way, play is a mindset thing. And yet for many adults these days, play is almost exclusively physical; sex or sport. For a decade or two in the mid-twentieth century we played happily with the bright toys of culture, but lately culture has become exceedingly earnest. These days our art, writing, intellectual life and architecture take themselves seriously indeed, even when – or perhaps especially when – they're being self-consciously ironic.

What is play? Defining it is pointless, of course, but you know when you're doing it. Play is fun, but not necessarily funny. It can be serious, but not usually purposeful. It can even be work, but it's never, ever predictable. Play is essentially curious, exploratory, open-ended. It's an adventure. And the more intelligent it is, the more fun. Play is intelligent adventure. And this is something in which good cities, without exception, excel.

Richard Goodwin is an architect-sculptor for whom the idea of porosity in cities has become a life's work. For Goodwin, traditional urban forms such as Italian hill towns and Greek fishing villages exhibit a porosity – which you might define as 'habitable texture' – that contemporary cities lack. His work ranges from endless experiment with forms of exoskeleton – body-wrappings, prostheses, bicycles, flying machines – to the deliberate colonisation of private urban space (in office buildings, for example) as if it were public, thus expanding, complicating and enriching – adding texture to – the public realm. Usually, in contemporary cities, the dynamic works the other way; not publicness invading private space, but private space invading and claiming public space.

The contemporary shopping mall is a classic instance, striving to ape the complexity and interest of a traditional market, but with one, overarching difference; the space is privately owned and entirely under private control. The air is cooled and conditioned and gently muzak-laced; the lighting, level changes, transparency and detail are minutely orchestrated to slow your gait within microseconds and lull you into buy-mode; and no one, other than the owner, has any right to be there. Everyone else is there on sufferance. Anyone undesirable, or homeless, or obviously poor, can be summarily shuffled out so that the mass-narcosis of consumerism never pops.

Of course, you argue, the poor have never 'owned' the city. And this is true. But it is ironic that the cities of democracy have become, if anything, less tolerant and less public – reserving more of their goodies for the moneyed – than ever.

And it may be that this super-clean, false at-homeness has leached out, shifting our expectations of city streets in general. Or it may simply be that the prioritisation of the private and personal model in all things – so that our relationship with god needs to be a friendly, first-name terms one, and our office spaces need to be casual, friendly, domestic and personalised – has come to apply to our city streets as well. Or it may simply be our growing obsession with personal safety, even as we live the safest lives known to human history, as though by eliminating threat we can overcome death itself.

Whatever the cause, city fathers the world over seem to have conceived the notion that a city can and should be rendered as clean and safe and non-threatening as your own living room. What's wrong with that? Two things. One, it's boring. Just as we now know that over-cleaning your own house can lead to increased levels of asthma and other allergies in children, over-cleaning the city – filling all the cracks and crevices where dirt or danger might gather – makes it boring. And boredom is the antithesis of explorability, the antithesis of play.

Nature and culture, order and chaos

Order – or, if you prefer, meaning – is in many ways the essence of art, including (or especially) architectural art. You might even argue that extracting order from nature is life's essential act. As Grosz puts it, 'each life needs to cast out the chaos but extract from it what it needs … [we] divide and organize chaos according to a plane of coherence … shielding ourselves from chaos with habit, cliché and doxa'.

Peter Zapffe, a Norwegian existentialist famous for completing his law finals in perfect rhyming couplets, defines civilisation as the 'strict regime of self-censorship' by which we keep ourselves sane. This is order, or art, or culture. But it depends on, and is nourished by, a constant supply, an up-bubbling of chaos. Chaos is threatening. But it is also something we seem to need. And this is the function of art. It allows us to taste chaos without the danger of immersion. In Grosz' words, art 'dips us into chaos in a controlled, temporary and ordering fashion'.

Art, then, straddles the crucial interface between order and chaos, forming a link or conduit between the two immiscibles, much as a soap molecule straddles the interface between oil and water. This is the transgressive nature of art. There is an essential naughtiness, or disobedience, by which art refuses to confine itself to the bounds of politeness. Art is essentially indiscreet; wild in the pursuit of truth, and profligate in its use. Which is why political correctness, as habitually imposed by arts-funding bureaucracies, is the kiss of death for all genuine artistic endeavour, including that most complex of art forms, the city.

'The citizen's job,' says essayist John Ralston Saul, 'is to be rude – to pierce the comfort of professional intercourse by boorish expressions of doubt. Politics, philosophy, writing, the arts – none of these, and certainly not science and economics, can serve the common weal if they are swathed in politeness.'

Cities need both chaos and order, and rely on a fine balance between the two. Too much chaos gives you Athens or Mexico City; too much order results in sterility – like Brasilia, Canberra, Singapore. It follows that any attempt to create a good city according to plan is in fact oxymoronic; an attempt doomed to failure. It's almost as if chaos is the raw energy which cities must constantly, actively, convert into the light-source – the lamp, if you like – of culture.

They used to say that the rat problem in ancient Rome – like the subway problem in New York – had got so bad, and the vermin so thoroughly entrenched in the largely unmapped system of pipes and sewers and tunnels and basements beneath the Imperial city, that there was no longer any hope of scoping the problem, much less of getting it under control. This, from the authorities' point of view, was a cause for great lamentation and beating of the breast. In fact, it was a sign of hope; hope that there is a degree of size and complexity beyond which cities cease to be control-capable. For just as the internet's main strength and potential for good in the world lies in its uncontrollability, by any one or for any purpose, so the best urban cultures carry in them the ever-present bubbling-up of chaos.

Why is this chaotic edge so important? Because creativity is about play, and play is about adventure, and adventure requires the unknown outcome, a sense of open-endedness, in order to be exciting. This means it is necessary to duck the yoke of control. If something can be controlled, you can be sure there'll be someone – some government, some regime, some orthodoxy – just busting to hop on the throne and do precisely that. Control it.

Controls are the forces of safety and comfort, the herd forces of cohesion and conservatism, and up to a point they're necessary. But they're also the forces of mediocrity; the forces that turn interesting street theatre, say, into the dull, safe, saleable West End sort so favoured by governments.

A city deprived of its bubbling undercurrent of chaos, or with its chaos so thoroughly plastic coated, so trapped by the bubble that there is no possibility of threat, holds also no possibility of excitement. When the mask becomes opaque and shiny, it's all over.

7 | **Feminism and future-eating**

Woman would not have the instinct for finery if she
did not have the instinct for the secondary role.

FRIEDRICH NIETZSCHE

Fat is a social disease, and fat is a feminist issue.

SUSIE ORBACH

Women, in myth, tradition and customary thought, are society's
unofficial eco-guardians. From the witches and soothsayers who
connived with nature against the androdoxy to the presumption that
the 'feminine' traits are the receptive ones, we take a fertility-based
earth–mother alliance pretty much for granted. And women's natural
tendency to accommodate rather than aggress, to nurture and manage
rather than slash and burn, and to assume a maternal, strategic view of
survival all gang up to support such an interpretation.

And so, from flaky eco-feminism through to everyday thought,
we presume that feminism, in empowering women, also empowers
nature. Indeed, gender-oppression is often seen as so like nature-

oppression that (it is assumed) nature and women might, as long-term co-oppressed, rise up together, two faces of some ancient goddess, to reclaim their place in the universe. But what if all this is wrong? What if the opposite were true, and feminism proved a primary, if unwitting, perpetrator of eco-crime? What if fat really were a feminist issue, only not in the way we thought? Not for how it looks, but for how it happens and what it signifies? What if women were the bad guys? What then?

● | Fat

It's not that women have, as the cliché goes, become men. We haven't morphed into grotesque paragons of aggression, whatever the growing incidence of bad, mad male-pattern girl-driving might suggest. No, it's more that, in ecologies as in diets, the really irreparable damage arises not from the one-off incident – the birthday binge, the catastrophic oil spill – but from the iterative, unexamined, habitual pattern. What does the damage is the daily grind that we consider harmless precisely because it is so normal.

The daily grind is, as we know, women's turf. So it's fitting, if ironic, that it is quotidian crime in which post-feminist womanhood has come to excel; lifestyle crime. The surprise is that feminism itself, which after all intends nature nothing but good, could be unwittingly implicated in her destruction.

While feminism is a broad church, its cults many and varied, the primary split is between those who want women to equal men on traditional men's turf, and those who claim equal status for their women's turf. In hunter-gatherer terms it's the difference between wanting to hunt with the men, and simply wanting equal recognition for gathering.

So far, so acceptable. The problem is that women's work is mostly dull and repetitive, while men's work, the hunt, ripples with adrenalin, novelty and adventure. This makes feminism's choice, at best, a choice between failures; failure through unequal competition and failure through drudgery. Perhaps it is no surprise that feminism, trapped between the dull and the doomed, has generally declined even to articulate the dilemma, drifting off instead into a fuzz of ideology, emotion and spin. Anne Moir and David Jessel, whose 1989 book *Brain Sex: The Real Difference Between Men and Women* tried to deal honestly with gender-based brain difference, still felt constrained to argue that 'women's work is only inferior on the male value system'.

We wish. In truth, housework will never be heroic. This is no male plot, but a simple, irritating fact. Even when it's genuinely important, like mothering; even ritualised to the level of sacrament or paid to the level of executive stress, women's natural work cannot be packaged as groundbreaking. Women may keep the home fires burning but, as a rule, it's still men who go out and light new ones. As a rule, it's men who *want* to. As Camille Paglia famously quipped, 'if civilization had been left in female hands, we would still be living in grass huts'.

Of course, women's standing has changed in recent decades, although how much is still a matter for debate. On the one hand, we now have a majority of working mothers; we have the pill and long daycare. We've had Golda Meir, Margaret Thatcher and Condoleezza Rice. But huge inequalities persist, especially in power, wealth and status. Any gathering of powerbrokers outside Norway and New Zealand will, still, be almost exclusively male, while, of that working-mother majority, most still manage house as well. Latest figures show the number of Australian males in full-time work is still almost twice that of females; participation rates hover around 72 per cent for males. For females it's around 57 per cent. In rank-and-file staff positions, Australian corporations typically show 60–65 per cent female employees; at senior executive level it's in the low teens and at board level, lower still. Further, recent reports show that, in the equal-pay fight, the current direction is less progress than egress; out the back door. Even in architecture, where almost half the students are female, the proportion at director level is around 1 per cent. Sometimes it seems women have taken on the burdens of equality, but none of its privileges; the appearance, but not the fact.

Nevertheless, more women have more money and more influence than ever before. Women may not – ever – wield vast political power, but spending power they do have, and it is changing the way we live.

Shopping is the most obvious arena of influence. In our hunter-gatherer brains, men (on the whole) hunt, women gather. Men shop, but usually under duress. Driven by need they do it fast, and badly. Women, on the other hand, *love* to shop. Shopping is for most women what socialising is for the true extrovert; not a chore but a pleasure, soothing in and of itself. So, while women have less time than ever, shopping time has become quality time. Retail therapy was invented by women, for women. America now has more shopping malls than high-schools, all of them, in the words of American retail anthropologist Paco Underhill, 'relentlessly female-driven' in arrangement and atmosphere. Compulsive shoppers – Andy Warhol notwithstanding – are almost always female. Psychologist Michael Kyrios told a recent European conference that compulsive shoppers share some common traits with problem gamblers, but the shoppers are more impulsive and *more likely to be women*. In recent studies, according to US sociologist Barry Schwartz, '93 percent of teenage girls surveyed said that shopping was their favourite activity'.

Without women, shopping-for-fun would be dead. Women shop naturally, easily and well, with a breadth and focus that leaves male shoppers gasping. As Underhill notes, 'men enjoy the mall as a form of recreation [but women] are at malls to shop'. With the increased dollar-power that feminism has delivered, women now shop harder and longer, more voraciously and voluminously, than ever. 'As women's roles change,' says Underhill, 'so does their shopping behaviour – they're becoming a lot more like men in that regard – but they're still the primary buyer in the American marketplace.' We may have 'female cops and firepersons and CEOs and cyber-entrepreneurs and vice presidential candidates,' says Underhill, but 'shopping is still and always will be meant mostly for females.'

And that's fine. In part, our shopping, even our over-shopping, is relatively innocent. We spend more because we can. This is understandable, if not entirely defensible. After all, it's not as if our needs have increased. Indeed, we have fewer unmet needs than any species at any time in history. And since gender equality increases in direct proportion to affluence, with post-industrial countries (other than Japan) consistently scoring highest on gender equality indicators, the very fact of feminism shows just how pretty we're sitting, materially speaking.

But it's not all innocent fun. There is a voracious side to consumption and here, too, women excel. Humanity's mythic history abounds with stories of voracious female monsters, from Sekhmet, the Egyptians' raging lion-goddess, to the central European Baba Iaga; from the carnivorous temptress of Sioux Indian mythology to warrior-maidens of eleventh century Bohemia, who would literally pocket their male prisoners until they agreed to marriage. The links between sex and eating are countless, not only via a shared sensuality but through the astonishingly direct morphological analogue: the business of feeding a mouth to nourish new life.

Myth and ritual teem with such imagery. The mouth–vagina analogy appears in a range of myths and beliefs, from Pliny's assertion that the male snake impregnates the female by putting his head into her mouth and being eaten, to the *vagina dentata* motif noted by Freud and others. This is startlingly resonant both with the medieval Christian belief that witches could grow fangs in their vaginas and with the more contemporary urban myth, prevalent among Vietnam War vets, that Viet Cong prostitutes concealed razor blades within their vaginas. Certain strands of medieval Christianity, according to some sources, equated female genitalia with 'the yawning mouth of hell', characterising the entrance to the underworld as 'the yoni of Mother Hel', and a variety of cultures have initiation rites involving ovens, mouths and cabins. As Italian academic Monica Resel Giordani notes, 'the motif of the swallowing, gulping, devouring monster is also well-known in Africa [and] usually the gulping monsters are female'.

For German philosopher Peter Sloterdijk, women's skills as 'gatherers by birth [makes them] much more compatible with capitalism than men'. The second part of this observation is hard to swallow (no pun intended), since capitalism clearly relies at least as heavily on the high-level corporate hunter as on the low-level consumer-gatherer. But Sloterdijk follows up with an intriguing second thought: 'In the consumer we can still see the calm, triumphal satisfaction of the gatherer who brings things home in her basket. Here the mysterious

feminine universal – the purse – has its roots. A man without a spear …
that's alright, but a woman without a purse, that's against nature.'

It is impossible not to be reminded here of the extraordinary
significance of the dilly-bag in Australian Aboriginal culture. It's
not just the elaborate methods, materials and decorative devices used
in the construction of the dilly-bag, but its recurrence in Dreaming
stories. Yingarna, the creator-ancestor of the Kunwinjku people of
western Arnhem Land, for example, carries fifteen dilly-bags attached
to her head, from which she dispenses – or births – the tribes and
languages of the Aboriginal peoples across the landscape. A similar
story explains the dispersal of peoples in central Australia, where an
old man carried his six sons in his dilly-bag, handing them out in
marriage to groups of young women, then stealing them back after a
single night, repacking them into his mobile 'womb' and taking them
to the next group of women. In Kurri Djang, the blue-tongue lizard
Dreaming from Arnhem Land, the dilly-bag offers a transformative
refuge from men with spears. It's that old sexual diagram: woman as
purse, man as projectile.

This biomorphic parallel between female sexuality and female
consumption suggests that a relentless bio-logic drives women to fill
things up, to fill houses and cars with children and stuff, and themselves
and children with food. Shopping is a classic filling activity: shopping
= eating = sex. Even the feelings are similar, with binge shopping
following the same neurotic patterns as binge eating. 'Self-esteem
problems,' says Kyrios, 'are prevalent in compulsive buyers, and they
use buying as self-medication for depression'. But the buzz of buying is
quickly followed by guilt. Shopping ultimately makes the shopaholic
feel worse, sending her into a downward spiral of joy and shame.

But it's not just biology. In a strange ironic twist, feminism
itself has become a direct expenditure-enhancer. As Clive Hamilton
notes in *Affluenza*, 'feminism has been a marketing bonanza'. This
brings us to the moral thicket that now surrounds feminism like
Sleeping Beauty's forest. Thorny and impenetrable, it remains largely
unexplored, since there be beasts that question the very possibility of
equality.

The traditional feminine traits that 'suit us' to drudgery are the selflessness virtues: caring, nurturing, soothing, supporting. Our mothers and grandmothers were brought up with ideals of duty, sacrifice and obligation. But because women's duties and obligations were owed, in large part, to men, feminism's rejecting of oppression impelled it also to reject selflessness, replacing altruism with assertiveness, duty and care with aggressive self-concern. For feminists of the baby-boomer generation, sloughing off selflessness merged with the natural process of parental rejection and the political fashion of rejecting orthodoxy in all its forms. None of that caring, spinsterish, self-abnegating stuff for us, went the self-talk. To hell with it. We're out there grabbing it, living our lives, as we should be. To be selfish was a designer-label that showed you were more modern than mother.

A telling juxtaposition in the *Sydney Morning Herald*'s *Good Weekend* magazine recently placed a profile of the grandmotherly Myra Pincott AC, National President of the Country Women's Association, next to a review of Naomi Wolf's latest rant. Whereas Pincott's most 'life-changing' book was a Simone Weil treatise holding that 'none of us has rights, only obligations', Naomi Wolf's obsession-du-jour was yet another aspect of self. Wolf, we're told, is 'restless, tired of politics, searching for spirituality, just trying to figure out what's made her unhappy – and now what makes her happy'. Focusing on the big issues, as ever, celebrity feminist examines navel.

Thus has feminism become just another princess game, making self-concern not only respectable but admirable. And commerce has exploited the new selfishness to the hilt, applying 'because you deserve it' advertising to every conceivable product, from cars to chocolates, and from lifestyle to lingerie. It's ubiquitous, and it's all aimed at women. Hamilton offers the example of the 'me ring', a concept invented by De Beers to create demand by designating women's right-hand ring-finger the 'bling finger'. Exploiting the elision between feminism and selfishness, De Beers market the me-ring both as a sign of independence (rather than commitment) and as 'a token of love from you to yourself'. As Hamilton notes, 'it would be difficult to find a better definition of narcissism', however neatly cloaked within the feminist aegis.

The shop, the purse and the womb room

Of course the practice of cloaking women's bodies, as much as their psyches, is age-old. It's a gesture at once at once protective and commodifying, as in the traditional nursery rhyme: *Peter Peter Pumpkin Eater / Had a wife and couldn't keep her / Put her in a pumpkin shell / And there he kept her, very well*. From ancient myth to modern psychology, from nursery rhyme to feminist theory, the identification of femininity with interiority, especially the domestic interior, is persistent. Cooking or burning in an oven was often part of mythic gender or coming-of-age rituals. Demeter, the Greek earth goddess, would put her son in a hot oven each night. Thetis did the same with her son Achilles, each hoping to destroy the mortal nature of their children and secure their immortality.

From prehistoric times the hearth has commonly been seen as the domestic womb, the house's warm productive centre, and the walls of the house as the maternal body. The big-roofed maternal house gives us that 'tucked-in' feel, safely back in the womb. As Macedonian folklorist Lidija Stojanovic says:

> to this family of images such as the oven, furnace, cauldron,
> pan, pot, hole dug into the earth, ie the pit, which show the
> primordial symbolism – *regressus ad uterum* – we would also
> add the symbols of house, a forest cabin, the stomach of the
> demon, beast or monster which also symbolise the mother's
> stomach, or more precisely the uterus, where the death of the
> neophyte represents the return to the embryonic stadium ...

This echoes the notion of the chalice as sacred-feminine that is the centring motif of the *Da Vinci Code* story. Again, the sexual symbolism is obvious. In three dimensions, the chalice is a receiving form, a bowl or uterus; in two dimensions it is a Y-form, like the fork that is the female part of traditional Aboriginal fork-and-ridgepole hut-building. Of woman as dark within, Camille Paglia notes in *Sexual Personae*:

> woman's body is a secret, sacred place [a] marked off space
> ... Every woman is a priestess guarding the temenos of the

daemonic mysteries ... The female body is the prototype of all sacred spaces from cave shrine to temple and church ... Woman is literally the occult, which means 'the hidden.' These uncanny meanings cannot be changed, only suppressed ... until then, we must live and dream in the daemonic turbulence of nature.

Emily Praeger, long-time Greenwich Village resident, wrote in the *Atlantic Monthly* that the events of 9/11 left her 'wounded in my sense of home'. And female victims of burglary and home-invasion typically feel a sense of violation bordering on rape. We may see this very identification of woman with interior as repressive, and of course purdah is the extreme form of such enforced and total interiority. Even so, it suggests that the fear we are so determined to banish, by filling our houses and lives with light and transparency, may not be fear from without so much as fear from within. Not a fear of 'them', but fear, in a deep sense, of ourselves, of what is within. Especially our mysterious, hidden, feminine selves.

Against this interiorisation of women, shopping can be a form of resistance. Writer Erika Rappaport documents how for eighteenth century women the 'ecstatic freedom' of walking in the street alone became a proto-feminist statement. In the modern era too, notes Paco Underhill, shopping was often 'what got the housewife out of the house'. Even now, in repressive cultures, shopping may be the only out-of-house activity women are allowed.

So it is interesting to note the increasing interiorisation of shopping as an activity. From the traditional street market where interiors were usually makeshift and temporary, to the modern mall where entire city blocks and precincts are interiorised to give the (usually female) shopper the illusion of being in a vast, sparkling, bejewelled, cathedral-like *home*. Women like malls because they're known, comfortable, clean and safe – from muggers and spitters, from sun, storms and mendicants. Here, at fantasy-home, women will relax, and when they relax, they will spend.

Malls titillate and relax, even while they make you feel needy, inadequate and dreamily disoriented. They're meant to. It's like chocolate. If you can be made to feel bad, in a small way, the more you want soothing, and the more you buy. One thing you don't see much of in a mega-mall, therefore, is social life. Whereas in a high street you might stop for a coffee, in a mall you bump into someone, you say hi and press on. This is because, from the first car-park moment, the place is designed as a disconnect, separating you from your reality and from your higher, warmer self. It's designed to put you in a bubble – a car-like bubble – of self-gratification.

This is another reason why the mall experience begins and ends at the car park. Grey, fumy and jammed with other irritable, bubble-wrapped humans, the car park is no pleasure dome. It's designed to do a kind of good-cop-bad-cop routine with the mall interior, to make you more susceptible to the shopping urge. And because it is important that we come to it through the gates of hell, the mall is the first architectural type in history that has an inside but no outside. The mall has interior design, heavily themed and fantasised, but it has no street presence, no public self, no architecture.

Unlike the grand shopping emporia of pre-war years, the mall doesn't even try to look attractive. The mall is that ultimate female form, an exteriorless within. A cavernous, fecund womb-space, or perhaps a great, grey, lumpy egg, as in those microscope photos, that is constantly serviced, pestered and penetrated by a zillion aggressive little trucks and needy, competitive, insistent little shoppers. Ugly as it is, the mall is wholly dependent on both the selective blindness and the collective solipsism of car-based suburbia, the constant supply of hungry little ticks wrapped in their Umwelten, helplessly drawn to warmth and blood.

This is recognised. Victor Gruen hoped to revitalise American towns by recreating the traditional Viennese plaza as the Edina mall back in the fifties, but he died a broken man because the opposite happened. The mall may have become *the* American way of life but is widely credited with destroying the physical and social fabric of American cities. Far from Europeanising America the mall, if anything, helped Americanise Europe.

Who shops at the mall? Everyone, but mostly women. In Underhill's words, 'Men dart in, look around, refuse to ask for help … and split. Boom.' For women, it's not just acquisition; the foraging itself is as soothing as a good massage. Some recent US research suggests this gender-patterning may change, that 'young men now shop like young women'. But the Neanderthal fact remains. Men hunt, women gather.

On shopping streets, reports Underhill, people walk at roughly six kilometres an hour, men outpacing women. In the mall, it's maybe half that, but there women walk faster than men. Women grow purposeful as the hypno-narcosis of the interior takes over and the urge-to-shop blossoms. Paid employment has increased women's spend-power even as it reduced their shop-time and the urge to spend more, faster, further enhances the cavern's narcotic effect. In mall-shopping especially, women are, in Underhill's words, 'the primary actors'.

So, if the shopping-gene sits on the X-chromosome, the unaskable question becomes: How much of the mall's environmental and urban destruction is female-led?

◉ | Surrogate selves: cars, houses, children

But it's not just shopping in streets and malls; not just stuff that fits in shopping bags and four-wheel-drives. Women are fast becoming the primary purchasers of essential shopping tools: the cars in which to carry the stuff and the houses (now known exclusively as 'homes' in deference to the idea of universal nesting) in which to keep it. To some extent, houses and even cars are traditional marketing-to-women territory. Now women's spend-power has made them – their habits, preferences, fantasies – a prime object of market research. A Wizard Home Loans' specially-for-women website coos, 'in just 20 years, women have become the new driver of the Australian property market', with 33 per cent of surveyed women having purchased homes in their own right and 43 per cent intending that way.

It's flattering, all this attention, the website having all the pastel unctuousness of a David Jones powder room. We're out of the closet, and the market itself has become a giant mirror in which to examine our own reflection. Less flattering is the coincident trend to fat – fatter children, fatter cars, fatter houses – all of them costly public health items, all blowing out in direct parallel with women's increasing influence and affluence. In Australia houses have doubled in size while families have halved; 67 per cent of men and 52 per cent of women aged 25 to 64 are overweight or obese, as well as a quarter of all Australian children. And car sizes are growing even faster than petrol prices, with 4WD sales doubling every decade. What's the connection? Is it that all of them – cars, houses, children – can be seen as extensions of the maternal self, alternative mouths for the feeding, alternative pockets to fill? Have our over-gratified instincts tipped over into narcissism, identified by Christopher Lasch back in the 1980s as the sin of our times? Is this what is fuelling not only finger-fashions but, more importantly, the apparently unstoppable trends towards fancier cars, fatter children and ever more bloated houses?

Start with children. The last century of child-rearing offers an object lesson, as the idea of original sin is gradually replaced by the more dangerous if less overt belief in original virtue. It's a 'just add water' approach to parenting, which has largely replaced discipline with gratification.

Between 1914 and 1942, as Margaret Mead and Martha Wolfenstein found in the 1950s, attitudes to infant-rearing shifted dramatically. From seeing overfeeding as a constant danger in the early part of the century, childcare norms came to regard the child's natural appetite as an adequate self-regulator. By 1947, Dr Spock was advising mothers to 'trust yourself' and enjoy; and as those babies, the boomers, have come to maturity, parenting manuals have typically advised that babies be fed on demand, never smacked, never criticised. Parents have been left holding a carrot, but no stick.

The mother's primary job, the argument goes, is to build the child's self-esteem, rather than to teach skills that might earn or justify such esteem. This has helped to build a society in which near-perpetual pleasure is both the norm and the expectation. Where pain is an affront, and to have an unsatisfied yearning seems almost an offence against nature.

Take, for example, the furore over *End Times*, an exhibition of crying-child photographs by US photographer Jill Greenberg. For her crime of giving children lollipops and taking them away to generate a few seconds' tears, Greenberg has been accused of child abuse and of inflicting permanent emotional damage. Why? Because, say critics, children should not be made to do or feel anything they don't like.

As blogger and activist Thomas Hawke commented:

> Jill Greenberg is a sick woman who should be arrested and charged
> with child abuse. Although the children are not sexualised, I
> consider what she is doing child pornography of the worst kind. It
> is the purposeful action of creating anger in a beautiful child for
> the sadistic purpose of making a name for herself as a pop artist.

Of course, Hawke himself could be working for Greenberg's publicity agent. But the mere fact that the story ran on every major news outlet in the Western world points to a hidden acceptance of the idea that negative emotions of any kind are somehow unnatural and damaging.

And so we watch our children become savages. We talk tough love and limit-setting, we adore Supernanny Jo Frost for daring to discipline our voracious little darlings. We pay thousands of dollars in school fees for institutions with 'traditional values'. But we shrink from disciplining them ourselves. On every street-corner, every beach, every bus, we see parents acting as their children's servants; carrying their bags, deferring, doing their bidding. Letting the kids make the running on everything from dinner to early morning television.

It doesn't work, even in its own terms. Piling on the pleasure in the hope of generating happiness seems to be profoundly counter-productive. We always knew that having what you wanted didn't make you likeable. Now we know it doesn't make you happy or successful either. Not only are Western levels of happiness declining in tandem with increasing affluence, we're deskilling as well. The *Atlantic Monthly* reports that recent studies also show that, although American and Australian eighth-grade students are more than twice as confident in their maths and science skills than their Asian counterparts, they lag 'far behind' in actual scores. As Bill Joy, founder of Sun Microsystems, noted recently of adolescents' blogging, livejournal and internet gaming habits: 'If I was competing with the United States I would love to have the students I was competing with spending their time on this kind of crap ...'

Still we go on telling ourselves 'we're doing it for the kids'. We give them what they want because 'it makes them happy' (even if it doesn't) and making them happy – not resilient, or clever, or even successful, but happy – *is our job*. As an unnamed McMansion-dweller on Channel Nine's *60 Minutes* beamed recently, 'My dream home is a little bit bigger – for my husband ... Already there's a kitchen, and a special frying room, but I'd like a third kitchen, specially for messy cooking. I would like to add a cool room, cigar bar, a snooker room for the kids.' Said another: 'Nothing makes me happier than to see the children play in the spa, come out, go and have a hit of tennis on the tennis court, go and watch a movie in the theatre. Nothing beats that. I'm sure I speak on behalf of any mother, you know, to see their children have such a good life.' Always for the husband, the kids. Never for me.

But we can't really blame the children. After all, we're having fewer and fewer of them, with family sizes having halved in pretty much the same time that house sizes have doubled. And who is buying these houses? Women. Now, though, it's not just the wife making decisions for the family but single women – unmarried, divorced, or never married – who account for an ever-increasing proportion of the housing market. In the US, our cultural source *du jour*, single women have become the second biggest category of home-buyer; after married couples, who still account for 59 per cent of the housing market, but well ahead of single men (11 per cent). And, reports the *Wall Street Journal*, their numbers are growing rapidly; from 16 per cent in 1993 to 21 per cent in 2003. Pam Liebman, president and CEO of The Corcoran Group in New York, notes that more women are house-shopping not just alone, but in the upper price ranges, between $1.5 and $6 million. Wendi Goldman, a forty-something Manhattan executive, is single and shopping for an apartment, 'something fabulous'. She doesn't *need* a bigger apartment. It's just that 'she is single and just wants more'. Australia is not far behind. Women, notes the Wizard website, prefer property over other investment options because 'property is safe'. Not only are Australian women not waiting for marriage before buying a house, they're not waiting for marriage before expanding that house, or buying a second one.

In a recent essay entitled 'Home alone: the dark heart of shelter-lit addiction', US academic Terry Castle details the new neurosis of 'interiors fanaticism', or house-porn. Afflicted individuals, of whom Castle confesses herself one, pore helplessly over shelter-lit (aka interior design magazines), fantasising about interiors they might one day have, or even, as it were, be. Such people are usually 'neurotic, refined, sad people, prone to secret melancholy and hypersensitive nerves', for whom, she argues, house-porn is classic consolation literature, bringing all the 'curious feelings of guilt, titillation, and flooding bourgeois pleasure – relief delivered through hands and eyeballs'.

But shelter-lit is a step further along the depravity scale even than standard pornography. As Castle notes, the idea that 'your house is you, so start revelling in it' is an article of faith in shelter-mag land, and has been gaining foothold at least since etiquette-advisor Emily Post wrote in 1930: 'your home's personality should express your personality'. These magazines, edited almost exclusively by women and filled with 'glib, repetitious, wonderfully brain-deadening express the inner you rhetoric' cater to what Castle describes as 'narcissism in a go-cup. The ladies say it's OK'.

Shelter-lit, then, combines the titillation of porn with the sad-proud neediness of narcissism. We all know women for whom the perfect house becomes an accessory so essential that getting it perfect and keeping it that way (the perfect children tucked into the perfect SUV on their way home to the perfect house) becomes an all-consuming obsession; an exercise every bit as obsessive-compulsive, as control-focused, as narcissistic as the anorexia it (arguably) replaces. Castle quotes interior decorator Rose Tarlow, who has become 'interested in a home only for myself', a kind of pink-and-white nun's cell where everything is perfect and 'peace prevails'. It's a common shelter-land fantasy, an interior 'unpeopled – stark, impervious, preternaturally still … seductive, sanitized, calm-verging-on-dead: mausoleum chic'. Anorexic, even.

And then there are cars. Castle's specification of the kind of insecurity that leads to shelter-lit addiction shows a remarkable resonance with the kinds of people who reportedly buy SUVs. As Malcolm Gladwell wrote in *The New Yorker* recently: 'According to [author Keith] Bradsher, internal industry market research concluded that SUVs tend to be bought by people who are insecure, vain, self-centered, and self-absorbed, who are frequently nervous about their marriages, and who lack confidence in their driving skills.' And Underhill points out: 'the car industry, perhaps the most backward and anti-shopper business in America, has realized for a few years now that women buy cars'.

At the heart of it, not surprisingly, are those same nurturing instincts about which we are so conflicted. Mixed with the new narcissism, our need-to-nurture makes a strange and toxic cocktail indeed. It is often thought that, in having children, women move from being self-centred to being other-centred. Psychically, however, children are less 'other' than an extension of self; a stretching, if you will, of the maternal skin around the brood. This is analogous to what psychologists Daniel Kahneman and Amos Tversky call the endowment effect; once something is yours, the value of it, to you, increases out of proportion with its value to anyone else, and the pain of anticipated loss is greater than the pleasure of its initial acquisition. It becomes, in a sense, a part of you.

Wimmin architects

Once, when I was eight, my mother got mad at my grandmother for installing in my autograph book the following aphorism: 'Happiness lies not in getting what one wants, but in wanting what one gets'. It was years before I saw the reason for the maternal fury: what might seem these days like ancient Buddhist wisdom (for application later) struck my mum as supine defeatism. A sniper-attack from doiley-land. Even now, this tension between changing the world and changing oneself to fit it better, or perceive it differently, is a constant subtext. In particular, given the sexes' opposite tendencies in this regard, it grounds the gender debate.

In this, architecture, despite occasional propagandic flurries to the contrary, is in the bleeding obvious box. Somewhere in the decades between graduation and maturity, women architects vanish. Always have, perhaps always will. But the propaganda – headlined, in the words of a recent Royal Australian Institute of Architects press release, 'No Glass Ceiling For Female Architects' – amounts to an assiduous misreading of the entrails.

And yet they are entrails we persist in perusing in our messy search for signs of growing equality – money, promotion, maternity leave, job satisfaction. As though the standard emblems and epaulettes of corporate success life were actually it, in a profession as peculiar as architecture. Probably the entire push reveals more about what we'd like to be true than about any material change in world order. A couple of female presidents in the RAIA, and suddenly we're hearing victory talk.

But, you counter, doesn't this in itself prove their point? That the girls are finally making it into the big top? Well, no, in a word. Even if female presidents were the rule, not the exception, measuring the feminisation of the profession in bits of gold braid could hardly be sillier. Architecture just ain't that kinda game. Nor, for that matter, is feminisation.

The RAIA press release referred to a 2004 study of Australian women architects headed by the late Queensland academic Dr Paula Whitman, also then president of the Queensland chapter of the Institute. Why is it, she and her colleagues wondered, that females comprise 40 per cent of architecture students but only 1 per cent of architecture's company directors?

Whitman's survey covered 500-odd female architects across Australia, half of them parents, most of them under 40 and working in a capital city. It found that 'more than one in four female architects are deliberately knocking back promotions at work'. Of these, 'more than half' are doing so voluntarily, because they either have 'different career aspirations' or don't expect greater job satisfaction to result. Further, said Dr Whitman, the survey showed that 'an overwhelmingly high number of female architects, almost 70 per cent, are willing to forgo career success to achieve balance in life … but still desiring improved remuneration'.

Even if it's true, though, even if *all* women architects were rhythmically refusing preferment, is this meant to make us feel better? Should we feel reassured, in pursuit of the equality grail, knowing that women architects are so ambitionless, so resigned or so (sigh, darling) content with their lot as to repeatedly eschew positions of influence? Is disempowerment okay when it's voluntary? Is *that* what we're saying?

It's a real danger. As US academics Linda Babcock and Sara Laschever pointed out in *Women Don't Ask*, 'this turns out to be a big problem for women: being satisfied with less'. Or, in Whitman's words, 'women say they are getting what they want [but] is what they want not very much? Do women [architects] have safe targets and low goals when it comes to their careers?'

The reasons for the limpness are more worrying still. Australian women architects, says Whitman, do not see gender as a barrier and do not blame externalities like systemic bias. Instead, they see motherhood, lack of time and 'negative personality characteristics (including low self-image, lack of confidence and discipline) as the biggest inhibitors'.

Say *what*? Here we have a bunch of highly educated, highly motivated prime-time females feeling it's okay that their careers are crippled by having children, or by their failure to perform the ego dance. Once again, that is, women are internalising blame in the time-honoured way – and this proves we're achieving some kind of equality? Ever hear of a bloke's career being inhibited because he happens to have a couple of kids, much less his being okay with that?

Beneath all this there's another, deeper misapprehension that escapes scrutiny altogether. Architecture is not a corporate deal. So architectural success is not measurable by the usual array of ticked boxes, salary targets and Key Performance Indicators. You can have all that, of course. But that's the point. You can have the lot, and still count for nothing within the profession. Why? Because while architecture calls itself a profession – has to, to get the work – it sees itself as an art. This explains architecture's standing oscillation between the slick side of the arts and the daggy edge of the professions. Explains, too, why its stars are not those who make the most money, or chair the most boards, or acquire the most Porsches.

So who is at the top? Well, the stars, of course. The design gurus; the Prometheus figures, the stealers of fire from heaven. And while their success is not measurable in the usual ways, there is a remarkable consensus, within architecture, as to who they are, and who they are not. Who they are, across the globe, is men. Who they are not – still *so* not (Gae Aulenti, Zaha Hadid, and one or two others notwithstanding) – is women. Even today, most female architectural principals, from

Denise Scott-Brown to Benedetta Tagliabue, either focus exclusively on domestic-scale work or practise with, and stand in the shadow of, their husbands. This is not changing. Not a jot. If anything, it's going backwards.

So it doesn't actually matter, in the end, how many women are experiencing sustained job satisfaction due to family-friendly policies in the workplace, blah blah. That women might be happy working in a corner of the lounge doing alts and adds for the friends and rels during school hours counts for zilch. This is not success, not within the accepted definition of the term, anyway. Satisfaction, perhaps. Contentment, sure. Balance, convenience, life-wisdom, whatever. But not professional success.

What it does not show is any form of attack on the glass ceiling. Indeed, it's back to the future, with women settling yet again for changing their expectations, not the world. Situation normal. And that women may be their own worst enemies in this makes it worse, not better.

All of which leaves us with the why, what to do about it and does it matter anyway questions. Why comes down to four short syllables: testosterone. Architectural stardom relies on focused and sustained (if often corduroy-cloaked) aggression of the kind that seldom comes naturally to women, especially women designers. Take, for example, publication. From Le Corbusier to Koolhaas, from Tschumi to Libeskind to Cox to Murcutt, they all know it: you don't get a place in the firmament if you don't publish. Publication is something at which Hadid, for example, excelled, decades before she had anything built. And yet, as Whitman's survey remarks with some concern, 'publication and/or public recognition was nominated as the *least* important goal of the women surveyed'.

So here's the unaskable question; if success as it is defined in architecture is not something women want, or not something of which they are (on the whole) capable, does that matter? Are women just ahead of the game, natural downshifters, too wise, too enlightened, to be bothered? After all, in Lily Tomlin's immortal words, 'the trouble with the rat race is that even if you win, you're still a rat'. Thing is, though, one reason they are immortal words – as opposed to dead and vanished – is that Tomlin's is a field in which women can shine *as women*.

So can architecture change to fit women better? If so, should it? Would architecture benefit? Would women, if recognition is genuinely not a priority for them? Is there some other way perhaps, which doesn't involve women either becoming pseudo-men or resigning themselves to second fiddle? It's a continuing story, for which history offers no guide. For me, it comes down to this. How will I feel when my daughters propose studying architecture? Answer? Mad, like my mum.

Safe and happy: twin pathologies

Safety is a big deal for women, perhaps quite rightly. Women, traditionally more vulnerable and with more, perhaps, to protect, are drawn to safety as men are drawn to risk. Women like big cars and big houses partly because they seem safe, while the male equivalent of problem shopping is problem gambling. Once again, the safety instinct has obvious evolutionary value, but only up to a point. With safety, as with our other appetites, you can have too much of a good thing. These days, safety has become an obsession bordering on pathology.

History may judge us harshly for indulging this obsession at a time when we are personally safer than at any point in history, and in a way that consistently sacrifices *being* safe long term for *feeling* safe, now. As the *Sydney Morning Herald* recently noted, 'the more safety-conscious Australia becomes, the more Australian parents worry about the perceived dangers to their children'. In Britain, similarly, a recent *Times* story showed that children are safer now than 30 years ago, with 75 per cent fewer child road-deaths, and no increase in child murders since 1976. Nevertheless, wrote *Times* journalist Carol Midgley:

> What is new and perhaps a little weird is that the more that medicine and child supervision and road, car and playground safety improve, the more our anxiety seems to grow. Study after study indicates that mothers and fathers are palpably more fearful for their children than they were 30 or 40 years ago.

We no longer let our kids walk or cycle home from school, play in the street as we did when we were kids, nor disappear from supervision for hours on end. No one knows why not, since safety itself has so dramatically improved. Melbourne psychiatric epidemiologist, Professor George Patton, says: 'parents are also being very protective of kids. Kids are engaged in a lot less physical activity ... because we are concerned about such things as child safety and prevention of injury'. But what has increased, at the same time, is youth suicide.

Our parental craving for (at least the illusion of) safety makes us buy 4WDs and SUVs despite their lamentable safety record. It makes us vote for grandfather figures despite their environmental wantonness; makes us invest in property, not shares, regardless of the market, makes us want bigger and bigger and bigger houses. New York cultural anthropologist Clotaire Rapaille notes of the epidemic:

> And what was the key element of safety when you were a child? It was that your mother fed you, and there was warm liquid. That's why cup-holders are absolutely crucial for safety. If there is a car that has no cup-holder, it is not safe. If I can put my coffee there, if I can have my food, if everything is round, if it's soft, and if I'm high, then I feel safe. It's amazing that intelligent, educated women will look at a car and the first thing they will look at is how many cup-holders it has.

Helicopter parenting and gated communities, victim mentality, nanny-statism and the liability crisis that kills street theatre and removes play equipment from public parks – all of it is based on a neurotic determination to feel 'safe', and to feel that our children are safe, whatever the cost. And the cost is a way of life – in particular a way of childhood – that, in being risk-deficient, is also excitement-deficient.

But is this contentment-cocoon really such a good life? Risk is probably the defining factor of play. The risk needn't be great. A baby playing with a ball, for instance, needs only the 'risk' that it might roll away, or do something otherwise unexpected, to maintain a level of engagement and fun. Play is essentially open-ended and adventurous; a known outcome is boring. Predictability, in large part, is what turns play into work. Like a path that is fully visible, known outcomes engender tiredness at the outset, so game quickly becomes chore. Safety, which absolutely requires predictability, makes everything dull.

And the result is that childhood simply isn't as anything like as much fun as it used to be. More stuff. More food. More treats. But way less fun. It's not just the removal of DIY fireworks, after-school street-play and cycling to school from our children's lives, though that's loss enough. There are schools in Sydney where kicking a ball is banned, everywhere, lest someone be hurt. Our children grow, fully loaded with unearned self-esteem but atrophied in the one muscle they may need most in the future we are making for them – the adversity muscle.

Our instinct is to barricade ourselves against a bewildering world in domestic environments so replete with swimming pools, games rooms and home theatres that we never have to leave except in a car that is effectively another house, on wheels. The result is that, driven by instinct towards security and instant gratification, we lock down, depriving ourselves of the very stimulus, the connectedness, we need.

Inside these fattened fortresses, these empires of cocooned contentment, we quickly lose our edge. Untested, under-challenged, we respond like chimps in a cage, becoming picky, bored and depressed. We shop, we buy, we eat. Or, in the thin-era of feminism, we feed our substitute-selves, namely our cars, our children, and our houses. All of it – the food and the lifestyle, the land-guzzling and the air-filthying – swells our eco-footprint well past Mother Earth's capacity, even short term, to cope. We are eating our children's future, and feeding it to them, reconstituted with fats and preservatives, on a pre-heated, guilt-rimmed plate.

Goddess

Equal pay or no, there is ample evidence for the feminisation of our culture and our world. Not just in shopping, sprawl and fat, but in extreme parenting generally, as well as nanny-statism, therapy culture, and the casualisation of the workplace and the church. To the workplace women have brought not just childcare and 'family-friendly' policies but also comfort as a value in furniture, clothes, relationships and even management techniques. We have also brought talk-culture, public emotionalism and consultation of all kinds – most of it aimed not at changing anything but at making people feel better, happier. Even churches have succumbed to the idea that a house of god should look and feel as comfortable and non-threatening as the home. Accompanying this is the idea of church as a 'community of relationships,' making god more bosom-buddy than teacher, boss or judge.

Sadly, much of this turns out to have little benefit in terms of our most heartfelt and long-term goals, namely the survival of our children and our planet, in all its lacy complexity. This is a double failure, a failure of courage and a failure of imagination. Fear drives us to over-eat, over-spend and over-barricade. Nestling down into our soft-feathered lives we abandon any quest for transcendence and settle instead for the mediocrity of comfort. This in turn dulls our imagination, protecting us from terror but also from any possibility of creative release.

Women may not, ever, control public life and yet they are blessed with an extra capacity for strategic vision, for clear-eyed empathy and for that extraordinary, transformative energy we call love. These are the essential ingredients of wisdom, the spark of goddess within each woman. Feminism is not about equal pay and childcare. It is about saving the future. It is here that women – not necessarily through established religious or cultural channels but through driving a grassroots push for survival – could lead the charge.

8 | Why so ugly? Archiphobia and the politics of Blubberland

Is there any architecture today? Are there any architects?...Are not we, who are at the mercy of all-devouring society... that knows no architecture, wants no architecture and therefore needs no architects!

BAUHAUS FOUNDER WALTER GROPIUS (1919)

Democracy an own goal?

Democracy, despite having generated the most fertile cultures of modern times and the most successful economies ever, may yet prove to be an own goal. Not only are its cities extraordinarily unlovely, even to their own inhabitants, but its societies suddenly seem as incapable of real adaptation as were the Easter Islanders, felling the last trees to erect the great stone idols that would outlive them. Democracy, long regarded as supremely responsive, has actually been the great guarantor of stability. But when the environment itself begins to change, stability becomes inertia. And when the ship of state is heading for the rapids, inertia is a problem. Democracy's greatest strength, in other words, is also its greatest weakness.

Like its ally capitalism, democracy also operates from desire. This is its great strength, since desire beats willpower every time. But it is also a potentially fatal weakness. Like capitalism, democracy is about what we want, and fosters the idea not only that we *can* have what we want, but that we *should* have it. That we have a right to it.

This comfortable elision between wants and rights is nurtured by advertising ('because you deserve it'), by litigation ('who can I sue?') and by the prosperity that, in installing physical comfort as a daily premise, underpins both. It is sustained by the nanny-state, which fosters quotidian blame-shifting, and by modern medicine, which has relegated death and even disease downstage left, whence they play the nasty reminder, not the constant presence.

Now, this very compulsion to desire-fulfilment has democracy in a trap. If we want to eat meat, with its huge eco-footprint, we do it. If we want to sprawl our cities across the landscape, live in a McMansion, drive an SUV, leave the lights or the hose or the TV on all night, we do precisely that. It may cost, us or the planet. But it's our right to make that choice. Even governments are intimidated to the point of being frightened to regulate. If it can't be achieved by the market, they weakly presume, it can't be achieved. If electricity other than coal-fired electricity is to be an option, it can only happen through carbon-tax, not through any sort of outright control. Government is like parenting – and what has gone wrong with contemporary parenting is pretty much what has gone wrong with government. Just as today's parents are reluctant to discipline for fear of causing negative feelings in their offspring, governments are reluctant to govern for fear of alienating their ever more demanding, ever more petulant electorate. We behave like a world full of spoilt babies so monstrous that even our politicians won't gainsay us.

In theory, democracy only guarantees such 'rights' insofar as they do not negatively impact our neighbours. But the reality is not so simple, either for the voter or for the politician-cum-decision-maker.

For the voter, there's not only the old conflict between the self and the herd, but the fact that even this conflict is murky. In modern democracies, anything that smells of the collective, from communism to harmless flower-power hippiedom, is still seen as dangerous.

Democracy runs on the pretence that we are not a herd at all, but a loose collection of log-cabin individuals, wilderness dwellers driven mainly by self-seeking, like a big family of only children. If this – call it collective solipsism – sounds like Adam Smith's 'invisible hand', it is. Which is why capitalism and democracy are so much in love.

But even the constant struggle between selfishness and altruism isn't simple, since each of us is both self and herd-animal. It's like agitating for more pedestrian rights and then getting frustrated, as a driver, at the traffic-calming that results. Like voting for lower taxes then getting fed up at hospital waiting-lists. In most such conflicts, most of us are on both sides; drivers as well as pedestrians; patients as well as tax-payers. So the conflict is less self-versus-herd than between competing self-interests; between selves.

The irony is that democracies, however individualising, reinforce our herd nature at every step. Just as capitalism pretends to enhance choice but actually reinforces sameness in everything from health insurance to fashion to lifestyle, so democracy enforces the lowest common denominator of mass-culture and mass-opinion even while appealing to each of us as an individual. This dumbing-down afflicts our culture across the board, from television to architecture to universities, which have abandoned education (it's elitist) to become cathedrals of customer service. But the tragedy goes further, since the one aspect in which we still enact our individual desires – if not our individual minds – is voting. As electors we limit our horizons to the back fence, reliably voting on self-interest alone, and economic self-interest at that – which is what gives pork-barrelling its power. Thus a terrible paradox has emerged: democracy as a form of mob rule that seems incapable of acting in the mob's best interests.

This is a form of miswanting, but one that is seldom recognised. And once again, it is driven by the salience syndrome; by our consistent failure fully to imagine the results of our actions, so that what is available, now, for me is always more desirable than what is distant, abstract or collective. Where the impact is attenuated by the 'it won't affect me' attitude – as with CO_2 emissions and dam levels – even self-interest is unreliable.

So we elect the wrong people – for their eyes, their teeth, their promises to our hip-pockets – then force them to do the wrong thing. Force them do what we want. And what we want is, it seems, more, and more, and more. An embarrassing factor in our current predicament is that it has arisen less from rising human numbers than from our steeply climbing impact-per-person. We consume more, pollute more and waste more than ever before, and we believe, deep down, that this is our right. We believe, to a degree that no society before has been privileged even to contemplate, that we can have our cake and eat it; that however much we consume there'll always be more in the tin. More energy, more air, more water, more space. We believe it because we want to believe it and, in the elision of want and right, we've forgotten there's a difference.

Governments kowtow to this belief. If they don't, we dump them. And so mass-wanting becomes mass-getting. Lifestyles that were once the privilege of the few are now available to the many. And this shift changes everything.

For the politician, as the election partying subsides and the role shifts from baby-patter to decision-maker, there is a morphing process comparable to first-time parenting. Initially, the elected person expects a degree of control, if not outright power. She expects efficacy to issue from her fingertips as lightning from the hands of Zeus. Gradually, over two or three trimesters, she realises that what it's really about is not doing right, but doing deals. That most of democracy's decisions are made not in its debating chambers or parliaments but in backrooms and restaurants and the narrow corridors of power. Not on the basis of principle or conscience, but as handshakes and horsetrades. That the only opinions that count are those of the shock-jocks and (to a lesser extent) editors. That public consultation is carefully designed to change nothing, while giving the public a fleeting illusion of engagement. And that justice is like a game of rock, paper, scissors; spin wins over fact every time. Postmodern government has become, like its critic Baudrillard, a simulacrum of itself.

Climate change – like fat, consumerism and sprawl – is essentially about discipline, or its absence. But as the issues become politicised, right-wing lobbyists present any call for discipline as a barely disguised socialist revival. Words like 'hair-shirt', 'self-hating' and 'doomsday' figure largely; many even argue that the entire climate-change scenario is a concocted leftist ruse. This is crazy and paranoid, but it is serious. And it rests on the assumption that anything other than pure self-interest – any call to decency, far-sightedness or even, heaven forbid, altruism – is totalitarianism in disguise.

The temptation is to point out the horrible irony that both the 'left' and 'right' of politics are stacked full of *soi-disant* Christians, who see no conflict between lip service and unbridled self-interest. The real issue is no longer one of left versus right. Those old tribal divisions are so not it. The real choice is between the business-as-usual coalition (call it BUCK) and anyone pushing survival with that thin but priceless veneer we call civilisation roughly intact. Which means a green and clean energy future, with just a touch of altruism. Call it GRACE. And the tragedy for the world is the diehard notion that there is a choice, that BUCK is a genuine option, that the next hundred years can continue just like the last hundred, that we can have BUCK without GRACE.

Getting what we (mis)want

Be careful what you want, as the saying goes, for you will almost certainly get it. And here's the mystery. If democracy gives us what we want, why is so much of its product – especially its built product – what we don't want? If we're living in democracy's built form, why is so much of it so destructive, so costly and so damn ugly? Was some kind of Mephistophelean trade-off undertaken by our ancestors back in the eighteenth century somewhere, where we exchanged an ugly physical reality for a fairer, more beautiful moral system? Or is there some other dynamic at work here? Canadian film-maker James Kunstler describes suburbia as 'the greatest misallocation of resources the world has seen'. Taking this thought even further: Is sprawl the greatest, most widespread and most destructive example of miswanting in history?

Sure, we want the suburban *dream*. Birdsong outside the bedroom window, sunshine on the breakfast table, grass where the kids play ball. This is the dream and, as its supporters tirelessly point out, it is humanity's living pattern of choice. Suburbia has become a universal dreaming; a universally sought-after medication. The bubble, fully updated with home theatres and quadruple garages, is now it; global lifestyle. There's no question, we want the suburban dream like we want the desert island dream. But do we want the suburban fact?

Paris, London, Rome. The world's most ancient and beautiful cities remain global tourist magnets although we know, but try to ignore, that they are beautiful only in their centres. Out there, where the masses live, are the concentric rings of increasing ugliness that calibrate the city's growth, revealing rising intensities of consumer ostentation just as the annular rings on a tree record ramping levels of CO_2.

These, the dream's side-effects, are what we didn't bargain for and almost certainly don't want, jointly or severally; the traffic jams and the water shortages, the poisonous air and the childhood asthma, the obesity, the neuroses, the depression. We didn't want the cookie-cutter houses pretending self-expression or the increasingly grandiose phoniness; didn't ask for the cold gaiety of the mall, the snaking, roaring motorways or the sad grey flannel of a suburban Sunday afternoon.

Suburbia is not democracy's only built product. The flipside of the suburban dream is the high-rise city centre, the concrete jungle, which for most people is even less lovable. Why then, given our unprecedented wealth, technology and individual power, as well as our near-universal admiration of old cities, do we seem incapable of producing living places – be they suburbs or downtowns – that we actually like? And why, further, was virtually every building, village, town or city that we admire produced by oligarchic or tyrannical systems that we revile? This is modernism's enduring mystery.

And yet, so strong is our desire to believe that an honourable process will give an admirable product, it is a question we are reluctant to ask, much less answer. Just as we want to believe that good buildings improve behaviour, we want to think that ugliness results from insufficient consultation, and that public engagement will necessarily, therefore, improve the product.

Sadly, both presumptions are demonstrably false. Public participation may be a good in its own right. Enhancing people's sense of engagement with their political Umwelt will plausibly have a genuine therapeutic effect. Whether it affects the built facts, however, and whether this effect, if real, is for the better, must be questioned. In fact, as it turns out, public participation is as likely to militate against good architecture and beautiful cities as against bad or ugly ones; to enhance mediocrity at the expense of both extremes. The reason for this goes back to questions of art, control and authorship.

Participation can be expected, if anything, to fit a building more finely to its users. This may do nothing for its qualities as architecture, however. It may even do less than nothing, according to the camel syndrome of committee design. There is an important if uncomfortable difference between architecture and a well-fitting camel; between functionality and excellence.

Just as a building may suit its users perfectly and still be a dog (or a camel), it may also be noticeably inconvenient and still a work of genius. Take, for example, architect Peter Zumthor's Bruder Klaus field chapel in Switzerland. On being invited to produce a chapel for the local farmers, Zumthor pointed out that he could offer only contemporary architecture and that his fee would probably outstrip the building's value. The farmers said fine, to both – so Zumthor waived his fee and did it for nothing. Arranging timbers into an attenuated teepee, he poured concrete around them in *tagwerk* (day's work) stages over 24 days to give diurnal growth rings in the concrete. The timber was then burned out from within, leaving a charred and textured interior that offers no sense of comfort, in the normal sense, but an immense and awe-full mystery, quite out of proportion to its physical size and of the kind that modern churches have generally found it impossible to capture.

Archiphobia

There is, in other words, a level at which architecture is and must be its own judge and jury. Certainly there are externalities; criteria to be applied, functions fulfilled. There's shelter from sun and rain to consider, circulation and ventilation, convenience of plan, structure and thermal mass. There is, however, a point at which the integrity of the work as a whole takes over, out-signifying all the external, quantifiable criteria that can be levelled at it. Externalities matter – but if the work's essential integrity is not maintained it will never be *architecture*.

Zumthor calls his sense of this overriding integrity thing a 'devotion to wholeness'. And you can see, from the architect's point of view, why it becomes a central concern. But why would you, as a client, care whether your building – your house or office or rowing shed – qualifies as architecture? In fact, you may not. You may require nothing more from your building than structure, ventilation and thermal mass. But there is something to be gained from architecture, all the same. Some sense of unity and completeness, of plan and section, the light and space and material textures, the cerebral and sensual qualities of the thing belonging fully together. A quality that can only properly be called beauty.

Beauty, as we have seen, is the architect's only unique contribution to the building process. Everything else – all the practical stuff – can be supplied, possibly better, by some other profession; by the legions of builders, plumbers, surveyors and engineers who make up the team. Beauty or, if you prefer, the infusing of a building with some coherent meaning, is what architects do. This makes architecture less a profession than a discipline and begins to explain, perhaps, why so many good architects go to pieces on a big budget. But it is also why architecture, at its best, brings a whisper of transcendence, a whiff, a promise of happiness. Of better lives that might be lived, better selves that might be realised. Without beauty, which alone qualifies it as an art rather than an elaborate constructive craft, architecture may as well give up and go home.

The beauty thing also gives architecture its characteristic aloofness and introversion, which may also explain one of the teeth-grindingly inconvenient truths with which architects daily grapple. Namely, that of all the countless buildings in a city, even a relatively affluent, educated and contemporary city like London or Sydney, only a microscopic percentage is architect-designed. Even people who understand the process, which is seldom straightforward, and who could easily afford an architect, which isn't costless, usually choose not to. Architects will argue, perhaps with some justification, that even on straight commercial grounds architecture adds value. That design has become a point of difference, a marketing ploy, and that architect-designed apartments (for example) sell better, faster and more profitably than the rest. There may be some truth in it. On the whole, though, architecture is a minute cog in the churning wheels of a development industry that is vast, unadventurous and unashamedly philistine.

Most people don't like what architects like, and don't much like what they make. This is partly because much of what architects make doesn't qualify, in the terms outlined above, as architecture. But even when it does, the unfortunate fact remains that what looks to architects like elegant simplicity, pared to the very essence, can look, to a non-architect's eyes, like a barn or a chicken coop. What architects see as quirky and interesting, with subtle, inverted reference perhaps to Palladio's Villa Rotonda or Koolhaas' Villa Dall'Ava in Paris, just doesn't thrill most people. They may want beauty, but as far as they're concerned, what architects do doesn't qualify. Indeed, to most people, most of what architects do looks just ugly or tacky or plain or stupid. This is archiphobia, and it works the other way as well. For most architects, mainstream taste is a form of living death.

The archophobia divide can often seem unbridgeable. But bridged it must nevertheless be, since architecture cannot exist without clients. Other arts can be performed alone in a darkened room. Painting, writing and music still need an audience, but the art itself is, broadly speaking, there on the page. Architecture, by contrast, does not exist until the play of light on stone, the flow of space, the choreography of colour and texture, is actually real. Design may be everything, but the design on paper is a ghost, nothing more; the art is in the making.

So if the gap is to be bridged, the question becomes, who should shift? Should architects bend away from what they intuit as 'true' architecture? Or should clients simply find a way of trusting their architect, accept something that they may not, ever, understand or even like?

This kind of trust-me-I'm-a-professional relationship, once a given in architecture, as in most professions, has (as noted in chapter 1) been reviled by postmodernism, which has tended increasingly to abandon push in favour of pull, an anti-authority, client-is-right approach. In architecture this was manifest as a cloak of populism, a 'mainstreet is almost all right' idea as popularised by writers like Robert Venturi and Charles Jencks back in the seventies. This enabled architects like

Melbourne's Peter Corrigan to take 'suburban' as a term of praise, albeit somewhat tongue-in-cheek, making an architecture from domestic red-and-yellow brickwork (thinly veneered in irony), and Ashton Raggatt McDougall to make architecture out of jokes and twirls and stuck-on photocopies. It generated, in fact, the entire Melbourne style.

But it's not the complete answer. For most architects, the abandonment of capital-A architecture for populism still felt like giving the whole game away. With the modernist revival of recent years, the stand-off remains, with architects feeling like misunderstood vestal virgins, tending the unappreciated architectural flame, and the public, unmoved, eating chips by the pool in the tight little mini-gardens of their McMansions.

One possibility, sometimes suggested, is that architecture's responsiveness, its capacity to empathise with its clients, might be enhanced if there were more women architects. In fact, it's more likely that this very responsiveness contributes to women's entrapment in the murky middle levels of the profession, as noted in chapter 7. But the subject always brings to mind the standard joke at architecture school, when the subject of being a woman on a building site comes up: Don't worry, they say, about what the builders think of you. They regard all architects as women anyway.

Legislating for taste

These days, as noted earlier, beauty, or at least non-ugliness, is more generally expected from architecture than from art. An ugly painting or performance work is *de rigeur* but an ugly downtown tower or university library provokes cries of 'how could it happen'-type rage. That this is only to be expected, considering the building's effect and endurance, only makes it the more surprising that no one seems to have any idea of how, reliably, to achieve beauty in architecture.

But the expectation remains, so strongly that our great and glorious leaders from time to time take it upon themselves to deliver. This is not new. It is, after all, the central and sustaining delusion of people in power that they are, in fact, in power. That's okay. We all have our fantasy lives. And you can understand the urge, the tear-welling frustration for any politician with eyes, stuck in the limo in the suburban traffic, forcibly confronting the sheer horror of modern urban reality. You can understand, too, that the politician's patent failure to shift the system to something more honourable should eventually manifest as a desire to change the way reality looks.

To some extent this is just basic packaging theory, extending the politician's standard addiction to 'point-at-ables'. Even Napoleon knew that empire alone wasn't enough; it had to be obvious, glittering and palpable. Palaces and boulevards for Napoleon, *grands projets* for Mitterand: point-at-ables are essential political kit.

In Australia, perhaps as a result of the continuing convict mentality, politicians from Governor Macquarie in 1821 to Jeff Kennett in 1999 have as often been ousted as lauded for investment in public works. Thus contemporary politicians pursue 'design excellence' more through competition and regulation than built example.

This, on the face of it, seems entirely reasonable. Who, after all, has not looked aghast on some gargantuan ugliness emerging from a construction site and wondered, *Who on earth let that happen? Can't such monstrosities be stopped, or at least the very worst of them prevented?* It's a nice thought, but how might the law be drafted? All buildings to be beautiful henceforth? If beauty is so elusive, so personal, so indefinable, how can you legislate for it?

One option is to adopt John Constable's very postmodern view, from 1843, that 'there is nothing ugly; I never saw an ugly thing in my life: for let the form of an object be what it may, light, shade and perspective will always make it beautiful'. On this take, whatever anyone chooses to build is fine. Beauty is entirely a bring-your-own affair. Most people, though – and in democracy most people are the ones that count – see it differently. Most people, without thinking too much about definitions, believe 'they' should filter ugliness out.

And this, indeed, is the intention. Proponents of aesthetic control usually argue that it's not about hard-and-fast rules: that the controls are designed as a loose sieve, filtering out the worst while leaving the best unfettered. The fact is, though, that such controls usually inhibit both extremes, the good and the bad, favouring only a generalised mediocrity.

Pattern books can work. In general they work where there is an educated client class, a coherent social philosophy and no mucking about with committees. The earliest pattern book of which evidence remains was a rather dull work by the Roman architect Vitruvius in the first century CE, designed to convey the classical canons to the ordinary Roman builder. A clutch of Renaissance theorists followed, including Alberti about 1450, Serlio in 1537, Palladio in 1570 and Scamozzi in 1615; all progressively updating Vitruvius and canonising the orders.

But the pattern-book genre really came into its own in the building boom that followed the Great Fire of London, where it offered the craftsman-builder a crucial leg-up. From there, the pattern book came into its own in the Georgian era and spread to Sydney, adapting itself through successive printings and copyings to generate the classic Sydney terrace house with its distinctive cast-iron lacework balcony.

Pretty, yes. But as an idea, the pattern book could hardly be less democratic. In standardising detail, material and composition, it gains in taste what it sacrifices in democracy's dearest qualities: ingenuity, individuality and creative freedom. London's modernist architectural sage John Summerson lamented in 1945, at the height of modernism, that the 'Palladian dictatorship' by which Georgian London had been shaped from 1730 to 1760 had suffocated thirty years of stylistic change.

Which takes us to the bigger issues; democracy, taste, free will and the nature of judgement. Why *is* most contemporary building so wretchedly hideous compared not only with the Versailles and Taj Mahals of the ancients but with ordinary Greek fishing villages and Sicilian hill towns? How is it that those old-time peasants, impoverished, ignorant and oppressed as they were, produced beauty, while we produce trash? What's going on?

Freedom, in a word. We take freedom, especially freedom of choice, as both an unmixed good and a god-given right. Perhaps, morally, it is. But the freedoms of democracy have done less than nothing for architecture and town-making. From Mykonos to Paris, beautiful, traditional towns – beautiful enough still to draw tourists centuries later – were produced under conditions that we would consider intolerably oppressive, with little or no personal choice on the part of builder, architect or user as to material, style, colour or decoration.

This link between beauty and tyranny is not just happenstance. It's directly causal. That's the odd thing. Beauty arose not despite the oppression but because of it. Traditional cities owe their beauty to the combined corsets of ignorance, poverty and social rigidity, material deprivation and technological constraint. Conversely, the visual cacophony of our latter-day burb is a direct result of capitalist democracy, as the crummy modern outskirts of all those picturesque medieval Euro-towns attest. Pattern books – or canons of beauty – can work, but only in homogeneous and oppressable societies without opinion, freedom or democracy.

Postmodernism, which in urbanist mode pretends to have the answers to this dilemma, has in fact exacerbated it by consistently elevating the personal and particular over the universal and transcendent. Three of the main postmodern winds – monetarism, relativism and spin – all blow constantly against the possibility of coherent city-making. Monetarism argues that leadership is pretty much down to the market, biobanking and carbon trading being classic examples. Why regulate when you can sit back and watch the dealers deal? Relativism argues that since all truth is just perception, and all perception is subjective, collective ideas and beliefs, like those on which urbanism and planning depend, amount to tyranny. And spin allows all this to masquerade as democratic public interest, when it's actually one on one. Dog eat dog.

Then again, perhaps postmodernism is simply democracy's logical extension, even its decadent endgame. It's a small step, over a few centuries, from allowing everyone their own vote to allowing everyone their own truth. To everyone thinking *their* truth is as valid as any other. Perhaps democracy has always carried the seeds of its own destruction.

The sad and prickly truth is that cities cannot be effectively planned, much less made beautiful, by democratic government. It's not just that bureaucrats are dullards, though this is certainly part of it. And it's not just the mediocrity of committees, though this too is a problem. It's systemic. Democracy makes effective planning impossible; a mercy for which, were it not for the looming environmental crisis, we should probably offer a heartfelt prayer of thanks.

● | Discretion

A common political response to the inimical mix of democracy and good city planning is to cry 'flexibility'. Flexibility, like freedom, is another presumed-positive, as if planning were a form of yoga. If rules produce mediocrity, goes the loose-approximation-to-reasoning, the obvious solution is to bend them.

That's the outer story. Beneath them are the inner whisperings. For the politician, there's that persuasive little voice – we've all heard it – suggesting everything would be fine if only *it were me* making the decisions. It's clearly delusional, but since politicians are usually narcissists, who willingly believe in universal love as long as it is directed universally at them, it carries a certain clout.

Plus, when you're in politics, especially when you achieve (by whatever means) what is known as 'high office', you quickly start to feel it's personal. You start to feel that all the bowing and scraping, all the back-slapping and forelock-tugging, all the business class and bonhomie and dinner parties and perquisites are because they like you, personally. Because you are something special. And that's when you start thinking you're above the law, that the normal rules don't apply, and that it's entirely reasonable to frame legislation around the presumption of your own omniscience and immortality.

But it's not just the pollies who love the idea of flexi-rules. For voters too, accustomed to a feelgood morality, there's the kneejerk notion, straight out of the baby-boomer parenting manual, that flexible rules are friendlier, happier and generally nicer to be near than rigid ones. That stiffness in rules is as reproachably Victorian as stiffness in parenting, teaching or religion.

Nothing could be further from the truth. The flexibility rhetoric is the all of 'merit-based decision-making', a phrase designed to push the buttons of a democracy-loving public by exploiting the implied link with meritocracy, and the false promise that in planning, as in society, excellence will naturally rise. But this is not the effect. Far from it. Flexibility requires statutes and regulations to be laced with fuzzball phraseology, systematically replacing categorical imperatives like 'shall', 'will' and 'must' with vague normatives like 'may', 'should' and 'ought'. Phrases like 'in the Minister's opinion' become commonplace, as do 'if practicable', 'where possible' and even 'as expedient'.

This makes flexibility sound like a concession to the people, a dent in government power. But the effect is the opposite, since it puts the onus on the developer to show that keeping the heritage fragment, or putting the car-park underground, is not practicable. This is the easiest thing in the world, pulling economic wool over the eyes of planning committees. Which only hides the real effect, namely, broadening the discretion of the decision-maker to vest immense, whimsical power in one person or committee. This, like the latest Planning Act in New South Wales, is trust-me legislation of the worst sort.

And yet many people think it's fine, especially if the decision-maker in question seems an okay kinda guy. *It's okay*, they think, *because he's okay*. But this is wrong; it's not okay, even if he is. The man himself could be Francis of Assisi, and still be succeeded by Idi Amin. He could be as pure as the driven snow, and this law would still place a big red 'press here' button on his chest for all to see. For all who can get close enough, lunch long enough, and donate lavishly enough, to press.

Which is how flexibility delivers the very opposite of its promise. The talk may be all transparency, accountability and consultation but the reality is different; a system of government from closed rooms and whispering corridors, moneyed access and the privileges of power, of public life being reduced to the rhythmic exchange of private favours.

Politics does have a personal face. A warm handshake and a kissed infant, permanently at the ready. But legislation, especially planning legislation, must be as impersonal as weather. To breach this principle is always dangerous, but especially in planning which, since it regularly delivers huge windfall gains to landowners, is really a high-stakes exercise in resource allocation. Even so, you might not mind if these extraordinary discretionary powers were directed to noble ends. Saving the planet, for instance, is a goal where the end may reasonably justify the means. But when the ends are no nobler than self-interest and cronyism, everything suffers.

In New South Wales, for instance, the state-wide planning loophole that is Part 3A of the Planning Act, passed by Parliament in 2005 and widened in 2006, gives the Minister vast and unprecedented discretion. On a whim the Minister can deem a particular project, or an entire class of projects – all marinas, say, or all high-rise apartment buildings – 'state significant', and so call them in from under the nose of local authorities. The Minister can approve such projects, regardless of Cabinet, regardless of departmental advice, regardless of established planning policy, regardless of public opinion and regardless of almost thirty years of environmental legislation. All specifically suspended for the purpose. No boxes need be ticked nor criteria met. Just the opinion of the Minister.

But, you counter, what of the relatively benign dictatorships that have generally been responsible for the cities we admire, the Romes and Parises, the Venices and Londons? Doesn't the advent of discretion in planning, the gathering of power to the Minister, simply emulate these regimes more closely? Weren't the monarchs, oligarchs, emperors and outright tyrants responsible for those cities' beauty all wearing the same big red 'press here' button?

Yes, that's true. They were. But it's also true that both the decision-makers and the button-pressers were not just rich but, on the whole, cultivated. They also tended to take a relatively long-term view of self-interest and to temper it with *noblesse oblige*. This, ironically, inclined them much more strongly to a well-mannered acknowledgement of the public realm than can be expected from democracy's protagonists. The patrons of London's Russell Square, developed by architect-builder James Burton for the Duke of Bedford between 1800 and 1814, or Regent Street, planned by John Nash for the Prince Regent in the same years, were engaged in a long-term public relations exercise, creating buildings and precincts as 'better selves', or masks, that would serve both as contemporary advertisements and future memorials.

The downside was a system that relegated a large part of the population to poverty. But the upside becomes apparent when comparing Bloomsbury, say, with new dockland developments in London or Melbourne or Sydney or San Francisco or New York, where hit-and-run development and shareholder-driven accounting means even major banks take short-term leases on buildings that no one expects, or indeed would wish, to last.

This tentative and temporary approach to city-building gets worse, not better, as our democracies mature, signifying perhaps a society uncertain about its beliefs and fearful of its future, and therefore unwilling to invest in either. A society driven by fear into myriad means of sustaining the status quo on a subsistence basis, rather than finding the courage and imagination to change it.

Sprawl

The sprawl debate is fast becoming political: sprawlers to the right, urbanists (or 'smart-growthers') to the left. To critique the boomburg, for either its aesthetics or its sustainability, is to provoke a torrent of letter-column inches in which bandwagoners leap to defend the democratic right of 'ordinary, successful people' to live in 'beautiful' (that is, huge) homes with 'a lock-up garage and plenty of bathrooms and bedrooms for everyone' – straight out of a fifties sitcom. Backing up their claims, in Sydney at least, is the strong McMansionville presence of 'Bible-based, evangelical Christianity' – and the proud fact that 40 per cent of McMansions are air conditioned.

Anyone with the temerity to criticise the McMansion is clearly a leftie inner-city trendoid with a water view, a weekender in Bowral and a 'spitting, blinding rage' against the family values that bind our society together. Class clichés at fifty paces. More worrying, though, is the sprawlers' steadfast refusal to consider that anything could matter more than what we want. Survival, say.

It's the same lower-chakra stuff that swells our obesity rates: *Duh, I wannit an I wannit now*. Underlying dumb growth are three presumptions: that what we want is automatically good for us, that all goods are individual goods, and that the ultimate good is freedom. Personal freedom, of which the ultimate icon is, of course, the car.

A more interesting question is how this elision came about in the first place? How did 'family values' come to equal the most wildly future-eating living pattern in history? The British Tories are now greener than Labour, exploiting a natural proximity between conservation and conservatism. But somehow this hasn't spread to Australia's conservative pollies, nor to the mums and dads. Don't we *see* that all the ensuites and games rooms in the cosmos cannot compensate for clean air and water? Where are Parents for the Planet? Why aren't the planners and politicians shouting this stuff from the ballot boxes?

'I am not an advocate of sprawl,' says US pro-sprawl consultant Wendell Cox, in Sydney recently to persuade us to build more motorways, 'I am an advocate of freedom.' Like, not anti-abortion, pro-life. Cox's first point is that, 'absent a material threat to other individuals or the community, people should be allowed to live and work how and where they like'. So far, so plausible. Less is certainly more on the governance front, and most cities could afford to brush up on elegant regime-design. It's stage two of Cox's argument that leaves you gasping. Namely, that since burbs and freeways are what people like, Sydney (and everywhere else) should have more of them. Lots more.

The obvious environmental riposte is that the destructiveness of sprawl (consuming arable land, destroying forest, filthying air, bankrupting public transport and attenuating services) busts Cox's 'absent material threat' principle wide open. The sprawl-threat is utterly material. You're breathing it. And that's the point being missed here. Neither ugliness nor climate change is class-specific. Ugliness may be liberated by wealth, new or old, but there is no doubt that the bloated and botoxed specials of well-heeled suburbia can be every bit as visually and environmentally destructive – and perhaps worse, morally – as the McMansions that ape them.

The pro-sprawl lobby glides on thin logical ice. Freedom is the first obvious crack. The classical view of freedom, as Cambridge philosopher Quentin Skinner noted recently, is what separates *liber homo* from slave: absence of coercion and independence from 'the arbitrary will of someone else'. Such a definition means that none of us is free, nor ever will be. We are, always, profoundly compromised by other individual wills and by the common will; our personal freedoms limited by every statute, tax, building, encounter, traffic light and drainage easement. This is not because government is evil (though that may also be the case). Nor because our fellow citizens are our enemies, but because we voluntarily curtail our individual rights in exchange for the immense advantages of the herd.

This voluntary relinquishment of rights suggests a more complex definition of liberty. Perhaps like Thomas Cranmer's sixteenth century paradox that 'service is perfect freedom'. This is usually seen as a thin-lipped, self-hating Protestant view of freedom. But, given Cranmer's take on service as the essence of human nature, it is possible – just possible – that what he had in mind was not that at all, but a richer, more complex and more paradoxical understanding. A view of service as sacrament or, in psychological terms, as self-actualisation in which to give is, literally, to receive. Such a view has underpinned a number of recent films, including Steven Shainberg's *Secretary* (2002), where the ambiguities of female sexuality make it possible for submission and control to be the same.

This paradox points to one of our ludicrous species' most lovable traits – that we need to give, quite as much as we need to take. We invented god, you might argue, not in order to be loved so much as always to have something to love. The best cure for depression is altruism. You can call this morality, or religion, or just ordinarily weird psychological fact. Freedom may lie in satisfying needs, but one of our needs is to subjugate our needs to those of others. Analyse that.

This is another aspect of masking. Just as the frog's skin crucially facilitates oxygen exchange, the mask facilitates life-sustaining flow. As Richard Sennett notes in *Conscience of the Eye*, flow cannot be achieved 'simply by tearing down the wall ... unity can be gained only at the price of complexity. The exposed, outer life of the city cannot be simply a reflection of the inner life'. The mask (be it skin, house or city) may be both inwardly protective and outwardly expressive. Further, there must be flow; throughness. Otherwise, like the boy in the bubble, we die.

Downshifting and sea-changing: the real costs

'For anyone who has ever loved too much, worked too hard or yearned for a new start, Take a sea-change to Salvation Creek ...' croons the in-air advertising over the cut-price chainstore's desultory morning shoppers. For anyone in any doubt as to whether 'sea-change' has made it into the popular unconscious, that should settle it. But how real is the dream, and what does it really cost?

The prettiest town left in Australia, personal view, is Hill End in New South Wales. The name is a mystery since it's hardly the end of the hills, in either direction. Arrival from the east is via a bumpy, grinding dirt road. From the west it's a bumpier, grindier dirt track that descends steeply, fords the Macquarie River, stutters with knee-deep ruts and threatens constantly to vanish up its own forestry trail. Once you get there, Hill End is all picturesque meandering streets and peeling picket fences, autumn colours and tiny stone churches. There's decent coffee and a genuinely *gemütlich* pub without a hint of gimcrack. But the journey itself is not for the faint-hearted. And that's important, since these wayfaring hostilities are the ramparts that have kept Hill End pretty while every other pretty town in Australia – from Broome to Esperance, Maroochydore to Byron Bay, from Kiama to Bega – has succumbed to the tide of asphalt and aluminium and plastic that passes for contemporary urban culture.

And what protects the ramparts? Landlubbery, in a word. While virtually every town within cooee of the sea has given way to the relentless roll-out of multi-lane roads and multi-car garages, warehouse shopping and warehouse-churches that signifies coming of age in Australian urbanism, inland towns like Hill End have been saved by neglect. Hill End has retained its charm because no one goes there. And no one goes there because there's no sea there. Meanwhile, the seaside places to which we do flock are traduced by that very flocking.

This is our dilemma. We want to escape, but we *all* want to escape, each other, together.

And the especial irony is this: although Australia is one of the few continents where that sort of mutual avoidance might (in theory) be possible, our escape destinations are not, in general, the wide open centre of the place. No way. We all want to escape to the long-but-skinny periphery – the sea edge.

Sea-change, for most of its practitioners, is a simple lifestyle choice: a human right, therefore, but one of private, rather than public significance. The beach promises, or seems to promise, every day in holiday mode. Mornings with sand between your toes and evenings like a superannuation ad, loving beach walks at sunset, the golden retriever/toddler grandchild frolicking in the wavelets.

The reality often involves long hours in traffic jams, alienation from family, friends and city culture and a serious-to-catastrophic drop in income. In glamorous Byron, for example, welfare is the second largest revenue stream, and double that of agriculture. Figures like this mean that sea-change strips often become areas of high demand but low satisfaction, as councils struggle to provide services and maintain amenity over a large area on an inadequate rates base. Slowly, as the reality sinks in, that old nature-culture dilemma reveals itself.

We love the beach. We love it for itself, and for the clean, honest, salty egalitarianism it seems to represent. And in loving it we want, naturally, to live there. But, as with suburbia, so with the beach. When the blow-ins blow in, land values rocket. Even locals who refuse to sell are often forced out by land taxes. Neither they nor their children can buy a future in the town that may have been theirs for decades. One by one, fibro shacks on leafy blocks are replaced by shiny apartment buildings that strain and bulge towards the view. The corner shop becomes a drive-in supermarket. Traffic lights arrive. Multiplex cinemas. Bathroom shops. Pretty soon, precisely because we love it so much, the whole beachside feel has gone, morphing before our eyes into the suburban reality we were so desperate to escape. What, if anything, can be done?

One possibility is 'slow architecture', the urban equivalent of slow food. Similar in some ways to the 'New Urbanism' ideas promoted by American architect Andres Duany and others, slow architecture doesn't necessarily produce beauty, but it does help impart an organic (rather than stylistic) coherence to a place. More significantly, since to build slow is usually to build for endurance, slow architecture reintroduces time into the built environment, a sense of eternity. And this – since it is a basic rule of thumb that good buildings can be fast or cheap, but not both – allows buildings to be affordable without being tacky. Slow architecture's first thoroughgoing manifestation in Australia is the new town of Tullimbar, in the southern highlands of New South Wales.

Tullimbar is the brainchild of Neville Fredericks who, as it happens, commissioned one of that crop of iconic houses which first brought Australia's Pritzker Award-winning architect Glenn Murcutt to the public eye, back in the early 1980s. Fredericks is a sheep farmer turned developer who became dissatisfied with the way his conventional subdivision projects became dreary reality with the inevitable installation of project homes.

Fredericks' solution is to build 'a country village that works'. It's intelligent, thoughtful and revolutionary. First, it's not about quick returns. Nothing will be sold off the plan; streets, landscapes and townscapes will be built first. Second, there are no shareholders. Fredericks' company is family owned, so they're free to interpret 'profit motive' their own way. Third, Fredericks and his daughter and general manager Jennifer Macquarie made a point of studying traditional local towns like Bega, Berry, Berrima and Thirroul, and interrogating the world's leading new-urbanist thinkers, then emulating their principles (like slowness, street address, scale and density) but not their forms.

Fredericks has had to fight for his experiment – against retailers who want to build hyper-marts (he insists on small non-chain stores), against Council, which wanted native street-trees, and against locals who wanted sprawl. And the first results are now visible. It's not breathtaking architecture but it is welcoming, villagey, leafy, affordable and dense. It's not autonomous, in energy or water, but it is carefully oriented, insulated and massed to minimise waste. The school is under construction and the four-storey town centre, mixing apartments, shops, commercial and retirement units, will follow.

Fredericks aims to offer higher-than-project-home quality, plus greater environmental sensitivity, for about half the cost of a typical architect-designed house within – and this is the main point – a fine-grained, slow-grown, village-scale country town. It's rather an aristocratic approach, admittedly. Slow architecture depends on land ownership, cultivation and a degree of altruism, all in the same hands. A bit of a stretch for your standard developer.

What, you might ask, about government? Isn't altruism what we have government for? If Neville Fredericks can do it, why can't the state? Or the feds? Would it work? Well, maybe. In the US, growth-management legislation designed to protect heritage and environment by limiting sprawl has been adopted over twenty years by thirteen states including Washington, Texas, Florida and California. Some, mostly planners, say it doesn't work; others, like developers, say it works too well. Either way, there is no similar legislation in Australia and, as things stand, no prospect of same.

Why not? Partly because of government reluctance to intervene in the sacred forces of the market, and partly because, although Australians tend to think of America as the source-of-all-things-trashy, it also has a number of structural civilising devices (like a meaningful constitution) that Australia lacks. In particular, Australia has no equivalent of either the 'third sector' or 'direct democracy'.

The third or not-for-profit sector in the US acts as a well-developed musculature around the body politic, generating vocal lobby groups on the sprawl issue such as Active Living by Design, devoted to promoting healthy cities, and Smart Growth America, a coalition of 100-odd different environmental, urbanist and anti-sprawl bodies. Smart Growth's mission statement, for example, says:

> Americans want fewer hours in traffic and more opportunities to enjoy green space. Housing that is both affordable and close to jobs and activities; healthy cities, towns and suburbs; air and water of the highest quality; and a landscape our children can be proud to inherit. Smart growth offers the best chance we have of attaining those goals. To that end: Smart Growth America's coalition is working to support citizen-driven planning that coordinates development, transportation, revitalization of older areas and preservation of open space and the environment.

Direct democracy is the initiative process whereby support from as few as 10 per cent of voters qualifies an issue for public ballot. This, says

Berkeley planning professor John Landis, is 'how most public policy decisions are made in the States'. In Australia, by contrast, although professional concern is probably as high, the electorate is almost entirely locked out of urban planning issues. Consultation is usually a farce, since there is no requirement for open reporting, let alone action on results, and politicians rely on the voters' hip-pocket nerve to ensure that planning issues never get to the top of the list. Planning is generally seen by politicians as yet another spigot for delivering windfall favours to political mates, rather than any genuine embodiment of the public interest.

At the same time, and largely for the same reason, most land releases fall to the huge tract-developers which on the whole are publicly-listed companies with a single bottom-line culture. Troubled residents can stand for council and fight every tree-lopping and road-widening through the grassroots democratic process. Or they can do what 80 per cent of Noosa-newcomers from Sydney and Melbourne reportedly do within two years of downshifting there: move back. Either way, it's exhausting and dispiriting.

The solution, as with so many cultural difficulties, lies in our preparedness to rise above narrow self-interest and become involved in culture-making at a broader, more communal, more altruistic level. Admittedly, many factors, including democracy and human nature itself, work against us here. Climate change, on the other hand, looks like giving us a shove in that direction that we cannot refuse.

9 | I have a dream ...

Art and morals are, with certain provisos ... one. Their
essence ... is love ... the extremely difficult realisation
that something other than oneself is real.

IRIS MURDOCH (1959)

As long as humankind proceeds in the fateful delusion of being
biologically fated for triumph, nothing essential will change.

PETER WESSEL ZAPFFE (1933)

It's a dream, sure. But it could happen. Maybe sooner than we think.
Imagine it. Petrol is now $10 or maybe $20 a litre. Water, half that or
more. Climate change has raised sea levels, shrunk dry land, shifted
ocean currents, changed rainfall patterns and warmed the atmosphere
by several degrees. Our children are now adults with their own kids. In
their all-out effort to prevent the billions of deaths that were predicted
earlier in the century, and to maintain civilisation in the face of chaos,
they have dramatically reinvented their living patterns.

In Australia, rain hasn't fallen in the eastern half of the country for a decade. Most of the land is now desert. Canberra, long since abandoned, is home only to the occasional band of kangaroos, which some people argue is no change at all. Sydney, Melbourne, Brisbane have all shrunk to little more than a tenth of their earlier size.

Along what remains of the eastern seaboard, moth-eaten as it is by the rising oceans, only the very wealthy remain, mostly elderly, living under enormous synthetic bubbles, some of them several kilometres in diameter, designed to prevent the escape of precious water vapour. The inhabitants grow what food they can inside the bubble, and fly in the rest from the other side of the country. Water comes by tanker and by trans-continental aqueduct. Air, on most days still too toxic to breathe, is filtered through special solar-powered pores in the bubble's skin. No one believes this arrangement can last for ever. Gradually the population is dying or drifting west, following the rain.

New cities have sprung up throughout Western Australia, concentrated in the new high rainfall north-west. The Kimberley has become Australia's breadbasket, its centre of agriculture, industry and population. With the arrival there of the multitudes, half a dozen new cities have had to be built rapidly, over just a few years. What are they like?

They're walled, for a start. Not literally, although some have planted forests, and in other cases people have started to construct stone walls, with proper city gates, for cosiness. Figuratively, though, the boundaries are clear, absolute and inviolable. Each city has a boundary, marked with a ring-road and milestones, beyond which development is statutorily prohibited. Out there, beyond the city bounds, is a ring of market gardens; most farmers live on their farms but since all farming is organic, again as required by law, daily hordes of farmworkers come by bus, bike and foot to their jobs in the fields.

Chemical pesticides, being petroleum based, have become prohibitively expensive. More than that, though, their deadening effect on the soil and their invasion of the food chain saw them all but outlawed, years back. Many argued for genetic modification and in some countries this has become standard. Australia, though, went the other way; pursuing smaller farms and more natural methodologies; mandating bio-pesticides and bio-fertilisers as petrochemical substitutes. Food-growing, with its required scholarship in plant and animal ecology, has become a highly respected occupation, like being a doctor in the Dark Age. Those with the knowledge of crop rotation, soil husbandry and chemical-free horticulture are revered almost as priests, and although the workers themselves are not immensely wealthy, their pay is adequate and their job satisfaction among the highest in the community. Meat is still produced, and eaten, but costs have encouraged people to incorporated more fruits and vegetables into their diets. From the garden-belt, food is taken by truck, usually, to the rail head. From there it is freighted into the city centres by magnetic rail, then distributed to shops and markets by fleets of the largely solar-charged battery-powered trucks and vans that have become commonplace.

Beyond the garden belt is wilderness. Out there, all land is Crown land. People are encouraged to visit, explore, camp, even lease the bush and coastal shacks that have sprung up as holiday destinations. They can travel by train or bus or bike. Even, if they choose the extra expense, by car. But speculation is discouraged and private land ownership forbidden outside the city. Large, conglomerate developments are also banned; people may build small holiday houses but only leasehold, and only for their own use. There are hotels, mostly of the small-cabin eco-variety. Leaseholders may sell, but only within a given percentage of what they paid. Certain coastal strips and hamlets are set aside for habitation in this way; the rest is wilderness. Downshifting, which before the Great Change was epidemic, has virtually ceased. It is still allowed, within any of the designated rural villages, but with the gentler, quieter cities, more accessible countryside and better diet, most people no longer feel the need. This, and the increased rainfall, have allowed great forests to spring up, karri and jarrah and giant river red gum, depending on microclimate. These forests help attract rainclouds, so the land around them remains healthy and animal life has started to regenerate. Here, notwithstanding the occasional bushfire, everything is peaceful and ordered according to the unbending rules of nature.

In the cities, by contrast, everything hums with energy. Physically, there is still a density gradient from inner to outer, as in old-style cities. But where twentieth century cities tended to abruptly change, with a high-rise core surrounded by a mat of low-density suburbia, the new cities show a more gradual transition from high-rise to mid-rise to low-rise (but still relatively dense) outer rings.

The city centre is dominated by tall and very tall buildings; downtown for office towers, uptown for residential. (The mixed-use ideal, still pursued in the lower-rise areas, has broadly been abandoned in the core, after experience in the old east coast cities suggested conflict over noise, lighting and privacy could prove insoluble.) Tax incentives designed to encourage distributed grids for electricity and water mean that every building has its own energy source – usually photovoltaics or the new, silent wind-driven micro-turbines – and its own rainwater tanks. In the case of towers, these tanks are usually vast underground affairs used as heat-sinks for summer cooling. Some have pioneered ingenious evaporative cooling technologies where the water is captured and recycled in a cooling system before being cycled through the greywater system; others provide a permanent water supply for vertical hydroponic gardens.

Strict caps apply to energy and water use as well as to greenhouse gas emissions but, extraordinarily, there are times when usage drops even below the caps. There are a number of reasons for this, over and above increased costs and awareness. All buildings must be at least 50 per cent renewable-dependent, and all water – including sewage – is recycled. Energy and water use per head have dropped to less than half old levels, partly because smartgrids, for both water and electricity, mean that every building, be it office tower, apartment building or single house, has wall-mounted meters showing real-time consumption (or production) and online access to historical and cost information. Usage costs and generation payments are scaled to reflect peak times, and users can see immediately the effect of switching a particular generator on or a particular appliance off. Users can also trade unused energy credits, in which there is a thriving market. This measure is controversial. Many of the ecologically minded believe it to be a mistake, since it encourages saving, on the one hand, even as it depends on sustained demand. But because such profits can be reaped only during peak times, and because all energy-credit profits are taxed to support the energy technologies sector, others defend the law.

Triggered by all this, a new corporate sport has emerged, where a building's gym is linked to the smartgrid. Office workers and residents compete in team-based power-generation marathons on cycle or walking machines. So addictive has this new sport become that whereas, at the start, tax incentives were used to encourage capital investment in generation technologies, now workers pick and choose jobs partly according to their team status.

Buildings are encouraged, further, to be traversable, covering horizontal and even vertical surfaces with gardens; rooftop orchards and wall-side herb or strawberry patches are common. Workers commonly step outside to gather food for lunch, and organise climbing expeditions around, across and through this semi-edible cityscape. This can get pretty exciting for here, in the centre, there is no height limit. Towers must comply with unwavering environmental standards; beyond that, they must provide structural soundness, basic function and street amenity. But over design itself there is no control, except that each year a plebiscite awards the building it regards as the most innovative, and the architect responsible automatically gets the next big job in town. Architects from all over the world compete to make the most interesting, most efficient and most fertile buildings. So skyline and cityscape are extraordinarily varied, with interesting forms, and buildings softened everywhere by greenery and human presence.

The city-centre streets are wide and shady, usually tree-lined or shaded with a vine-covered pergola. Since there is little seasonal differentiation, year-round shade, whether from planting or tall buildings, is generally welcome. The streets are also relatively wind-sheltered, since the broken-up masses of the buildings, and their rampant greenery, enormously reduce the wind-generation effects for which old-style smooth-skinned skyscrapers were renowned.

Private cars are banned in the city centre. This, which began as an emergency measure after global oil peaked, is no longer strictly necessary since solar-powered electric cars, while still not cheap to buy or run, have become widely available. But by then people had grown so attached to the social benefits of the car-free city centres (clean air, increased safety but, above all, quiet) that reintroducing them became politically impossible. People who do own cars, individually or in clubs, stable them on the city fringe.

In the city centre the main streets are between four and six lanes wide; one for public transport, one for taxis and mopeds, and two full lanes dedicated to bicycles. Even so, the cycle lanes are often crowded, since most people choose to get about this way, both for fitness and for the sheer pleasure of it, now that the streets are quiet and serious accidents almost unheard of. All office buildings have showers, and many people keep their work-wardrobes at work; street garb has therefore taken on a more casual air.

Around the central blocks a light rail system describes a complex loop, one car every two minutes, 24/7. Where there are six lanes, the centre strip is undercut by deep stormwater swales connecting to an artificial aquifer beneath the town. Above ground, the centre strip is given over to cafés and restaurants, interspersed with fruit trees, vegetable gardens and grapevines. The necessity to guard these gardens has given rise to a new job niche, the city night-watchman, and this in turn encourages pedestrian activity throughout the night, as well as the day.

Within these main blocks the city is criss-crossed by narrow laneways, accessible only to pedestrians and bicycles. Some of these lanes tunnel through the arcaded bases of tower buildings, others are open to the sky, but all are overtly public space, never closed, and lined with shops, cafés and bars.

These changes are supported by regulation. A special city ordinance requiring retail along all street frontages has decimated retail rents from the old days. This, more than compensated for in value terms by the extra tower heights, has combined with the huge fuel prices to replace the old street-level monoculture of banks and chain stores with a vast and variegated array of on-street retail outlets, including the fresh produce markets that have sprung up at every street corner. People shop on foot; daily for food, and locally for almost everything, so streets constantly bustle with shoppers. At the same time, since it is no longer viable to import vast quantities of alcohol, most wines and even spirits are locally produced, and licensing laws having been changed to encourage small hole-in-the-wall wine bars and licensed cafés. Running a small bar or shop has therefore become something many people, often cooperatives or groups of students, do for a few years, semi-experimentally, before going on to other things. This has entirely transformed not only the streets, occupying what would, in the old cities, have been leftover or unused basement nooks, but also the music and performing arts scene. Casinos and large pokie-dominated pubs still exist, but are relatively rare, having been outpaced by the all-night café culture, in which a thriving live music, street poetry and performance art scene has become an essential element.

In the uptown residential district, as in any global city centre, residents are generally youngsters, students, empty-nesters and that third of the population now living as one-person families. Added to this demographic range is a further category of people for whom it might be more comfortable and practical to live outside the city centre but who choose the uptown lifestyle as status symbol. Living lean and green has become a prestige gesture, and quite a number choose it simply for the cachet.

Outside the city centre, the inner residential neighbourhoods are medium density and medium rise; most are six- and eight-storeyed apartment blocks based largely on the nineteenth century Belgravia model. The buildings look, more or less, like rows of tall terrace houses, brick-built for high thermal mass, arranged around a central square. In the centre of the square – sometimes encircled, sometimes quartered by leafy streets – is a large fenced garden, heavily planted with mature trees and shrubs and easily mistaken for a small park. The garden is kept locked but all residents of the square are entitled to a key, so on evenings and weekends it becomes an unofficial meeting point, where people garden, exercise and walk their dogs. In some gardens tiny café-kiosks have been allowed to spring up; others are home to the weekly or even daily fresh local produce markets.

Inside, each apartment building is organised around a common staircase. Most have a basement flat, with borrowed light from the street and mews, and one or two storeys of attic flats in the roof. Since access is walk-up, by common stair, the older and less fit favour the ground-floor apartments. Others go for the extra view and sunlight of the upper floors. The very wealthy, of course, may own entire buildings, or even install their own solar-powered lifts, while the poor may inhabit the attics.

Further out again the housing devolves into two- to four-storeyed terrace housing, traditionally formed on the outside but designed within to maximise light and a sense of space, much like the classic late twentieth century Paddington terrace-house renovation. Out here, private cars are not banned but many choose not to own them and those who do may share, often stabling their cars on the periphery, using them strictly for special trips. Car clubs, like the corporate sport teams, are another tribal venue, since most car owners belong to one and there is competition to have – and be seen to have – the cleanest, greenest fleet of vehicles.

Within each of the housing forms, further, whether high rise, medium rise or terrace housing, a certain volume is devoted to community utilities: high-intensity power generation, water recycling, neighbourhood composting and worm farms to supply the local gardens. This stuff, farming, has become important and personal. The cost of fuel, land and labour for the new organic farming has more than doubled the cost of bought food, so most people grow at least some of their own vegies. Every horizontal surface is colonised by horticulture, and quite a few vertical ones; everywhere where the sun falls that isn't already used for sun or water collection. Roof gardens have become elaborate and luxuriant. Some people even manage to run chooks and the odd goat on their roof, although a number of bodies corporate remain adamantly opposed. The growing business has become a source of great personal pride; some public health professionals even credit it with the near-total disappearance of the epidemic depression that afflicted what people now describe, for all its techno-affluence, as the Dark Age.

Here, as in the core, energy use has dropped sharply, partly because both awareness and energy costs have risen sharply but also because the new housing types, in sharing walls, minimise external surface for heat loss and gain, effectively insulating each other. Their luxuriant roof gardens give extra insulation, as well as softening the cityscape, so the houses are relatively easy to heat and cool.

Throughout the city, the ownership pattern is mixed; some people own their dwellings, others rent. This is not a class distinction but a simple choice, facilitated once again by statutory change. Across the country, capital gains tax exemptions have been removed from the private home. So while people may still invest speculatively in their homes, the incentive to prefer this over other forms of investment, and thus to inflate the size and value of the family home, has gone. McMansions are seen as dinosaurs; baggage that no one wanted to remember, much less bring in the move west. At the same time, statutory rent control has meant that many people choose to rent throughout their lives so, instead of speculating on their own home – and being forced to sell in order to fund their superannuation – they invest in enterprise.

This, in turn, has had the surprising spin-off benefit of funding not just the small bars and cafés of the city centre but many other otherwise unsupported industries. The new Australia has at last become the clever country. Not only does it no longer send its intelligentsia and creatives overseas, it now draws such people from elsewhere, since there is so much free money to invest in good ideas.

Australia's range of exports has thus broadened beyond recognition. But the new investment pattern has also enriched the culture, and this effect is further enhanced by the new lifestyle as people gradually lose the suburban habit of concentrating their lives as much as possible within the private bubbles of office, car and home.

Instead, it has become sophisticated for people of all ages, not just those engaged in the sexual hunt, to spend a much higher proportion of their life in the public realm. Many people have come to think of their neighbourhood as an extended living room; spending large chunks of ordinary leisure-time out, in streets and public spaces, rather than at home in front of television. The consequent blossoming in patronage of the city's public parts has not only enhanced the numbers and quality of cafés and restaurants, shops and cinemas, pools, parks, galleries, theatres and sports venues, but has also given rise to a completely new crepuscular phenomenon, which people describe as an Australian *passaggiata*. In the tropical dawn people gather in the city's central square, which in one case overlooks the vast expanse of Lake Argyle and, as flamingos rise in flocks, the people do tai chi or yoga, or drink coffee, or simply sit and watch.

Household shopping has been transformed. The gargantuan Dark Age supermarkets and mega-malls, which proved unworkable without air-conditioning, refrigerated storage, chemical pesticides and fossil fuel transport, have all but disappeared. Some smaller versions exist, but even they are finding life difficult, as people, literally voting with their feet, make clear their preference for locally grown chemical-free produce. Because people shop daily and on foot, instead of weekly by car, packaging is vastly reduced, and much of it is recycled paper or glass. The mountains of waste plastic from double and triple packaging have shrunk, and the occurrence of polymer-migration into food has virtually ceased. Meat is still eaten, of course, being grown on the agricultural outskirts and brought into town by rail or truck. But the farms are smaller and more labour intensive, since non-organic farming methods are banned. Meat prices have therefore tripled, so most people eat less of it.

This simple regime – increased cycling and walking, less meat, cleaner air, less plastic packaging, fewer dietary chemicals – has transformed public health. Diabetes, obesity, colon cancer and heart disease, once rampant, have returned to their pre-modern levels. Depression is rare and alcohol-related crimes and diseases, while by no means eliminated, have roughly halved in incidence. Commentators disagree as to why; some put it down to increased fitness levels, others to the lower levels of stress and depression, others still to the fact that the small-bar phenomenon has made drinking a more civic and civilised activity, taking it out of the booze-barn environment and so more integrated with society at large. Childhood asthma is unusual and childhood obesity virtually unknown. Most kids cycle to school and after school are allowed to play in the quiet local streets and neighbourhood gardens. Private health insurance is no longer mandatory, because governments find it possible again to fund full healthcare. People are poorer materially, but healthier and, on the whole, happier; longevity and quality of life are higher than ever.

With the general increase in fitness levels, and decreased kilojoule intake, few people any longer struggle to lose weight – although anorexia, too, is almost unknown. This has become a standard source of humour since, while capitalism is stronger than ever, there is a single, global stock exchange and a single global currency, called the *joule* in recognition of the fact that money is the ultimate in embodied energy. Human energy, nature's energy, food energy; all come together in the joule. Far from struggling to lose joules and kilojoules, therefore, people now struggle to gain them and keep them.

So it's not that human nature has changed. We're still as shortsighted and greedy as ever, with the occasional spark of the divine. But a new belief system has evolved, mainly from necessity. From survival. It's not really a religion, in the old sense of rules and strictures. Like many belief systems of the past, it has swiped elements from other theologies, with echoes of Zoroastrianism, of Sufism, of Buddhism and of Christianity audible in the new liturgy, but there is an element of humility in the face of nature that is entirely new, at least for a millennium or two. Deifying Mother Earth, the new religion makes heavenly disciples of sun and rain, worshipful shrines of fertility and compost and sacred objects of water tanks and worm farms. The rules of eco-living have become scripture, with spring and harvest the holiest days in the calendar. The highest sacrament is a ritual receiving of the rains, while the various categories of modernist hubris and solipsism – waste and pollution, greed and gluttony, avarice, envy and sloth – are the updated deadly sins.

The priests of the new religion are not only mostly women, but mostly mothers. Their highest, most transcendent value is altruism, which they hold to be no more than enlightened self-interest since it perfectly exemplifies the most sacred principle, that to give is to receive. This is taken by some to show that the new religion is just Christianity reworked. In fact it is modelled closely on the roundness of nature, where the identity of giving and receiving creates and sustains the cycle of life. Thus, where Christianity elevated male virtues of aggression and dominion over nature and over others (as distinct, in its view, from nature), the new religion – closer, perhaps, to Christianity's truncated Gnostic strand – sees humanity as one of many glorious animal species, and the feminine virtues of giving and receiving, of empathy and service, as the highest goods. From these flow the other, secondary values – courage, imagination, beauty and truth – by which we can escape the prison of ego to participate in nature's great tapestry.

The churches of the new religion are not formulaic in construction. Built of tree trunks or concrete, carved from clay or solid rock, they tend to encourage light from on high, in the old way, but at the centre is neither vestal flame nor man-god but water, pure life-giving water, an appreciation of which came to us in the Great Drought. The purpose of these buildings is to help us remember and fully see these elements of our dependence, and to give form – rather than modernist denial – to our deep, mortal immersion in eternity. So, while human nature is unchanged, being every bit as venal, self-concerned, vain and weak as it always was, there has been a small shift in consciousness, a tiny dawning of the realisation that self-concern, to be sustainable, must also encompass sacrifice. That to give is to receive.

Accordingly, and partly in emulation of nature's unbending rule-book, the legislative regime underpinning the new society has been rethought, and drastically simplified to contain statutes that are as few and as simple as possible, and give minimum discretion to politicians. This allows everyone to understand the law, at least in principle, often unassisted by legal teams. It has also, unexpectedly, allowed business to thrive in an environment of certainty, largely free of the tedium and expense of long lunches and favours to elected members.

Business life has been transformed in other ways too, since although globalism continues through the single currency and the internet, international air travel has become prohibitively expensive – and morally unacceptable except in the most compelling circumstances. This single factor was predicted to have the direst consequences for Australia, as the tyranny of distance, presumed sleeping, was once again snarling in the yard. In the event, though, this very factor has had a surprising spin-off. Australia is one of the few countries with enough land to abandon its old cities and start again, afresh. It is also blessed with unparalleled quantities of all the renewable energy sources: sun, wind, waves and geothermal. This, along with new technologies for storing and transporting energy, has allowed Australia's economy to boom where other, older, less adaptable economies – economies with less stored blubber – have withered. Suddenly the focus of the planet has shifted, and Australia has found itself, far from being the end of the universe, at its centre. Australia, the lucky country, at last.

In the rest of the world, things are less rosy. For a while, two or three decades, it seemed the wealthy, developed countries would suffer least from climate change. This was an irony lost on no-one: that these countries, having led the world into catastrophe, would be least scathed. At first, indeed, there were even benefits for Britain, northern Europe and the USA, as growing-seasons lengthened and tourism picked up much of the demand from the heat-ravaged Mediterranean and now decimated tropics. The Isle of Skye became the new balmy seaside paradise.

Gradually, though, this picture started to shift. A number of factors were influential. Extreme weather events – floods, cyclones and heatwaves – took a direct and increasing toll on these hitherto stable ecosystems and their dependent economies. Heatwaves, killing tens of thousands, and bushfires of the kind once unheard of in northern Europe became more or less annual events. Insurance premiums rocketed, as did the costs of providing medical care in populations hit for the first time by tropical diseases such as malaria, dengue fever and sleeping sickness; brown peoples' revenge, some said, on whites.

At the same time, cheap nuclear power became an impossibility since the great rivers, including the Rhine, the Loire and the Mississippi, were now generally too warm to provide cooling. In any case, the constant threat of superstorms increased anxiety over the stations' safety; an anxiety further intensified by scientific predictions that the destabilised arctic land-mass, a result of the fast-thawing Canadian and Siberian permafrost, had brought the risk of major earthquake to the northern continents. Soon, station after station had been decommissioned, generating a huge international stalemate over responsibility for storing existing nuclear waste in these newly unstable continents.

Then the migrations began. First, just a trickle: refugee-laden boats arriving from low-lying countries such as Tonga and Tuvalu, too poor to defend themselves against the rising seas. Slowly, though, as cyclones like Katrina became regular visitors to the southern US states, the trickle swelled to a flood unequalled since before the Irish potato famine. Even the wealthy Netherlands, with centuries of experience in holding back the oceans, found itself inundated. Briefly, a new tradition of 'Dutch stilt-housing' sprang up, but in the end it became impossible to design these leggy, high-centre-of-gravity dwellings to withstand the increasingly frequent superstorms.

Africa quickly became a dustbowl, the massive loss of life exacerbated by reduced global aid as the wealthy countries, newly unconfident, looked to their own. Then South America, hit by the dual disaster of extreme drought and vanishing glaciers, ran out of water. The picture is now a patchwork of extremes: while the Argentinian pampas became subject to extreme flooding, the Amazon – once one of the world's wettest ecosystems – dried up. Gradually, the mighty river stalled; its vast, maternal delta silted and stagnant, unable to reach the sea, despite the heightened water levels. The towering Amazon rainforests, once the planet's richest biodiversity reservoir, shrank into mythology; with tens of thousands of species becoming extinct just as scientists began to apprehend their extraordinary medical properties. Entire populations dependent upon the Amazon for fishing, transport, water and agriculture dwindled, dying or moving slowly north like vast herds of buffalo towards the Mexican border.

China, whose determined pursuit of economic growth at any cost was blamed by many for finally tipping the world into catastrophic climate change, has suffered massive population loss through floods and storms. Its economy, once the latest Asian 'tiger', is in tatters. Inflation is rife. Many families who had re-immigrated to taste the glories of the 'new China' are now anxious once again to leave before they become too poor to do so.

In North America and Europe people watch these vast population movements with dismay, monitoring them via satellite. The nightly newscasts show the great desperation-driven herds of humanity spreading across countries and continents like stains, moving ever closer, leaving devastation in their wake. An early willingness to accommodate refugees has hardened, although debate still rages as to whether it is moral, or even possible, to resist. Much effort and expense is invested in walls and weaponry. This, go the dark mutterings, is globalism's fruit. This is greed, the hubristic end of humanity's Icarus story.

Others, though, see a new beginning here; a new opportunity for spiritual advancement and political cooperation. And there are (mainly in those places where technology has abetted survival) glimmerings, shreds of evidence for this strange optimism, as people increasingly find what is called 'new happiness' or sometimes, in a play on old-style scientism, 'illogical positivism' in sharing their already reduced food, shelter and territory with others. Humans have proved immensely, staggeringly adaptable. Many give credence to a new, muscular form of nature worship that seems to have spread from the reinvented southern cities. Further, there is an unaccustomed sense that adaptation and even hardship can be for the better. No-one knows whether the planet or its dominant primate will survive but, increasingly, people surprise themselves by feeling lucky; lucky to be alive but lucky, too, not to have missed this most dramatic shift of consciousness in the history of the species.

Bibliography

Note that entries are listed in order of appearance within each chapter.

Introduction

Michael Bywater, *Big Babies or, Why Can't We Just Grow Up?*, Granta, London, 2006, p. 2
Dr Who, in conversation with the Nestene Consciousness, Episode 1, 'Rose'
John Flynn, 'Receiver of wisdom', interview with John Crace, *The Guardian*, 2 January 2007

Chapter 1

William B Irvine, *On Desire: why we want what we want*, Oxford University Press, 2006, p. 2
Dylan Thomas, 'The force that through the green fuse drives the flower', *The Poems of Dylan Thomas*, New Directions, New York, 1952
John F Schumacher, 'The happiness conspiracy', *New Internationalist*, July 2006, pp. 30–1
'If It Makes You Happy', from the album *Sheryl Crow*, 1996
Christopher Lasch, *The Culture of Narcissism: American life in an age of diminishing expectations*, Norton, New York, 1979, p. 240
Stefanie Reinberger, 'Bitter could be better', *Scientific American*, June/July 2006, pp. 57–61
The Hedonistic Imperative, <http://www.hedweb.com>
Ian Thorpe, quoted in profile by Janet Hawley, *Sydney Morning Herald*, *Good Weekend* magazine, 24 March 2007
Adele Horin, 'We can find happiness in this urban life', *Sydney Morning Herald*, 18 February 2006
Mark Kingwell, Department of Philosophy, University of Toronto, 'Limits and Thresholds: On the Power of Interiority', talk delivered at University of Technology Sydney, 8 August 2003

James O'Neill, quoted in *Sydney Morning Herald*, 21 February 2007

Franklin Foer, 'The talented Mr Chavez', *The Atlantic Monthly*, May 2006, p. 100

Frank Furedi, introduction to *The Culture of Fear*, précis in *Sydney Morning Herald*, 4 May 2002

Tim Kasser, *The High Price of Materialism*, MIT Press, Cambridge, MASS, 2002, pp. 38–9

Alvin Toffler, *Future Shock*, Bantam Books, New York, 1970, p. 63

Ashish Kumar Sen, 'The malling of America', *Span* magazine March-April 2005, p. 3, US Department of State website

Victor Gruen, *Centers for the Urban Environment: survival of the cities*, Van Nostrand Reinhold, New York, 1973

William James, *The Principles of Psychology*, Dover, New York, 1958

The Edge, <http://www.edge.org>

Robert Epstein, 'My date with a robot', *Scientific American*, June/July 2006, pp.69–73

Viktor Frankl, *The Doctor and the Soul*, Vintage Books, New York, 1973

Barry Schwartz, *The Paradox of Choice: why more is less*, Harper Collins, New York, 2004, p. 10

Fred Hirsch, *Social Limits to Growth*, Harvard University Press, 1976

Jay Katz, *The Silent World of Doctor and Patient*, Johns Hopkins University Press, 1984

Avner Offer, *The Challenge of Affluence: self-control and well-being in the United States and Britain since 1950*, Oxford University Press, 2006

D Gilbert and T Wilson, 'Miswanting: some problems in the forecasting of future affective states', in J Forgas (ed.), *Thinking and Feeling: the role of affect in social cognition*, Cambridge University Press, 2000

John Ratey, *A User's Guide to the Brain*, Little, Brown & Company, New York, 2001, p. 75

Francis Bacon, *The New Organon*, L, [1620], p. 45, quoted in Simon Blackburn, *Truth: A Guide*, Oxford University Press, 2005, p. 107

Sonja Lyubomirsky, quoted in Marina Krakovsky, *The Science of Lasting Happiness*, www.ScientificAmerican.com, 18 March 2007

George Vaillant, *Adaptation to Life*, Harvard University Press, 1977

Viktor Frankl, *Man's Search for Meaning*, Simon & Schuster, New York, 1946

Raymond Tallis, 'Art (and philosophy) and the ultimate aims of human life', *Philosophy Now*, September/October 2006, pp. 7–11

Irving D Yalom, *The Schopenhauer Cure*, Harper Collins, New York, 2005, p. 340

Chapter 2

Terry Castle, 'Home alone: the dark heart of shelter-lit addiction', *The Atlantic Monthly*, March 2006

Tristan Tzara, quoted in Arthur C Danto, *The Abuse of Beauty: aesthetics and the concept of art*, Open Court, Chicago and La Salle, 2003, p. 39

Hans Urs von Balthasar, *The Glory of the Lord: a theological aesthetic*, Vol. I, T&T Clark, UK, 1986, p. 18

Alexander Nehamas, *Only a Promise of Happiness: the place of beauty in a world of art*, Princeton University Press, 2007

Oscar Wilde, preface to *The Picture of Dorian Grey*, Ward, Locke & Company, London, 1891

John Updike, *Seek My Face*, Alfred A Knopf, New York, 2002, p. 46

John Armstrong, 'Beauty and the beast', review of Alexander Nehamas' *Only a Promise of Happiness*, *Sydney Morning Herald*, 10 March 2007

Dave Hickey, 'Enter the dragon', in *The Invisible Dragon: four essays on beauty*, Art Issues Press, Los Angeles, 1993

Ronal Jones, review of the Hirshhorn's 'Regarding Beauty: a view of the late 20th century', *Art Forum*, January 2000

Alain de Botton, *The Architecture of Happiness*, Hamish Hamilton, London, 2006, p. 21

John Berger, *Ways of Seeing*, BBC and Penguin, London, 1972, p. 139

Mark Kingwell, 'Limits and Thresholds: On the Power of Interiority' lecture given at the IDEA Conference, University of Technology Sydney, 8 August 2003

Iris Murdoch, 'The sublime and the good', *Chicago Review*, XIII, August 1959, pp. 42–55

Leon Battista Alberti, *On the Art of Building in Ten Books*, trans. N Leach, J Rykwert and R Tavenor, The MIT Press, Cambridge, 1988, Book 6.2

Abbé Batteux, *The Fine Arts Reduced to a Single Principle*, 1746

Johann Winckelmann, *History of Ancient Art* [1764], quoted in Martin Gayford and Karen Wright, *The Penguin Book of Art Writing*, Penguin, Harmondsworth, 1999, pp. 260–1

Arthur C Danto, *The Abuse of Beauty: aesthetics and the concept of art*, Open Court, Chicago and La Salle, 2003, p. 40, quoting from Kant's *Critique of Judgement* (5: 353)

Matthew Arnold, *Culture and Anarchy*, edited by Samuel Lipman, Yale University Press, New Haven, 1994, p. 34

Adolf Loos, 'Ornament and Crime', lecture to the Second International Congress for New Building, Frankfurt, 1908; in Adolf Loos, *Ornament and Crime: selected essays* [1929], Ariadne Press, Riverside, CA, 1998

Adolf Loos, afterword to *Ornament and Crime*, 1929, p. 176

Harold Rosenberg, 1973, quoted in Martin Gayford and Karen Wright, *The Penguin Book of Art Writing*, Penguin, Harmondsworth, 1999, p. 562

Kristen J Navara, Alexander V Badyaev, Mary T Mendonca and Geoffrey E Hill, 'Yolk antioxidants vary with male attractiveness and female condition in the house finch (*Carpodacus mexicanus*)', *Physiological and Biochemical Zoology* 79:6

Paul Johnson, 'Ravishing blondes did not queue up to become Mrs Einstein', *The Spectator*, 12 July 2003

Joan Jacobs Brumberg, *The Body Project: an intimate history of American girls*, Vintage Books (Random House), New York, 1997, p. 75

Taki, *The Spectator*, 31 March 2001

John Armstrong, 'Beauty and the beast', *Sydney Morning Herald*, 10 March 2007, p. 36

Dr Garry Stevens, *Why Architects are Flashy Dressers*, <http://www.archsoc.com>, Dr Garry's Key Centre for Architectural Sociology

Alain de Botton, *The Architecture of Happiness*, Hamish Hamilton, London, 2006, p. xx

Iris Murdoch, *Metaphysics as a Guide to Morals*, Chatto & Windus, London, 1992, pp. 306–7

Stratford Caldecott, *An Introduction to Hans Urs von Balthasar*, Vol. 5, Second Spring, UK, 2002

Chapter 3

Ivan Illich, *Deschooling Society*, Harper & Row, New York, 1970

Paul Keating in interview with the author, 28 May 2007

Tara Pepper, 'A master of elegy (Lucian Freud)', *Newsweek*, 8 July 2002

Dave Hickey, 'Enter the dragon', in *The Invisible Dragon: four essays on beauty*, Art Issues Press, Los Angeles, 1993

Daniel Kuntiz, *The Other Beauty Myth*, <http://www.Salon.com>, 10 January 2000

Shirley Fitzgerald, *Sydney 1842–1992*, Hale & Iremonger, Sydney, 1992

Randy Kennedy, 'Could be a Pollock, must be a yarn', *New York Times*, 9 November 2006

David Boyle, *Authenticity: brands, fakes, spin and the lust for real life*, Flamingo, London, 2003

Ray Robinson, president of American Church Builders Inc, <http://www.acbi1.co>

Nan Stalnaker, 'Fakes and forgeries', in Berys Gaut and Dominic McIver Lopes, *The Routledge Companion to Aesthetics*, Routledge, London, 2001, p. 397

Francis Bacon, *The New Organon*, XLIX, [1620], p. 44, quoted in Simon Blackburn, *Truth: A Guide*, Oxford University Press, 2005, p. 1

Fr Timothy Radcliffe, 'The Crisis of Truth Telling in Our Society', The 19th Eric Symes Abbott Memorial Lecture, 2004, delivered in Westminster Abbey (broadcast ABC Radio National, 23 February 2005)

Sam Harris, *What We Believe but Cannot Prove*; *The Edge*, <http://www.edge.org>

Pat O'Shane, *The Weekend Australian*, 7–8 November 1998

David Hare, *Obedience, Struggle and Revolt: lectures on theatre*, Faber & Faber, London, 2005, p. 73

Chapter 4

Camille Paglia, cancelled preface to *Sexual Personae*, in *Sex, Art and American Culture*, Vintage Books, New York, 1992, p. 103

Arthur Koestler, *The Act of Creation*, Arkana, London, 1989, pp. 308–9

Aristotle, *de Anima*, II.1

John Ward Anderson, 'French doctor defend ethics of first face transplant,' *Washington Post*, 3 December 2005

John Ratey, *A User's Guide to the Brain: perception, attention and the four theatres of the brain*, Little, Brown & Company, New York, 2001 pp. 314–18

Jorge Luis Borges, afterword to 'El Hacedor', 1960

M Garland, *Artifices, Confections, Manufactures*, Royal College of Arts, London, 1957

Paco Underhill, *The Call of the Mall: how we shop*, Profile Books, New York, 2004, p. 57

Christine Chaseling, *The June Dally Watkins Book of Manners for Moderns*, Dally-Chase Publications, Sydney, 1969, p. 7

Sydney Morning Herald, 26 October 2006

Petronella Wyatt, 'Living dangerously, singular life', *The Spectator*, 7 September 2002

Oscar Vladislas de Lubicz Milosz, 'Melancolie' (French-Lithuanian writer)

Jun'ichiro Tanizaki, *In Praise of Shadows* (trans. Thomas J Harper and Edward G Seidensticker), Leete's Island Books, Stony Creek, CT, 1977, p. 28

Richard Sennett, *Flesh and Stone: the body and the city in western civilisation*, WW Norton & Co, New York, 1994, p. 34

Jung, quoted in 'Jung, men, women and God', in W McGuire and RFC Hull (eds), *CJ Jung Speaking: interviews and encounters*, Princeton University Press, 1987

Margaret Visser, *The Rituals of Dinner: the origins, evolution, eccentricities and meaning of table manners*, Penguin, Harmondsworth, 1991, p. 79

Giambattista Vico, quoted in Alain de Botton, *The Architecture of Happiness*, Hamish Hamilton, London, 2006

Paul Scheerbart, *Glasarchitektur* [1914, p. 11], quoted in Reyner Banham, *The Architecture of the Well-Tempered Environment*, The Architectural Press, London, 1969, pp. 125–6

Walter Gropius 1919, the first Bauhaus Proclamation, in Reyner Banham, *Theory and Design in the First Machine Age*, The Architectural Press, London, 1960, p. 277

Le Corbusier, *Towards a New Architecture* [1923], trans. Frederick Etchells, Dover, New York, 1986

Bruno Taut 1927, quoted in Reyner Banham, *Theory and Design in the First Machine Age*, The Architectural Press, London, 1960, p. 266

Frank Lloyd Wright 1931, quoted in Reyner Banham, *Theory and Design in the First Machine Age*, The Architectural Press, London, 1960, p.125

Lazlo Maholy-Nagy, quoted in Adrian Forty, *Words and Buildings: a vocabulary of modern architecture*, Thames & Hudson, London, 2000

Chapter 5

Robin Boyd, *The Australian Ugliness*, Cheshire, Melbourne, 1960

Sam Cassis in *60 Minutes* report, 'The Castle,' Channel 9, 26 February 2006

Michael Stanbridge, 'Australia, you're rolling in it,' *Sydney Morning Herald*, 27 March 2006

Sarah Silverman, quoted in Dana Goodyear, 'Quiet depravity: the demure outrages of a standup comic', *The New Yorker*, 24 October 2005

Pascale Hunter, 'Mauritania's "wife-fattening" farm', BBC News, 26 January 2004

'Not so little Britain', BBC News, 1 September 2004

UK Department of Health statistics, quoted in Simon Nixon, 'Jumping on the low-fat bandwagon', *The Spectator*, 13 May 2006

Mark Steyn, 'A broadside in the war on blubber', *Daily Telegraph* (UK), 1 June 2004

'As Sydney's waistline expands, health workers should talk the walk', *Sydney Morning Herald*, 21 November 2003

Paul Gross, Director of the Institute of Health Economics and Technology Assessment, reported in Ruth Pollard, 'Obesity bill more than health budget,' *Sydney Morning Herald*, 2 March 2006

Paul Zimmet, quoted in 'McMansions to blame', *The Age*, 8 September 2006

Tony McMichael, 'Our big, fat cultural problem needs a wider solution', *Sydney Morning Herald*, 5 May 2006

Professor Paul Knox, lecture delivered at the University of Sydney, 23 March 2006

Professor Tony Capon, lecture delivered at the Sydney Town Hall, 25 September 2006

Julie Robotham, 'Health fears as young become screen zombies', *Sydney Morning Herald*, 7 December 2006; study by Dr Louise Hardy, NSW Centre for Overweight and Obesity, University of Sydney, in *Journal of Paediatrics and Child Health*, 42 (11), 709–714

Third National Health and Nutrition Examination Survey: RE Anderson, CJ Crespo, SJ Bartlett, LJ Cheskin and M Pratt, 'Relationship of physical activity and television watching with body weight and level of fatness among children: results from the Third National Health and Nutrition Examination Survey', *JAMA*, 1998, 279: 938–942

'School's out and the weight piles on', *The Daily Telegraph* (Sydney), 2 March 2007

Gina Kolata, 'Ideas and trends', *New York Times*, 29 October 2006

John Huxley, 'Bigfoot alive and thriving on the North Shore', *Sydney Morning Herald*, 1 August 2005

Mark Steyn, 'A broadside in the war on blubber', *Daily Telegraph* (UK), 1 June 2004

Edward O Wilson, 'A brave new world', *Cosmos*, Issue 3, 2005, pp. 64–9

Andy Warhol *The Philosophy of Andy Warhol: from A to B and back again*, Penguin, Harmondsworth, 1975

WH Auden, 'Thanksgiving for a Habitat', 1962

'First Home Ownership', Australian Productivity Commission Enquiry, Report, March 2004, p. 128

Stephen Crafti, *Beach Houses Down Under*, Images Publishing, Melbourne, 2006

Harry G Frankfurt, *On Bullshit*, Princeton University Press, 2005

Susan Sontag, 'Notes on camp', in Susan Sontag, *Against Interpretation and Other Essays*, Farrar, Straus & Giroux, New York, 1964

Roger Scruton, 'Kitsch and the Modern Predicament', *City Journal*, <http://www.city-journal.org>, Winter 1999

'Excerpts from the Aspen Ideas Festival', *The Atlantic Monthly*, October 2006, pp. 47–52

Milan Kundera, *The Unbearable Lightness of Being: A Novel*, Harper & Row, New York, 1984, p. 248

Harvey Cox, *The Secular City*, Macmillan, New York, 1966, p. 49

Richard Sennett, *The Conscience of the Eye: the design and social life of cities*, Norton, New York, 1992

Richard Sennett, *Flesh and Stone: the body and the city in western civilisation*, Norton, New York, 1994

Chapter 6

David Owen, 'Green Manhattan', *The New Yorker*, 18 October 2004, reprinted in *Australian Financial Review*, 21 January 2005

On New York oil usage: 'Cities fuel hope the US can kick its oil addiction', *Sydney Morning Herald*, 30 May 2007

George Taylor in Paul Ashton, *The Accidental City: planning Sydney since 1788*, Hale & Iremonger, Sydney, 1993, p. 44

On the Netherlands: S de Vries, R Verheij and P Groenwehen, 'Natural environments: healthy environments', in *Environment and Planning A*, 2003, vol. 35, pp. 1717–31.

Richard Florida, 'The nation in numbers: where the brains are', *The Atlantic Monthly*, October 2006, p. 35

Gary Banks, David Robertson and Edward Shann, Australian Productivity Commission, First Home Ownership Report, March 2004

2006 State of the Environment Report, HS-14, Indicators of Health and Wellbeing

Billie Giles-Corti, 'The Impact of Urban Form on Public Health', paper prepared for the 2006 Australian State of the Environment Committee, Department of the Environment and Heritage, Canberra

TF Smith and M Doherty, 'The Suburbanisation of Coastal Australia', paper prepared for the 2006 Australian State of the Environment Committee, Department of the Environment and Heritage, Canberra

David Nicholson-Lord, 'Drink fresh snow,' *Adbusters: Journal of the Mental Environment*, Jan/Feb 2006, #63, vol. 14, no. 1

John Ratey, *A User's Guide to the Brain*, Little, Brown & Co, New York, 2001, p. 156

Antonio Sant'Elia and Filippo Tommaso Marinetti, quoted in Ulrich Conrads, *Programmes and Manifestoes on Twentieth Century Architecture*, Lund Humphries, London, 1970, pp. 36–8

Alvin Toffler, *Future Shock*, Bantam Books, New York, 1970, pp. 75–6

Mark Kingwell, 'Speeding to a standstill', interview with Joe Gelonesi, *Arts & Opinion*, vol. 2, no. 2, 2003

Marinetti's Foundation Manifesto, in Reyner Banham, *Theory and Design in the First Machine Age*, The Architectural Press, London, 1960, p. 101

Kelly Burke, 'I'll recycle – but leave my family car alone', *Sydney Morning Herald*, 22 November 2006

Jakob von Uexkull, *A Stroll Through the Worlds of Animals and Men: a picture book of invisible worlds*, monograph, International University Press, New York, 1934

Sam Allis, 'Vehicular conversation: talking has a different tone in confines of a car', *Boston Globe*, 3 September 2006

Michael Pollan, *The Omnivore's Dilemma: the search for a perfect meal in a fast-food world*, Penguin, Harmondsworth, 2006, p. 110

Barbara Wallraff, 'Word fugitives', *The Atlantic Monthly*, October 2006, p. 152

Toru Sato, *The Ever-Transcending Spirit: the psychology of human relationships, consciousness and development*, iUniverse, Lincoln, Nebraska, 2003, p. 42

Richard Sennett, *The Conscience of the Eye: the design and social life of cities*, Norton, New York, 1990

Richard Sennett, *Flesh and Stone: the body and the city in western civilization*, Norton, New York, 1994

Johan Huizinga, *Homo Ludens: a study of the play element in culture*, Beacon Press, Boston, 1955

Elisabeth Grosz, 'Chaos, Territory and Art: Architecture from the Outside,' lecture given at Sydney University, 25 August 2005

Paul Zapffe, quoted in Gisle Tangenes, 'The view from Mount Zapffe', *Philosophy Now*, March/April 2004, p. 33

John Ralston Saul, *The Doubter's Companion: a dictionary of aggressive common sense*, Penguin, Victoria, 1994, p. 237

Chapter 7

Anne Moir and David Jessel, *Brain Sex: the real difference between men and women*, Michael Joseph, London, 1989, p. 151

Fiona Smith, 'Leaders smooth path to the top', *Australian Financial Review*, 8 August 2006, p.61

Paula Whitman, Kerry Brown, Miriam Warr, Whay Lee, Pamela Whitman and Sarah Briant, *The Career Progression of Women in the Architectural Profession*, preliminary findings presented to the Royal Australian Institute of Architects, August 2004

Paco Underhill, *The Call of the Mall: how we shop*, Profile Books, London, 2004

Michael Kyrios, reported in Kirsty Needham, 'Retail therapy: beware cure hiding a disease', *Sydney Morning Herald*, 22 October 2005

Barry Schwartz, *The Paradox of Choice: why more is less*, Harper Collins, New York, 2004, p. 18

Ronald Inglehart and Pippa Norris, *Rising Tide: gender equality and cultural change around the world*, Cambridge University Press, Cambridge, 2003

Monica Ressel Giordani, University of Trieste, review of Catherine Atherton (ed.), *Monsters and Monstrosity in Greek and Roman Culture. Nottingham Classical Literature Studies*

Midland Classical Studies, vol. 6. Bari: Levante, 2002, p. 135. ISBN 88-7949-290-X. EUR 25.00. *Bryn Mawr Classical Review*, 2003.04.15

Peter Sloterdijk in 'Gendered like Beckham', interviewed by *Der Spiegel*, 3 June 2006, reprinted in *Harpers Magazine*, September 2006, p. 17–18

Dreaming stories: S May and A Murphy, 'Some baskets are special ones', in L Hamby (ed.), *Twined Together: Kunmadj Njalehnjaleken*, Injalak Arts and Crafts, Gunbalanya, NT, p. 25; Roland Robinson, *The Feathered Serpent*, Angus & Robertson, Sydney, 1956

Clive Hamilton and Richard Denniss (eds), *Affluenza: when too much is never enough*, Allen & Unwin, Sydney, 2005, p. 27

'Your time starts now'; and Julia Baird, 'Claws out for a wolf exposed,' *The Sydney Morning Herald, Good Weekend* magazine, 20 May 2006

Lidija Stojanovic, *The Archetype of Initiation of the Threshold of the Third Millennium*, <http://www.folklore.ee/rl/pubte/ee/cf/cf/15.html>

Camille Paglia, *Sexual Personae: art and decadence from Nefertiti to Emily Dickinson*, Penguin, Harmondsworth, 1990, p.23

Emily Praeger, quoted in Terry Castle, 'Home alone: the dark heart of shelter-lit addiction', *The Atlantic Monthly*, March 2006

Erika Rappaport, S*hopping for Pleasure: women in the making of London's East End*, Princeton University Press, New Jersey, 2000

Margaret Mead and Martha Wolfenstein (eds), *Childhood in Contemporary Cultures*, University of Chicago Press, 1955

Benjamin Spock, *Baby and Child Care*, Simon & Schuster, New York, 1945 <http://www.thomashawke.com>, 13 April 2006

'Math and science education in a global age: what the US can learn from China', *The Atlantic Monthly*, October 2006, p. 45

Unnamed resident, *60 Minutes* report 'The Castle', Channel 9, 26 February 2006

Jennifer Lisle, *Single Women Become a Force in Home-Buying*, <http://www.Wallstreetjournal.com>, 24 November 2004

Terry Castle, 'Home alone: the dark heart of shelter-lit addiction', *The Atlantic Monthly*, March 2006, p. 188

Malcolm Gladwell, 'How the SUV ran over automotive safety,' *The New Yorker*, Culture & Commerce section, p. 28, 12 January 2004

Linda Babcock and Sara Laschever, *Women Don't Ask: negotiation and the gender divide*, Princeton University Press, New Jersey, 2003

Carol Midgley, quoted in Steve Meacham, 'Protection force,' *Sydney Morning Herald*, 9 September 2006

George Patton, quoted in Steve Meacham, 'Protection force,' *Sydney Morning Herald*, 9 September 2006

Clotaire Rapaille, *The Culture Code: An ingenious way to understand why people around the world love and buy as they do*, Broadway Books, New York, 2006

Chapter 8

James Howard Kunstler, *The End of Suburbia*, television documentary, 2004

John Constable, recorded in CR Leslie, *Memoirs of the Life of John Constable RA* [1843], quoted in Martin Gayford and Karen Wright, *The Penguin Book of Art Writing*, Penguin, Harmondsworth, 1999, p. 258

Professor Quentin Skinner, 2006 Vice-Chancellor's Distinguished Lecture: 'How Many Concepts of Liberty?', University of Sydney, 19 July 2006

Steven Shainberg director, *Secretary* (2002), based on the 1988 short story 'Bad Behaviour' by Mary Gaitskill

Richard Sennett, *The Conscience of the Eye: the design and social life of cities*, Norton, New York, 1992

Smart Growth, <http://www.smartgrowthamerica.org>

Index